Human Rights and the Law

Neera Bharihoke

SERIALS PUBLICATIONS
NEW DELHI (INDIA)

First Published – 2009

ISBN: 978-81-8387-230-0

Published by

SERIALS PUBLICATIONS
4830/24, Prahlad Street, Ansari Road
Darya Ganj, New Delhi-110002 (India)
Phone: 23245225 Fax : 91-11-23272135
E-mail: serials@satyam.net.in

Contents

	Preface	*vii*
1.	Human Rights and Right to Health: An Indian Scenario DEVESH KUMAR SAHU & B. M. MUKHERJEE	1
2.	Human Rights-Global Refugee Trends S. SRI KRISHNA & S. ANIL KUMAR	13
3.	Human Rights and Refugee Law: A Study of Indian Approach Towards Tibetans ANUPAM AHLUWALIA	25
4.	Human Rights of Refugees: An Appraisal R. D. VIJAYASEKHAR & K. SRINIVASA RAO	39
5.	Principle of Non Refoulement and Refugees Under International Perspective MARUTHI T. R.	55
6.	Refugees And Human Rights: A Study of Sri Lankan Tamil Refugees Y. GURAPPA NAIDU	71
7.	Obscuring the Asylum-Seeker in the Refugee: A Note on the Ambit of Non-Refoulement in Refugee Law RENUKA DHINAKARAN & VYDYANATHAN LAKSHMANAN	91
8.	Development of International Standards on Rights of Disabled Person B. S. PATIL	105
9.	Remedies Under International Law to Victims of Human Rights Violations KULJIT KAUR	121

10. Human Rights of Children 133
S. N. YOGISH

11. Child Health and Nutrition in India– Plight and Right 149
V. BASIL HANS

12. Breast Feeding as Human Right of the Child 169
ALOK PANDEY

13. A New Paradigm for Law and Justice 177
J. P. MISHRA

14. Role of the United Nations in the Development of Human Rights 193
KULJIT KAUR

15. Problems of Refugee Women and the International Law 203
MS. SUNEET KASHYAP

16. The Limitations of Fundamental Human Rigths in Nigeria: A Critical Analysis 213
BASHIR LEKE IJAIYA

17. Legal Aid and Justice: Panacea for Poverty Reduction 229
BASHIR LEKE IJAIYA

18. Status of Women Domestic Workers in Tirunelveli City-A Study 245
R. EZHIL JASMINE

19. Organizational Performance Assessment: Effectiveness, Efficiency, Productivity 271
RITA REZAEE

20. Overview to Evaluation: Types, Methods and Strategies 285
RITA REZAEE & SHIRAIN IRANFAR

21. Relevance of Humanrights in the 21st Century 297
P. MUTHAIYAN & K. SELVANATHAN

Index 303

Preface

Mention of human rights brings to a person's manifestation its many facets, their meaning, concepts, contents etc. The related issues and notions also bring to spotlight the beneficiaries of human rights, protection of their rights, their rehabilitation etc. Refugees, migrants, disabled people, displaced people, domestic workers are the classes or groups who are more susceptible to human rights violation. Their vulnerability is attributable to landlessness, poverty, lack of employment opportunities, ruthlessness of society towards them etc. Their problems and grievances can be addressed and vindicated by strengthening of legal, social as well as economic infrastructure and to build the same wherever these are lacking.

Regardless of the stage of a country's economic development, significance of human rights cannot be undermined. *P. Muthaiyan* and *K. Selvanathan* in their paper titled *'Relevance of Human Rights in the 21st Century'* have highlighted how the contents and contexts of human rights have undergone metamorphosis in the new era of globalization and liberalization and have concluded by providing as to how the aspirations of such human rights content can be achieved by human rights education as well as introducing of courses of human rights in India.

Refugees, migrants, disabled people and displaced people are the classes or groups who are more susceptible to human rights violation. Refugees are externally displaced persons and asylum seekers who are victims of involuntary relocation. Persecution or violence in their countries of origin, innumerable instances of violation of human rights force people to run away from their home countries and seek refuge. They have to resurrect their new lives in the host countries. Host countries too have to strike a balance between tribulations of sovereignty, migration control, national security on one hand and international obligations on the other hand. *R.D.Vijayashekhar K. Srinivasa Rao* in their paper titled *'Human Rights of Refugees: An Appraisal'* has explained the concept of human rights vis-à-vis refugee, their status under International Law and under Refugee Convention 1951. They have discussed as to how the problem of refugees continues to challenge the international community.

There is a complex and rapidly evolving field of international refuge and refugee law. Principles and concepts of refugee protection have been spelled out under the 1951 United Nations Convention on Human Rights (UNCHR) and other forms and instruments of protection under various Conventions. These are measures towards finding solutions to the problems of the refugees and to provide an international platform for their protection. *Ms. Suneet Kashyap* has in detail scripted the plight of female refugees and the plethora of their problems in her paper titled *'Problems of Refugee Women and the International Law'*. Women refugees are more susceptible to sexually transmitted diseases and infections and are also subjected to sexual and gender based violence. She has also suggested what all requires to be done to tackle their problems.

S. Sri Krishna and S. Anil Kumar in their paper *'Human Rights-Global Refugee Trends'* has brought to focus how governments and humanitarian organizations are finding it extremely difficult to cope with the situations created by problems related to refugees protection and rehabilitation. The data referred to in their paper of voluntary repatriation, resettlement and local integration of refugees is very informative.

Refugee inflow in India has been regulated by an ad hoc system of executive action dictated and determined by the government's policy towards the country of origin of the refugees. *Y. Gurappa Naidu* in *'Refugees and Human Rights: A Study of Sri Lankan Tamil Refugees'* has discussed the infiltration of Tamil refugees from Sri Lanka in India, the assistance programmes for them and the position of the refugees after the assassination of former Prime Minister Rajiv Gandhi in 1991. The paper also provides information on their repatriation as well as human rights violation and problems of refugees. *Anupam Ahluwalia* in paper titled *'Human Rights and Refugee Law: A Study of Indian Approach towards Tibetans'* has after reviewing the international law related to refugees discussed the inflow of Tibetan refugees in India and how Indian government has worked towards their shelter and rehabilitation.

India is not a party to either UNCHR, often referred to as Refugee Convention or its 1967 Protocol. India has also not enacted any national legislation to govern the protection of refugees. However, India has signed a number of international conventions that indirectly hinge upon its obligations towards refugees e.g. Universal Declaration of Human Rights, 1948 (UDHR) the International Convention on Civil and Political Rights, 1966 (ICCPR) the International Convention on the Elimination of all Forms of Racial Discrimination, 1966 (CERD) etc. This piecemeal approach has thus enabled India to escape to meet the international obligations laid down under UNHCR and has at times also lead to depriving the hapless refugees of their basic rights and needs.

United Nations Convention on Human Rights (UNCHR) and other forms and instruments of protection under various Conventions are measures towards finding solutions to the problems of the refugees and to provide an international platform for their protection. International refugee protection, its standards, the rights of the refugees, non-refoulement principle, different kinds of asylum raise a plethora of issues and it becomes necessary to stimulate research and thinking on refugee law. *Renuka Dhinakaran* and *Vydyanathan Lakshmanan* in their paper titled *'Obscuring the Asylum-*

Seeker in the Refugee: A Note on the Ambit of Non-Refoulement in Refugee Law' have discussed the problems faced by refugees in implementation of non-refoulement principle for their protection. Non-refoulement principle prohibits contracting parties to UNCHR from returning a refugee in any manner whatsoever to the frontiers of the territory where he would be subjected to persecution. The paper also skillfully articulates the problems posed by migration of refugees into a nation. *Maruthi T.R.* in the article *'Principles of Non-Refoulement and Refugees under International Perspective'* has discussed nature, scope and extent of applicability of the non-refoulement principle, how it has been interpreted and what its exceptions are. The paper also highlights the difficulties faced in implementation of the principle due to insufficiency of legal instruments in domestic laws of the countries for protection of refugees as well as because of difficulty in implementation of existing legal provisions enacted for refugees.

The book focuses on the human rights of not only the susceptible economically weaker groups but also of human rights of any individual of a society. The very first paper, titled *'Human Rights and Right to Health: an Indian Scenario'* by *Devesh Kr. Sahu* and *B.M.Mukherjee* enlightens on how development of health is integral process for overall growth of socio-cultural, economic, educational, political and environmental factors. Suggestions of right based approach to health lays down important guidelines for making right to health a meaningful right. The paper written by *S.N. Yogesh*, namely *'Human Rights of Children'* generates awareness of child rights and its various components, their violations in the form of child abuse, child trafficking, child labour etc. and disregard by providing statistical data of India, China, Taiwan and other global economies. Similarly *V. Basu Hans* in his article *'Child Health and Nutrition in India- Plight and Right'* presents the bewildering picture of deprivation of right to health, hygiene and nutrition in India while presenting an overview of the international and national commitments.

Suggestions at the end of the chapter serve as valuable steps which need to be taken for fulfillment of these commitments.

The least talked about human right of any individual in the whole world, namely right to be breastfed has been presented articulately by *Alok Pandey* in his article *'Breast Feeding is Human Right of the Child'*. He creates consciousness towards this not so well-known right under the auspices of international law as well as under Indian Constitution. *R. Ezhil Jasmine* draws attention to plights of women domestic workers in her paper *'Status of Women Domestic Workers in Tirunelveli City- A Study'*. Domestic workers are susceptible to human rights violation because of landlessness, poverty, lack of employment opportunities and ruthlessness of society towards them. The magnitude of their problems is complex and huge and is attributable to their belonging to lower stratum of society as well as their destituteness. The paper discusses the plight, the problems, and occupational diseases of women domestic workers in Tirunelveli city.

Another vulnerable victim of human rights violation or that of denial of human rights is the disabled person. *B.S.Patil* in the paper titled *'Development of International Standards on Rights of Disabled Person'* has documented the International Conventions, Declarations and Norms dealing with human rights as a whole and the rights of disabled persons in particular and has emphasized that the attempts of the State and Organizations for the protection of the human rights of the disabled persons are motivated by the international concerns.

Kuljit Kaur in the paper titled *'Remedies under International Law to Victims of Human Rights Violation'* has highlighted the competence of human rights tribunals to afford remedies to violation of human rights as well as the types of remedies available and the problems at the stage of implementation of these remedies. In another paper by the same author titled *'Role of the United Nations in the Development of Human Rights'* role of United Nations the legal development of human rights and their protection through the institutions of United Nations has been discussed.

Bashir Leke Ijaiya in the article *'The Limitations of Fundamental Human Rights in Nigeria: A Critical Analysis'* has highlighted how the fundamental rights enshrined in the Nigerian Constitution have limitation imposed on them by the same Constitution for good or worse, by weighing the human rights of an individual against the welfare of the society as a whole.

Judicial system has a vital role in assuring the protection of human rights. Providing legal rights or human rights on paper without any implementation machinery in place or the machinery being apathetic, unwilling or inclined is worthless for victims who suffer human rights encroachment and intrusion. *J.P.Mishra* in his paper *'A New Paradigm for Law and Justice'* has highlighted that in the wake of new emerging developments because of liberalization, there is need for improvements in the existing laws. There is need for enacting new laws where there is no legislation and also there is a need to change the implementation machinery as well as procedure for implementation and the change in outlook of judicial machinery while delivering justice.

Justice delivery system, no doubt, needs to play a pro-active role by monitoring the implementation of these rights and to take punitive measures against the slacking, erring and defaulting individuals/ authorities. Equally important is the access to justice by all. The State needs to provide free legal aid to indigent and impoverished individuals/ groups. *Bashir Leke Ijaiya* in the paper titled *'Legal Aid and Justice: Panacea for Poverty Reduction'* emphasizes on this aspect by defining legal aid, poverty and its causes and consequences. The article also discusses the rationale and scope of legal aid laying stress on the legal needs of the poor and their right to access to justice.

Article by *Rita Rezaee* titled *'Organizational Performance Assessment: Effectiveness, Efficiency, Productivity'* provide important guidelines for all policy circles and academicians for assessing productivity and cost efficiency. The author concludes by providing the litmus tests for Organizational Performance Evaluation. Article by *Ritu Rezaee* and *Shirain Iranfar*, titled *'Overview to Evaluation: Types, Methods and Strategies"* informs the readers of how evaluation is different from traditional social research and what are the requirements for achieving valuable results through evaluation by management ability, group skills etc.

Problems and grievances of victims of human rights violation or deprivation can be vindicated by strengthening of legal, social as well as economic infrastructure and to build the same wherever these are lacking. Darwin's theory of the survival of the fittest has to give way to equality and non-discrimination so that the fruits of development are made available to all regardless of residence, sex, colour, age, creed, class or caste. Fundamental Rights and Directive Principles of State Policy reflect the commitment of Indian Constitution towards securing a dignified, non-discriminatory and healthy and secured life for all the persons. There is a complex and rapidly evolving field of national as well as international law in the direction of protection of the right of a human to be human and also for prevention of the violation of human rights.

Concerted and co-ordinated efforts of awakened society, legal provisions, recognition and enforcement of international obligations under various treaties, committed implementation machinery, a strong pro-active and corrective judicial system can together play a cohesive role for effective availability of human rights to all humans.

NEERA BHARIHOKE

Human Rights and Right to Health: An Indian Scenario

DEVESH KUMAR SAHU* & B. M. MUKHERJEE*

BACKGROUND AND RATIONALE

Human rights and public health are powerful and modern approaches with intrinsic connections, which share the common objective of protecting the health and the well being of all being of all individuals. The Calcutta Declaration adopted at the Regional Public Health Conference in 1999 had, in its agenda for action, recommended using a rights approach to health. Upholding human rights and the dignity of all human beings and adoption of an intergenerational approach are important prerequisites for improving public health and ensuring sustainable development.

The 1978 Alma-Ata Declaration called on nations to ensure essential primary health care availability. The World Health Assembly, in 1998, stressed the will to promote health by addressing its basic determinants and prerequisites. Arbitrary restrictive measures that fail to consider other valid alternatives are abusive of human rights principles and in contradiction with public health 'best practice'. Discrimination in health systems, and unsound human development policies and programmes exacerbate disparities in health. Equal

* Department of Anthropology, Pt. Sundarlal Sharma (Open) University Chhattisgarh, Bilaspur.

** Department of Anthropology & Tribal Development, G.G. University, Bilaspur.

treatment within societies and within health care settings should be the norm.

The goal of extending the benefits of sustainable health over an expanding life span, to all members of the human family, is the cardinal tenet of public health. The Declaration of Human Rights eloquently upholds the right to life as an inalienable entitlement of all human beings. As the mutually nurturing relationship between health and development becomes increasingly clear, protection of health (as an essential requirement for enabling human beings to develop to their full potential) becomes integral to the mandate of human rights. Such a shared vision and shared mission pave the way for a natural alliance between the advocates of public health and the defenders of human rights. Purposeful partnership between the two groups, catalyzed by a conjoint consultation, would be very productive for public health.

The major determinants of health lie outside the health system. Human rights provide a useful tool for advancing public health goals, and a framework for analysis and research into complex health problems. A systematic human rights analysis uses an analytical and action-oriented framework, with indicators relating compliance with health promotion and human rights principles, could guide evidence-based health policy and programme development.

HUMAN RIGHTS

Human rights are legally guaranteed by human rights law, protecting individuals and groups against actions that interfere with fundamental freedoms and human dignity. They encompass what are known as civil, culture, economic, political and social rights. Human rights are principally concerned with the relationship between the individual and the state. Governmental obligations with regards to human rights broadly fall under the principles of respect, protect and fulfill.

RIGHT TO HEALTH

The development of health is not a fragmented process, it is integral in its nature which includes the overall growth and development of different socio-cultural, economic, educational, political and environmental factors. Until 1983 there was no formal health policy in India. The resolution on fundamental rights of the Indian National Congress in 1931 mentions all the fundamental rights except health. However, for the first time the health issue was raised by the Sokhe Committee which recommended a centralized authority to provide services for mothers and children, the need for a national level minimum infrastructure, and the need to train para-medical workers and traditional dais to provide natal, ante and post natal services.

Subsequently, the far better known Bhore Committee observed, 'if the nation's health is to be built, the health programme should be developed on a foundation of preventive health work and such activities should proceed side by side with those concerned with the treatment of patients. In the context of the global debate on alternative strategies during the 1970s, the signing of Alma Ata declaration of 'health for all by the year 2000' and the recommendations of ICMR-ICSSR joint panel report, the government of India decided to have a formal National Health Policy (NHP). It was felt that a comprehensive and integrated approach is needed for the future development of medical education and training, research and health services which would serve the actual needs of the people specially the vulnerable groups by establishing an effective and efficient health care system.

The major emphasis of the NHP was to have a strong and stable infrastructure of primary health care with an aim to attain health for all by 2000 AD. The main focus was on preventive and promotive health care services along with curative health care, close co-ordination between the health related services and activities such as nutrition, drinking water supply and sanitation; the active involvement and participation of voluntary organizations and the community;

the provision of essential drugs and vaccines; qualitative improvement in health and family planning services and medical research aimed at the common people's problems.

In the Sixth and Seventh Five Year Plans the aim was to achieve the target of one primary health centre for 30,000 people and one sub centre per 5000 people in the plains and one primary health centre for 20,000 people and one sub centre for 3000 people in tribal and hilly areas. There was also a focus on universal immunization of expectant mothers and all eligible children by 1990. Special programmes were launched for maternal and child survival, safe motherhood and reproductive and child health during the Seventh Plan period.

In spite of the NHP there has been a shift in emphasis towards the more curative aspect of health. However, there have been several successes on the health front, notably the decline in crude death rate, infant mortality rate and the increased life expectancy. There are also some achievements with regard to expansion of medical research and training, expansion of health care services especially of primary health centres. The number of PHCs increased from 20,719 to 21,854 and sub centres from 1,31,469 to 1,33,730 during the Eight Five Year Plan. But lack of funds, non-availability of trained para-medical and medical staff and other supportive services have made them non-functional. There has also been some success in the sphere of nutrition during the Eighth Five Year Plan.

The number of children of 'normal' nutritional status has increased from 1975-79 to 1988-90 yet far behind the set goal of health for all by the year 2000. The other targets, related to fertility, immunization and national disease control programmes are much below the projected figures. Decentralisation and demystification-mentioned in the NHP-have taken place to some extend but there has been no community participation. The public health system has not been able to provide much epidemiological surveillance services recommended by NHP.

WHAT IS MEANT BY "THE RIGHT TO HEALTH"?

The right to health does not mean the right to be healthy, nor does it mean that governments must put in place expensive health services for which they have no resources. But it does require governments and public authorities to put in place policies and action plans which will lead to available and accessible health care for all in the shortest possible time. To ensure that this happens is the challenge facing both the human rights community and public health professionals. The right to the highest attainable standard of health was first reflected in the WHO Constitution (1946) and then reiterated in the 1978 Declaration of Alma Ata and in the World Health Declaration adopted by the World Health Assembly in 1998. It has been firmly endorsed in a wide range of international and regional human rights instruments.

The right to the highest attainable standard of health in international human rights law is a claim to a set of social arrangements, norms, institutions, laws, and an enabling environment that can best secure the enjoyment of this right. The most authoritative interpretation of the right to health is outlined in Article 12 of the ICESCR, which has been ratified by 145 countries (as of May 2002). In May 2000, the Committee on Economic, Social and Cultural Rights, which monitors the Covenant, adopted a General Comment on the right to health. General Comments serve to clarify the nature and content of individual rights and States Parties (those states that have ratified) obligations. The General Comment recognized that the right to health is closely related to and dependent upon the realization of other human rights, including the right to food, housing, work, education, participation, the enjoyment of the benefits of scientific progress and its applications, life, non-discrimination, equality, the prohibition against torture, privacy, access to information, and the freedoms of association, assembly and movement. Further, the Committee interpreted the right to health as an inclusive right extending not only to timely and appropriate health care but also to the underlying determinants of health, such as access to safe and potable water and adequate sanitation, an adequate supply of safe food, nutrition and housing, healthy occupational and environmental conditions, and access to health-related education and information, including on sexual and reproductive health.

The four criteria by which to evaluate the right to health are as follows:

(a) **Availability:** Functioning public health and health-care facilities, goods and services, as well as programmes, have to be available in sufficient quantity.

(b) **Accessibility:** Health facilities, goods and services have to be accessible to everyone with out discrimination, within the jurisdiction of the State party. Accessibility has four overlapping dimensions.

- Non-discrimination;
- Physical accessibility;
- Economic accessibility (affordability);
- Information accessibility

(c) **Acceptability:** All health facilities, goods and services must be respectful of medical ethics and culturally appropriate, sensitive to gender and life-cycle requirements, as well as being designed to respect confidentiality and improve the health status of those concerned.

(d) **Quality:** Health facilities, goods and services must be scientifically and medically appropriate and of good quality.

THE PRINCIPLE OF FREEDOM FROM DISCRIMINATION RELATE TO HEALTH?

Discrimination manifests itself in a complex variety of ways, which may directly or indirectly impact upon health. For example, the Declaration on the Elimination of Violence against Women recognizes the link between men and women.

Vulnerable and marginalized groups in societies tend to bear an undue proportion of health problems. Overt or implicit discrimination violates a fundamental human rights principle and other lies at the root of poor health status. In practice, discrimination can manifest itself in inadequately targeted health programmes and restricted access to health services. The prohibition of discrimination does not mean that differences should not be acknowledged, only that different treatment and the failure to treat equal cases equally must be based on objective and reasonable criteria intended to rectify imbalances within a society.

In relation to health and health-care the grounds for non-discrimination have evolved and can now be summarized as proscribing "any discrimination in access to health care and the underlying determinants of health, as well as to means and entitlements for their procurement, on the grounds of race, colour, sex, language, religion, political or other opinion, national or social, origin, property, birth, physical or mental disability, health status (including HIV/AIDS), sexual orientation, civil, political, social or other status, which has the intention or effect of nullifying or impairing the equal enjoyment or exercise of the right to health.."

RIGHTS-BASED APPROACH TO HEALTH

A rights-based approach to health refers to the processes of:

- Using human rights as a framework for health development.
- Assessing and addressing the human rights implications of any health policy, programme or legislation.
- Making human rights an integral dimension of the design, implementation, monitoring and evaluation of health-related policies and programmes in all spheres, including political, economic and social.

Substantive elements to apply, within these processes, could be as follows:

- Safeguarding human dignity.
- Paying attention to those population groups considered most vulnerable in society. In other words, recognizing and acting upon the characteristics of those affected by health policies, programmes and strategies, children (girls and boys), adolescents, women, and men; indigenous and tribal populations; national, ethnic, religious and linguistic minorities, internally displaced persons; refugees; immigrants and migrants; the elderly; persons with disabilities; prisoners; economically disadvantaged or otherwise marginalized and/or vulnerable groups.
- Ensuring health systems are made accessible to all, especially the most vulnerable or marginalized sections of the population, in law and in fact, without discrimination on any of the prohibited grounds.
- Using a gender perspective, recognizing that both biological and socio-cultural factors play a significant role in influencing the health of men and women, and that policies and programmes must consciously set out to address these differences.
- Ensuring equality and freedom from discrimination, advertent or inadvertent, in the way health programmes are designed or implemented.
- Disaggregating health data to detect underlying discrimination.
- Ensuring free, meaningful, and effective participation of beneficiaries of health development policies or programmes in decision-making processes which affect them.
- Promoting and protecting the right to education and the right to seek, receive and impart information and ideas concerning health issues. However, the right to information should not impair the right to privacy, which means that personal health data should be treated with confidentiality.

- Only limiting the exercise or enjoyment of a right by a health policy or programme as a last resort, and only considering this legitimate if each of the provisions reflected in the Siracusa principles is met.
- Juxtaposing the human rights implications of any health legislation, policy or programme with the desired public health objectives and ensuring the optimal balance between good public health outcomes and the promotion and protection of human rights.
- Making explicit linkages to international human rights norms and standards to highlight how human rights apply and relate to a health policy, programme or legislation.
- Making the attainment of the right to the highest attainable standard of health the explicit ultimate aim of activities, which have as their objective the enhancement of health.
- Articulating the concrete government obligations to respect, protect and fulfils human rights.
- Identifying benchmarks and indicators to ensure monitoring of the progressive realization of rights in the field of health.
- Increasing transparency in, and accountability for, health as a key consideration at all stages of programme development.
- Incorporating safeguards to protect against majoritarian threats upon minorities migrants and other domestically unpopular groups, in order to address power imbalances. For example, by incorporating redress mechanisms in case of impingements on health-related rights.

CONCLUSION

Human rights provide a standard against which to evaluate existing health policies and programmes, including highlighting the differential treatment of individual groups of people in, for example, manifestations, frequency and severity of disease, and governmental responses to it. Human rights norms and standards also form a strong basis for health systems to prioritize the health needs of vulnerable and marginalized population groups. Human rights moves beyond averages and focuses attention on those population groups in society which are considered most vulnerable (e.g. indigenous and tribal population; refugees and migrants, ethnic, religious, national and racial monitories), as well as putting forward specific human rights which may help guide health policy, programming, and health system processes (e.g. the right of those potentially affected by health policies, strategies and standards to participate in the process in which decisions affecting their health are made).

REFERENCES

Basu, S. K. (ed.) (1994), *Tribal Health in India.* New Delhi: Manak Publishers.

Caldwell, John C. and Santow Gigi (eds.) (1991), Selected Readings in the Cultural, Social and Behavioural Determinants of Health. *Health Transition Series* No. 1, The Australian National Univeristy.

Kalla, A. K. and P. C. Joshi (ed.) (2004), *Tribal Health and Medicine.* New Delhi: Concept Publishing Company.

Myrdal, G. (1952), *Economic Aspect of Health.* Chronicle of World Health Organization, 6.

National Human Rights Commission (2001), *Regional Consultation on Public Health & Human Rights: Report & Recommendations,* New Delhi.

R. M. R. C. (1996), *Glimpses of Tribal Health,* Jabalpur: R. M. R. C.

Thomas, Jhon K. (ed.) (2005), *Human Rights of Tribals,* Delhi: Isha Books.

Ministry of Health and Family Welfare (2005), *National Rural Health Mission: Meeting People's Health Needs in Rural Areas.* New Delhi, Ministry of Health and Family Welfare, Government of India.

Ministry of Health and Family Welfare Government of India (2005), *Report of the National Commission on Macroeconomics and Health* Ministry of Health and Family Welfare Government of India.

UNFPA, 2005, *The State Of World Population 2005.* UNFPA, 2005.

Verma, Justice J. S. (2002), *Human Rights Redefined: The New Universe of Human Rights. Journal of the NHRC,* Vol. 1, 2002, 1-17.

Human Rights-Global Refugee Trends

S. Sri Krishna* & S. Anil Kumar**

One of the biggest political and human tragedies of the Twentieth century has arisen in the shape of more than fifty million refugees and displaced persons in the world today. This century is referred to by many as the century of the uprooted and themoneless men. It has marked by a seemingly unending number of mass fights of people fleeing their native lands, seeking a new life in foreign countries. Human rights violations are a major factor in causing the flight of refugees as well as an obstacle to their safe and voluntary return home. The refugee problem today is a central issue of hot discussion in all international forums. The impact of this problem is increasingly becoming more pronounced. The last five years have witnessed some significant changes in the scale, scope and complexity of the global refugee question. During that period, millions of people have been forced to abandon their homes as a result of political terror, armed conflict and social violence. And, recent experience in the Balkans, Central Africa and parts of the former Soviet Union has demonstrated Governments and humanitarian organizations a like are finding it increasingly difficult to cope with the multiple demands generated by these emergencies. There are few areas of international law of such current importance where the

* Professor and Head, Department of Political Science & Public Administration, Sri Venkateswara University, Tirupati-517 502 (A.P.), INDIA.

** Lecturer, Department of Political Science, S.V. Arts College, Tirupati-517 502, (A.P.), INDIA.

law and institutions are so undeveloped and where the enormous pressures for growth are producing developments at such speed.

Coming to Indian scene one may see that India is one of the few countries in the world which has experienced refuge situations on a gigantic scale during last five decades. It has given humanitarian assistance and protection to millions of refugees who come from its neighboring countries, namely, from Tibet, Bangladesh, Pakistan, Sri Lanka and Afghanistan. Recently, it has also granted political asylum to hundreds of refugees from Myanmar. But, it is important to note that India has not yet ratified the 1951 United Nations Convention on the Status of refugees, and also its protocol of 1967, which are only principal instruments of the present international refugee law. India has handles the issues at the political and administrative levels. Of course, it is very crystal clear from the experience that India has nobly adhered to the international standards of protection of refugees as its humanitarian obligation. But still there remain some unresolved legal questions as to the determination of the refugee status, such as, to whom India should grant asylum or what would be the merits it should take into consideration while granting asylum to refugees. Moreover, form the past experience it is found that for a solution, India has always followed the policy of bilateral negotiation with the country of origin and as a result has not allowed any foreign agency including the UNHCR to interfere into the problem. Recently, a lot of allegations have been made by various national human rights organizations against the Indian government in their policy of repatriation and humanitarian assistance.

By the end of 2004, the global number of refugees reached an estimated 9.2 million persons. This constitutes a net decrease of approximately 356,000 refugees (-4%) since the beginning of 2004, when 9.6 million refugees were recorded.

About half (54%) of all refugees benefit from UNHCR assistance programmes. The number of refugees directly assisted through UNHCR fell by 175,000 persons (-3%) to 5.0 million refugees by the end of the year.

This is the fourth consecutive year in which the global refugee population has dropped, although not as sharp as in the two previous years. Over the fourth-year period, the global refugee population has fallen by 24 per cent Decreases in the refugee population are often the result of refugees having access to durable solutions, in particular voluntary repatriation.

In regional terms, Southern Africa recorded the largest reduction in the refugee population during 2004 (-20%), followed by West Africa (-12%) (See box below).

Refugee Population by UNHCR Bureau, 2004

UNHCR Bureau	*Begin 2004*	*End 2004*	*Annual Change*
-Central Africa & Great Lakes	1,257,900	1,267,700	0.8%
-East and Horn of Africa	768,100	770,500	0.3%
-Southern Africa	306,200	245,100	-20.0%
-West Africa	531,200	465,100	-12.4%
Total Africa*	2,863,400	2,748,400	-4.0%
CASWANAME**	2,827,300	2,735,200	-3.3%
Americas	623,900	598,400	-4.1%
Asia and Pacific	823,600	836,700	1.6%
Europe	2,454,800	2,317,800	-5.6%
Total	9,593,000	9,236,500	-3.7%

*Excluding North Africa

** Central Asia, South West Asia, North Africa and Middle East.

Reductions in the refugee population were also reported in Europe (-6%), the Americas (-4%) CASWANAME (Central Asia, South-West Asia, North Africa and Middle East) (-3%). A few regions recorded increases, including Asia and Pacific (+2%), Central Africa and the great lakes region (+1%), and East and Horn of Africa (-0.3%).

Africa and CASWANAME each hosted almost 30 per cent of the global refugee population at the end of 2004. Europe hosted 25 per cent of all refugees, followed by Asia and the pacific (9%), and the Americas (7%).

Most beneficiaries of UNHCR programmes are located in developing countries. Almost 90 per cent are living in countries covered by the UNHCR Bureau for CASWANAME (47%) and Africa (40%).

In 2004, the Islamic Republic of Iran became the main asylum country, accounting for 11 per cent of all refugees under UNHCR's mandate. The increase is mainly explained by a revision of the refugee figures in the country following a registration exercise undertaken during 2003. Following the repatriation of some 424,000 Afghan refugees, Pakistan dropped from being the main country of asylum at begin-2004 to the second largest by end-2004 (-15%). Germany stayed as the third largest asylum country of 2004. The united Republic of Tanzania and the USA (UNHCR estimate) remain as the fourth and fifth largest asylum countries despite experiencing decreases of seven per cent each during 2004. Chad saw a major increase of 78 per cent in the number of refugees during 2004 making it the ninth largest asylum country in the world (18th at begin-2004) (see box below).

Afghanistan continues to be by far the largest country of origin of refugees under UNHCR care. By the end of 2004, 2.1 million Afghan refugees were reported by 78 asylum countries, constituting 23 per cent of the global refugee population. Despite continued repatriation, the number of Afghan Refugees dropped by only two per cent during the year.

Main Countries of Asylum, 2004

Country of asylum	*Begin 2004*	*End 2004*	*Annual Change*
Islamic Rep. of Iran	984,900	1,046,000	6.2%
Pakistan	1,124,300	960,600	-14.6%
Germany	960,400	876,622	-8.7%
Tanzania	649,800	602,100	-7.3%
United States[2]	452,500	420,900	-7.0%
China	299,400	299,400	0%
United Kingdom[2]	276,500	289,100	4.6%
Serbia and Montenegro	291,400	276,700	-5.0%
Chad	146,400	259,900	77.5%
Uganda	230,900	250,500	8.5%

* UNHCR estimate.

** UNHCR estimate based on recent arrivals.

Other major refugee origins experiencing important decreases during 2004 were Burundi (-9%) and Iraq (-15%). The strong fall in the Burundian refugee population reflects the repatriation of refugees from the United Republic of Tanzania (89,000) (see table below):

Main Origin of Refugees, 2004

Origin	*Begin 2004*	*End 2004*	*Annual Change*
Afghanistan	2,136,000	2,084,900	-2.4%
Sudan	606,200	730,600	20.5%
Burundi	531,700	485,800	-8.6%
DR Congo	451,500	462,200	2.4%
Somalia	402,300	389,300	-3.2%
Palestinians*	350,600	350,600	0%
Vietnam	363,200	349,800	-3.7%
Liberia	353,100	335,500	-5.0%
Iraq	368,600	311,800	-15.4%
Serbia and Montenegro	296,600	250,600	-15.5%

* Under UNHCR mandate, only..

Significant decreases in the refugee population, often as a result of durable solutions, were also recorded for refugees from Angola (-101,000) Bosnia and Herzegovina (-62,000), Iraq (-51,000), Serbia and Montenegro (-33,000), and Liberia (-18,000).

However, some refugee nationalities recorded an increase in the population during 2004. The number of Sudanese refugees increased by almost population during 2004. The number of Sudanese refugees increased by almost 125,000 persons (+21%) due to mass outflows, mainly to Chad. The number of refugees from the Russian Federation increased by 11,000 (+12%) while the number of Indonesian and Colombian refugees increased by more than 11,000 (+72%) and 9,000 (25%) respectively.

REFUGEE ARRIVALS

During 2004, some 232,000 prima facie refugee arrivals were reported, creating new refugee emergencies in various asylum countries. The level of new outflows in 2004 was 20 per cent lower than in 2003 when 290,000 refugees fled their country en masse.

Eleven asylum countries reported the arrival of more than 1,000 prima facie refugees during 2004, including Chad (131,000), Burundi (20,700), Yemen (16,600), Uganda (15,500), Rwanda (14,100), the Syria Arab republic (12,000) and Liberia (5,500).

There were four countries of origin which produced more than 10,000 prima facie refugees in 2004. Sudan (147,000), the Democratic Republic of the Congo (38,100), Somalia (19,100) and Iraq (12,000).

VOLUNTARY REPATRIATION

Based on reports from countries of asylum (departure) and origin(arrival), it is estimated that some 1.5 million refugees repatriated voluntarily to their country of origin during 2004. In all, there were a total of 27 voluntary repatriation movements involving more than 1,000 refugees.

The main countries of origin to which refugees returned during 2004 including Afghanistan (940,000), Iraq (194,000), Burundi (90,000), Angola (90,000), Liberia (57,000), Sierra Leone (26,300), Somalia (18,000), Rwanda (14,000), the Democratic Republic of the Congo (13,800) , and Sri Lanka (10,000).

The past three years saw an almost unprecedented level of voluntary repatriation, mainly due to the return of more than 3.5 million Afghans from Pakistan and the Islamic Republic of Iran. In total, more than five million refugees were able to return home.

RESETTLEMENT

In 2004, almost 30,000 refugees were resettled from their previous asylum countries with UNHCR assistance. The main nationalities benefiting from UNHCR facilitated resettlement were refugees from Liberia (5,610), Sudan (5,050), Somalia (4,870), Afghanistan (2,710), the Islamic Republic of Iran

(2,190), Myanmar (1,900), Ethiopia (1,490) and the Democratic Republic of the Conngo (1,290).

Some 68 UNHCR country offices were engaged in facilitating resettlement departures during 2004. The largest number of refugees resettled with UNHCR assistance departed from Kenya (5,640), Cote d'lvoire (4,480), Egypt (4,110), Turkey (2,290), Thailand (1,580) in addition some 9,100 others of concern to UNHCR were resettled with UNHCR-assistance, the Islamic Republic of Iran (830), the United Republic of Tanzania (810), Lebanon (710), Pakistan (640), the Russian Federation (590), and Ethiopia (590).

In 2004, 15 countries received refugees resettled under UNHCR-auspices. The main countries which resettled refugees through UNHCR were USA (63%), Australia (19%), Canada (13%), Sweden (2%), Norway (1%), Finland (1%), and Denmark (1%).

Immigration countries resettle refugees through UNHCR as well as bilaterally. Taking into account both, the US admitted the largest number of resettled refugees (52,900 during US Fiscal Year), followed by Australia (16,000) and Canada (10,500).

LOCAL INTEGRATION

In many countries, refugees have the opportunity to integrate locally because the host country has provided them with access to land or the labour market. In other countries, refugees remain confined to camps where they depend on assistance from the international community. Using UNHCR beneficiary statistics, it is possible to determine the degree to which refugees depends on the international community for their survival. Industrialized countries, where assistance is generally provided by the host country, are not included in this analysis.

By the end of 2004, 71 percent of the 6.5 million refugees hosted by developing countries have access to assistance provided by or through UNHCR. The proportion of refugees benefiting from international assistance varies greatly, reflecting the different opportunities provided to refugees by the host country for local integration and self-reliance. Major asylum countries where less than 75 per cent of the refugee population depends on international aid include the United Republic of Tanzania (67%), Guinea (65%), Zambia (54%), Sudan (49%), Armenia (21%), the Democratic Republic of the Congo (16%), India (7%), and China (4%).

Naturalization, the final and crucial step towards obtaining the full protection of the host country, is not available to refugees in all asylum countries. Moreover, the provision of citizenship to refugees is under-reported. During 2004, UNHCR was informed about significant numbers of refugees being granted citizenship by the host country in the Russian Federation (8,400), Armenia (4,150), Mexico (1,430), Kyrgyzstan (1,060), Ukraine (250), and Belize (130).

LEGAL STATUS

It is estimated that 41 per cent of the refugee population under UNHCR care has been granted protection under the 1951 Convention and /or its 1967 protocol. An additional 18 per cent of the refugees are recognized under the 1969 OAU Convention; where as 12 per cent have been granted UNHCR mandate status. The legal status of more than a quarter (29%) of the refugees is unclear.

The majority of the world's refugees (64%) have been granted refugees status on a group or prima facie basis, whereas almost one third (30%) have been granted refugee status following individual determination.

A large majority of refugees in Africa (86%), CASWANAME (87%) and Asia and Pacific (72%) are prima facie refugees, which contrasts starkly with Europe (24) and the Americas (1%), where most refugees have been granted refugee status following individual screening. These regional differences in recognition are explained in large part by the nature of the refugee situation (mass displacement versus individual asylum-seekers) as well as by the level of economic development (individual refugee status determination is resource intensive).

GENDER AND AGE

About half of the world's refugees are female (49%). The proportion of female refugees varies greatly, depending on the nature of the refugee situation, the region of asylum, age, etc. For instance, in countries with mass refugee situation, the proportion of female refugees tends to be around 50 per cent. The percentage of females among asylum-seekers is significantly lower. Women are over-represented in the older age category (60 and over), reflecting the higher life expectancy of women in general.

Some 47 per cent of the persons of concern to UNHCR are children under the age of 18, whereas 13 per cent are under the age of five. Half of the refugees (47%) are aged between 18 and 59, whereas six per cent are 60 years old or more. Considering that most demographic data are available on more.

ASYLUM-SEEKERS

During 2004, a total number of 676,000 first instance or appeal applications for asylum or refugee status were submitted to governments or UNHCR officers in 143 countries. The number of applications during 2004, decreased by 19 per cent compared to 2003 were 830,300 applications were lodged globally, most claims were registered in Europe (444,000), followed by the Americas (84,000) Africa (82,000), Asia and the Pacific (35,000) and CASWANAME (31,000).

Countries receiving the largest number of new asylum claims during 2004 were France (58,500), the United Kingdom *(40,200), Germany (35,000), the United States (27,900), South Africa (32,600), Canada (25,800), Sweden (23,100) and Australia (24,600).

The Category of asylum-seekers in the total population of concern to UNHCR consists of those asylum-seekers whose claim has not yet been decide or who are otherwise registered as asylum seekers. The number of undecided asylum cases, both at the first instance and on appeal, decreased by 16 per cent to reach 839,000 by the end of the year. If the number of asylum applications is stable or increasing, a fall in the backlog of asylum cases generally indicates that asylum procedures have become more efficient. In a situation where the number of applications is going down, the explanation of decrease in the backlog is more ambiguous.

At the end of 2004, the largest of undecided cases at the first instance and on appeal was reported by the United States (263, 700), South Africa (115,200). Germany (86,200), Austria (38,300), the Netherlands (28,500), Sweden (28,000), and Canada (27,200). Many countries were able to reduce the number of undecided cases during 2004 United States (-88,200), Germany (-42,000), the Netherlands (-16,000), and United Kingdom and Canada down some 14,000 each. Increases in the backlog were reported by South Africa (+31,200), Cyprus (+4,900), and Australia (+4,700).

OTHER OF CONCERN TO UNHCR

The total number of others of concern to UNHCR (internally) displaced or IDPs, returned IDPs, stateless, etc.) increased from 5.3 million at the end of 2003 to 7.6 million by the end of 2004 (+43%). This increase primarily reflects the revised Government IDP figure in Colombia as well as the newly reported IDPs of concern to UNHCR in Sudan (660,000). Furthermore, increased reporting on stateless persons has been included for various countries which make a direct comparison difficult.

Excluding the Colombian IDP figures, the number of IDPs of concern to UNHCR increased by 489,000 persons (+10%) during 2004.With the exception of Colombia (+240,000) and Sudan which reported IDPs for the first time during 2004, all other IDP situations of concern to UNHCR decreased in the number of persons affected. This includes IDPs in Sri Lanka (-33,700), the Russian Federation (-*33,400), Liberia (-33,100), Afghanistan (-24,700), Georgia (-23,100), and Bosnia and Herzegovina (-17,000). The IDP situation in Burundi was no longer reported by the UNHCR office.

A number of IDP situations, however, appear to be protracted with few durable solutions being achieved in 2004. This includes the situation in Colombia (2 millions), Azerbaijan (579,000), and Serbia and Montenegro (248,000).

STATELESS PERSONS

In addition to refugees, UNCHR has been tasked by the United Nations General Assembly through various resolutions to contribute to the reduction of statelessness and further protect stateless persons. In particular, UNHCR has been asked by the United Nations General Assembly to regularly inform the international community on the magnitude of the problem of statelessness.

In March 2004, UNHCR published an analysis of the replies made by 74 states to a questionnaire on the steps taken by States to reduce statelessness and to meet the protection needs of stateless persons. One finding of the survey is that many States referred to the difficulty of identifying stateless persons. As of 2004, UNHCR is further reinforcing its collection of statistics relating to stateless persons by devoting a special table to these populations (Table 14a). Although UNHCR is not in a position to provide reliable statistics on the total number of stateless persons, it has indicated countries with confirmed individuals and groups of stateless persons but where the numbers are not available. Stateless persons reported in the category other of concern to UNHCR only includes persons who are not already included in the other categories of concern to UNHCR (e.g. refugees, asylum seekers, IDPs).

UNHCR is aware of 42 countries with stateless persons in this category by the end of 2004. For the 30 countries where date was available as per end 2004, the total number of stateless persons was estimated to be 1.5 million.

Human Rights and Refugee Law: A Study of Indian Approach Towards Tibetans

ANUPAM AHLUWALIA*

A refugee is itself a product of human rights violation and if subsequently he is not given the required attention and protection it will be a further violation of his human rights. Refugees are result of mass movement of people suppressed by opposite regime or result of ethnic or religious discrimination. No person becomes a refugee by choice. It is the circumstances in his home land which force him to take shelter in some other country. These are the people who seek asylum in the other countries but deep in their hearts lies a will and wish to go back home.

From decades the issue of refugee law has been a matter of concern but unfortunately refugee law is often treated like a "second cousin,' as many human rights activists remain wary of engagement with refugee advocacy, especially individual claims to refugee status. Human rights lawyer and scholars have viewed refugee law as too embedded in domestic immigration law and institutions. The great innovation of the international human rights movement of the past half-century was to bring human rights "out of the confines of domestic legal systems" and into the realm of international law and institutions[1].

* School of Legal Studies, Guru Nanak Dev University Regional Campus, Ladhewali Jalandhar, Punjab.

Under the Convention relating to the status of Refugees, the responsibility to provide international protection–a surrogate to the ruptured, national protection–is placed on states that are parties to the Convention. Thus, refugee law is implemented by states and, refugee regime seems different from the international human rights regime. For example, there is no regularized monitoring of states, compliance with their obligation to provide surrogate protection, although the United Nations High Commissioner for Refugees (UNHCR) serves an important supervisory function. No refugee-specific, international institutions hear inter-state complaints or individual communications.[2]

It is worth mentioning here that in the past two decade the refugee law has matured a lot. Judicial bodies, including states' highest courts, are revieweing more refugee cases. There is also growing sophistication within some administrative systems[3]. Furthermore, several states' administrative bodies and courts engage in productive dialog with one another: by borrowing, adapting, and building on each other's jurisprudence and instruments such as national guidelines, they are beginning to create a complex and rich body of "transnationalized" international law.[4]

Non-binding norms articulated by the UNHCR influence the standards for protection in both legalized and non-legalized settings. Moreover, a growing number of states (e.g., South Africa and countries in Eastern and Central Europe) are specifically incorporating the Convention into domestic law and developing domestic infrastructures for refugee status determinations.[5]

In many respects, refugee law crosses the threshold justifiability and enforceability past which human rights law has found it difficult to proceed. Refugee law provides an enforceable remedy–available under specific circumstances–for an individual facing human rights abuses. Determinations of refugee status entail conceptualized, practical applications of human rights norms. Increasingly, refugee law is confronting issues on the forefront of the human rights agenda, especially questions of gender and women's rights.

In order to redress the issue of human rights of refugees many instruments have been framed at international level.

MEANING OF REFUGEE

A refugee is a person-seeking asylum in a foreign country in order to escape persecution. Some regional legal instruments further those seeking to escape generalized violence in the definition of a refugee. Those who seek refugee status are sometimes known as asylum seekers and the practice of accepting such refugees is that of offering political asylum. The most common asylum claims to industrialized countries are based upon political and religious grounds.

Refugees are a subgroup of the broader category of displaced persons. They are distinguished from economic migrants who have left their country of origin for economic reasons, and from internally displaced persons who have not crossed an international border. Environmental refugees (people displaced because of environmental problems such as drought) are not included in the definition of "refugee' under international law. Strictly speaking: a refugee is someone who seeks refuge out of fear of other people as opposed to any other motivational cause.[6]

Under international law, refugees are individuals who:

- Live outside their own country of nationality or their own habitual residence due to some fear.
- Are individuals who have a well-founded fear of persecution because of their race, religion, nationality, membership in a particular social group or political opinion, in their home land and
- are unable or unwilling to avail themselves of the protection of that county, or to return there, for fear of persecution.

HUMAN RIGHTS AND THE REFUGEE

Definition of Refugee

A Refuge is a person who takes refuge in a country other than the country of his or her origin owing to genuine fear of persecution on grounds of religion, nationality, association with some social or political group or groups or political opinion.[7]

THE HUMAN RIGHTS AT ISSUE

Human Rights are the rights which a human being acquires irrespective of colour, race, caste, creed or nationality. They are of universal character and civil, political, economic, social and cultural rights belong to all human beings. Every human being is a subject of human rights and so are the refugees and the civil, political, economic, social and cultural rights belonging to all human beings refugees and internally displaced people.

Refugees also enjoy certain human rights specifically linked to their particularly vulnerable status, including the right to seek asylum, to freedom from forcible return, to freedom of movement, to a nationality, and to receive protection and assistance in securing their basic economic, social and cultural rights. The Human Rights that a Refugee is entitled to have and to claim include the following types of rights which are indivisible, interdependent and interrelated.

- Right to life.
- Right to a nationality.
- Right to seek and enjoy asylum from persecution.
- Right not to be forcibly returned to the country he or she is fleeing if such a return would pose a threat to the life, security, or freedom of the refugee.
- Right to freedom to choose residence, freedom of movement, freedom to leave any country, including his or her own, and to return to his or her country.

- Right to freedom from discrimination based on race, colour, sex, language, religion, region, nationality, or any other status.
- Right to identity and travel documents.
- Right to freedom from arbitrary detention, equal protection of the law and equal access to the courts.
- Right to freedom from genocide and "ethnic cleansing.
- Right to protection from torture or ill-treatment.
- Right to protection from economic and sexual exploitation, particularly for refugee women and children.
- Right to an adequate standard of living, including adequate food, shelter and clothing.
- Right to education.
- Right to the highest possible standard of health.
- Right to live in a healthy and safe environment.
- Right to work and to basic labour protections.
- Right to sustainable development.
- Right to peace.

In order to protect the different human rights of these homeless people a concern had been shown at the international level for the past so many decades and it has been the result of this concern only that a number of instruments have been made in order to grant protection to the refugees.

INTERNATIONAL INSTRUMENTS AND THE HUMAN RIGHTS OF THE REFUGEES

There is a large body of instruments at the international level which aim at providing and protecting the human rights of the refugees. The most important among them is **Convention Relating to the Status of Refugees, 1951,**[8] The Convention was approved at a special United Nations conference on 28 July, 1951. It was initially limited to protecting European

Refugees after World War II but 1967 protocol removed the geographical and time limits, expanding the Convention's scope. Denmark was the first state to ratify the treaty (on 4 December, 1952) and there are now 145 signitaries to either or both the Convention and Protocol.

The Convention provides that, "the contracting States shall apply the provisions of this Convention to refugees without discrimination as to race, religion or country of origin.... The ....States shall accord to refugees within their territories treatment at least as favourable as that accorded to their nationals with respects to freedom to practice their religion...As regards housing, the .....States......shall accord to refugees...treatment.....not less favourable than that accorded to aliens generally in the same circumstances..... The...States shall accord to refugees the same treatment as is accorded to nationals with respect to education......the same treatment with respect to public relief and assistance.....the same treatment......in respect of....remuneration, hours of work.....minimum age of work,.......social security..... Each...State shall accord to refugees......the right to choose their place of residence and to move freely within its territory subject to......regulations applicable to aliens generally...... No....State shall expel or return ("refouler") a refugee in any manner whatsoever to the frontiers of territories where his life or freedom would be threatened on account of his race, religion, nationality, membership of a particular social group or political opinion.....The...States shall.....facilitate the assimilation and naturalization of refugees......"[9]

THE UNIVERSAL DECLARATION OF HUMAN RIGHTS, 1940

"No one shall be subject to arbitrary arrest, detention or exile.....Everyone has the right to freedom of movement and residence within the borders of each State.....Everyone has the right to seek and to enjoy in other countries asylum from persecution.....Everyone has the right to a nationality...."[10]

PROTOCOL ADDITIONAL TO THE GENEVA CONVENTIONS OF 12 AUGUST 1949, AND RELATING TO THE PROTECTION OF VICTIMS OF INTERNATIONAL ARMED CONFLICTS

"Persons who, before the beginning of hostilities, were considered as stateless persons or refugees.....shall be protected persons...., in all circumstances and without any adverse distinction."[11]

GENEVA CONVENTION RELATIVE TO THE PROTECTION OF CIVILIAN PERSONS IN TIME OF WAR

"The Detaining Power shall not treat as enemy aliens exclusively on the basis of their nationality....of an enemy State, refugees who do not, in fact, enjoy the protection of any government."[12]

CONVENTION RELATING TO THE STATUS OF STATELESS PERSONS

The States shall accord to stateless persons within their territories treatment at least as favourable as that accorded to nationals with respect to freedom to practice their religion. A stateless persons shall have the same treatment as a national in matters pertaining to access to the courts...;....treatment......not less favourable than that accorded to aliens generally.....as regards...employment...As regard housing,.....treatment.......not less favourable than that accorded to aliens generally......The ....States shall accord to stateless persons the same treatment.....accorded to nationals with respect to elementary education....;.....the same treatment with respect to public relief and assistance....;..the same treatment....in respect of..... remuneration,....hours of work....minimum age of employment...., and the enjoyment of......collective bargaining. Social security (legal provisions in respect of employment injury, occupational diseases, maternity, sickness, disability, old age,....unemployment, family responsibilities....Each...State shall accord to stateless persons.....the right to choose their place of residence and to move freely within its territory....The.....States shall not expel a stateless person lawfully in their territory save on grounds of national security or public order. The expulsion of such a stateless person shall be only......in accordance with due process of law."[13]

CONVENTION ON THE REDUCTION OF STATELESSNESS

A...State shall grant its nationality to a person born in its territory who would otherwise be stateless....; shall grant its nationality to a person, not born in the territory....who would otherwise be stateless, if the nationality of one of his parents......was that of that State....A ......State shall not deprive a person of his nationality if such deprivation would render him stateless.....A...State may not deprive any person or group of persons of their nationality on racial, religious or political ground."[14]

CONVENTION ON THE PREVENTION AND PUNISHMENT OF THE CRIME OF GENOCIDE, 1948[15]

"The....Parties confirm that genocide...is a crime under international law which they undertake to prevent and to punish."

CONVENTION ON THE ELIMINATION OF ALL FORMS OF DISCRIMINATION AGAINST WOMEN, 1979 (CEDAW)

"State Parties shall grant women equal rights with men to acquire, change or retain their nationality....States parties shall grant women equal rights with men with respect to the nationality of their children."[16]

CONVENTION ON THE RIGHTS OF THE CHILD, 1989

The child shall be registered immediately after birth and shall have the right to a name, the right to acquire a nationality....

States Parties shall take appropriate measures to ensure that a child who is seeking refugee status or who is considered a refugee in accordance with applicable international or domestic law and procedure shall weather accompanied or unaccompanied by his or her parents or any other person receive appropriate protection and humanitarian assistance in the enjoyment of applicable rights set forth in the present Convention and in other international human rights or other humanitarian instruments to which the said sates are party....States Parties shall provide as they consider appropriate, cooperation in any efforts by the United Nations and other competent inter governmental organizations or non-governmental organizations cooperating with the United Nations to protect and assist such a child and to trace the parents or other members of the family of any refugee child in order to obtain information necessary for re-unification with his or her family. In cases where no parents or other members of the family can be found, the child shall be accorded the same protection as any other child permanently or temperorally deprived of his or her family environment for any reason as set forth in this convention"[17]

INTERNATIONAL COVENANT ON CIVIL AND POLITICAL RIGHTS, 1966

Each State Party to the present convention undertakes to respect and to ensure to all individuals within its territory.....rights....without distinction of any kind, such as race, colour, sex, language, religion, political or other opinion, national or social origin, property, birth or other status......Everyone lawfully within the territory of a State shall.....have the right to liberty of movement and freedom to choose his residence. Everyone shall be free to leave any country, including his own...No one shall be arbitrarily deprived of the right to enter his own country. An alien lawfully in the territory of a State Party....may be expelled....only......in accordance with law and shall....be allowed to submit the reasons against his expulsion and to have his case reviewed by......the competent authority.......All persons shall be equal before the courts and tribunals….All persons are equal before the law and are entitled any discrimination to the equal protection of the law…."[18]

INTERNATIONAL COVENANT ON ECONOMIC, SOCIAL AND CULTURAL RIGHTS, 1966

The States Parties….recognize the right of everyone to an adequate standard of living for himself and his family, including adequate food, clothing and housing…;….recognized the right of everyone to the…..highest attainable standard of physical and mental health….; the right of everyone to education……Primary education shall be compulsory and available free to all….[19]

TIBETAN REFUGEES IN INDIA

By virtue of art 51 (c) of the Constitution of India shall endeavor to foster respect of international law and treaty obligations in the dealings of organizing people with one another. Thus India is also under an obligation to provide protection to the refugees and since its independence India has beep providing protection to refugees coming from Bangladesh, Afghanistan, Nepal and Tibet.

The incoming of Tibetan refugees started in mass in March 1959 after the Chinese suppression of Dalai Lama the religious, spiritual and political leader of Tibetans. Most of Tibetans who have crossed to India since than have traveled on foot across the difficult and snowy journey through the rough Himalayan ranges. Though the Chinese side of the border was sealed in the year 1960, but till day the escape of Tibetan refugees in India is continuing. More than 40 years of the exodus from Tibet began the number of Tibetan refugees in India is more than 100,000 in India now[20]. These refugees were first accommodated in transit camps at Missarami in Assam and Buxa in West Bengal. It is noteworthy here that till that time international agencies like UNHCR were not involved. The 1962 Sino–Indian border was marked as turning point. That was the first time when a request was sent at international level by the Indian authorities to help the refugees and it was then only that the UNHRC played a role by giving assistance to Tibetan refugees in the year 1964. Although it did not established its formal presence in the Indian capital till 1969.

Since then Indian authorities have worked for the welfare of these refugees. They have been allotted lands for settlement. Registered refugees have been given ration cards, identity papers, travel documents, etc. although they are considered foreigners[21]. They have been given the basic rights of citizens but are not allowed to contest or vote in Indian elections. Those who have married Indian nationals may apply for the citizenship and for those who are now born in the territory of India automatically acquire citizenship by birth.

Indian Government has tried to do the best for the shelter and rehabilitation of these refugees at the same time the government has tried to preserve the separate identity of Tibetans both at cultural level as well at political and administrative levels. Tibetan government is exile has been established at Dharamshala in Himachal Pradesh.

More than a period of four decades of the initial flight of the group of these people as refugees the permanent solution of this problem is still not visible but the fact remains that in spite of the positive changes in their lives still most of the Tibetans live on a hope to return back home one day.

SUGGESTIONS

1 Asylum seekers need access to full and fair asylum procedures. They are often prevented from having their refugee claims heard because of legal and physical restrictions and procedural obstacles. The procedure should be made simple and approachable to the asylum seekers and they should be provided with human rights documentation and analysis in support of their claims, so that they can fight for their rights effectively.

2. Efforts should be made to influence refugee policy internationally by promoting international responsibility

sharing, humane levels of international humanitarian assistance to refugees and internally displaced persons, and seeking safe conditions of asylum and durable solutions for refugees.

3. Special treatment should be given to the women and children refugees.
4. Efforts should be made to implement the provisions of the treaties to the fullest so that what all has been intended at national and international level is practically applied as well.

NOTES AND REFERENCES

1. Louis B. Sohn, The Human Rights Movement: From Roosevel's Four Freedoms to the Interdependence of Peace, Development and Human Rights 4 (1995) (lecturer published by Harvard Law School Human Rights Program). *See also* Steiner & Alston, *supra* note 9, at vi.
2. Walter Kalink however, also notes the extensive, positive impact of the UNHCR on the protection of asylum seekers and favourably contrasts the Refugee Convention with other human rights treaties in this regard, *See* Kalin, Supervising the 1951 Convention on the Status of Refugee: Article 35 and Beyond, Part I (paper submitted for expert roundtables under the "second track" of the UNHCR Global Consultations on International Refugee Protection) (on file with author). "Unlike the [Refugee] Convention and 1967 Protocol, these treaties do not have an operational agency with a world-wide presence and 'protection officers' in a large number of countries working to ensure that these instruments are implemented." *Id.* at 1.1.
3. This is true in the United States, where the Board of Immigration appeals recently has been issuing a greater number of reasoned decisions, which provide better guidance for decision-makers. *See, e.g., In re* S-P, 21 I. & N. Dec. 486 (U.S. BIA 1996) (relying extensively on State Department human rights reports and providing criteria for identifying a persecutory motive); *In re* H, 21 I. & N.Dec. 337 (U.S. BIA 1996) (explaining the meaning of the past persecution standard, and specifying the burdens of proof in such cases); *see also* Carolyn P. Blum, *License to Kill: Asylum Law and the Principle of Legitimate Governmental*

Authority to 'Investigate Its Enemies," 28 Willamette L. Rev. 719 (1992) (discussing some problems in earlier jurisprudence). The New Zealand Refugee Status Appeals Authority has a long-standing, distinguished reputation as a refugee decision-making body. *See* Mark Symes, Caselaw on the Refugee Convention ii (2000) [hereinafter Refugee Caselaw].

4. One of the best examples of such transnationalization is the interpretation of "particular social group" to include sex and gender. *See* Deborah Anker, *Refugee Status and Violence Against Women in the 'Domestic Sphere,'* 15 Geo. Immigr. L.J. 391, 391-92 (2001).
5. *See* 1998 Refugees Act 130 (GG6779) (S.Afr). In May 2001, the Hungarian Parliament passed four pieces of legislation affecting the regulation of asylum as well as migration matters. *See http://www.helsinki.hu/eng/indexm.html* (describing amendments to the 1998 Act on Asylum, including changes to determination procedures).
6. *www.freedictionary.com*
7. *Muntaquim Khawaja Abdul, (2004) Protection of Human Rights,* Ist Edn, Law Publishers (India) Pvt. Ltd, p. 297.
8. Came into force on 22nd April, 1954.
9. Articles 3, 4, 21, 22, 23, 24, 26, 33 and 34.
10. Articles 9, 13, 14 and 15.
11. Article 73.
12. Article 44.
13. Articles 4, 16, 17, 21, 22, 23, 24, 26, 31.
14. Articles 1, 4, 8, and 9.
15. Article 1.
16. Article 9.
17. Articles 7 and 22.
18. Articles 2, 12, 13, 14 and 26.
19. Articles 11, 12 and 13.
20. The Tibetan Refugee Community in India.
21. Under the Foreigners Act, 1946.

Human Rights of Refugees: An Appraisal

R. D. Vijayasekhar* & K. Srinivasa Rao**

REFUGEE means a person in exile. They are the persons who leave their States in which they have permanent residence only to escape persecution or military action. Refugees are vulnerable groups whose human rights are violated. According to Article 1 of the Convention Relating to the Status of Refugees of 1951, refugee means any person who owing to well founded fear of being persecuted for reasons of race, religion, nationality, membership of a particular social group or political opinion, is outside the country of his nationality and is unable, or owing to such fear, is unwilling to avail himself of the protection of that country, or who not having a nationality and being outside the country of his former habitual residence as a result of such events, is unable or, owing to such fear, is unwilling to return to it. The Refugee Convention 1951 is also known as Geneva Contention of 1951. This convention aimed at protection of the refugees. Article 1 of the African Convention provides that the term refugees shall also apply to every person who, owing to external aggression, occupation, foreign domination or events seriously disturbing public order in either part of or the whole of his country of origin or nationality, is compelled to leave his place of habitual residence in order to seek refuge in another place outside his country of origin. The Convention on Governing

* Assistant Professor, Dr. Ambedkar Law College, Tirupati, Andhra Pradesh.

** Assistant Professor, Department of Human Rights and Social Development, SV University, Tirupati, AP.

the Specified Aspects of Refuge problems in Africa, the term Refugee shall apply on that every person, who due to foreign attack or aggression, or occupation, or in one's own original country or a part of it, due to the incidents of occurrences disturbing the public affairs of that country or part of it, are compelled to leave their homeland and to ask for shelter and nationality of another country or another part of the same country. Genocide acts of a certain country or community or organization are the main causes of creating the problem of refugees. Genocide is the heniest form of war crimes for which the German leaders were prosecuted in Nuremburg Trial. But the same countries have been taming the terrorist countries as their hounds to safeguard their interests and to cow down their victims to follow them in the name of world peace and prosperity. That is an anomalous state of affairs. Thus refugee is a person or persons who have left their homeland or place of residence due to unavoidable and oppressive circumstances and are not prepared now to go back to their homeland or original place of residence.

Refugees are a subgroup of the broader category of displaced persons. They are distinguished from economic migrants who have left their country of origin for economic reasons, and from internally displaced persons who have not crossed an international border. Environmental refugees (people displaced because of environmental problems such as drought) are not included in the definition of "refugee" under international law. Strictly speaking a refugee is someone who seeks refuge in a foreign country out of fear of other people as opposed to any other motivational cause. The practical determination of whether a person is a refugee or not is most often left to certain government agencies within the host country. This can lead to abuse in a country with a very restrictive official immigration policy; for example, that the country will neither recognize the refugee status of the asylum seekers nor see them as legitimate migrants and treat them as legal aliens. On the other hand, fraudulent requests in an environment of lax enforcement could lead to improper classification as refugee, resulting in the diversion of resources from those with a genuine need. At least in the United States, a significant percentage of asylum/refugee seekers did not meet the international standards of special-needs refugee, for whom resettlement was deemed proper. A claim for asylum may also be made onshore, usually after making an unauthorized arrival. Some governments are relatively tolerant and accepting of onshore asylum claims, other governments will not only refuse such claims, but may actually arrest or detain those who attempt to seek asylum. A small number of governments, such as that of Australia, have a policy of mandatory detention of asylum seekers.

NANSEN PASSPORT

The suitable action under international law in favour of the refugees was not taken seriously till 1920s. However, Dr. Fridtjof Nansend tried to collect world public opinion to create international machinery for the protection and assistance to refugees. The League of National took initiative to establish a High Commission for Russian Refugees and appointed Dr Fridtjof Nansen as the first High Commissioner on August 20, 1921. He devised a travel document which is known as *Nansen passport.* It gave the holder the right to move more freely across and beyond national boundaries. The same has been adopted by more than fifty States. After the demise of Nansen in 1930 the task of protecting he refugees was entrusted to the Nansen International Office for Refugees.

Statistics of refugees: According to United Nations there are about 13 million people who have fled from their homelands after recent wars or other political turmoil. According to Bernand D Sami's statistical report in Africa the total number of refugees are 4,341,480, while in Asia their number is 4,808,624. Refugees in Europe account for 3,166,039 and in Latin America it is 88,430. Refugees in North America number 720,119, while in Australia their number is 74,954. The total number of refugees in the world today is 13,199,646. Generally the nationals leave their country in order to escape persecution or military action. They are known as political refugees. They are not ordinary migrants or economic refugees. The nationals become political refugees due to political persecutions. They alone can be treated as qualified for the status of refugees. The status of refugees can never be confused with the displacement from one area to another within the borders on account of civil disturbances or apprehension of such disturbances.

HUMAN RIGHTS AND REFUGEES

Human Rights are universal, and civil, economic, social and cultural rights belong to all human beings, including refugees and internally displaced people. Refugees also enjoy certain human rights specifically linked to their particularly vulnerable status, including the right to seek asylum, to freedom from forcible return, to freedom of movement, to a nationality, and to receive protection and assistance in securing their basic economic, social and cultural rights. The Human Rights of Refugees include the following indivisible, interdependent and interrelated human rights:

- The human right to seek and enjoy asylum from persecution.
- The human right not to be forcibly returned to the country he or she is fleeing if such a return would pose a threat to the life, security, or freedom of the refugee.
- The human right to freedom of movement.
- The right to freedom to choose his or her residence.
- The right to freedom to leave any country, including his or her own, and to return to his or her country.
- The human right to freedom from discrimination based on race, colour, gender, language, religion, nationality, ethnicity, or any other status.
- The human right to equal protection of the law.
- The right to equal access to the courts, and freedom from arbitrary.

- The right to prolonged detention.
- The human right to a nationality.
- The human right to life.
- The human right to protection from torture or ill-treatment.
- The human right to freedom from genocide and "ethnic cleansing".
- The human right to an adequate standard of living.
- The right to adequate food, shelter and clothing.
- The human right to work and to basic labour protections.
- The human right to the highest possible standard of health.
- The right to access to health care.
- The human right to live in a healthy and safe environment.
- The human right to education.
- The right to free and compulsory elementary education.
- The right to secondary and higher education.
- The right to freedom from all types of discrimination at all levels of education.
- The human right to protection from economic and sexual exploitation, particularly for refugee women and children.
- The human right to participation in decision-making which affects a refugees life, family, and community.
- The human right to sustainable development.
- The human right to peace.

STATUS OF REFUGEES UNDER INTERNATIONAL LAW

Prior to the establishment of United Nations, the League of Nations for the first time appointed a High Commissioner for

Russian Refugees in 1921. The decision relating the appointment of such High Commissioner was taken on 27th June, 1921. Later the High Commissioner was appointed to deals with the following problems of refugees. They are:

- To decide the legal status of refugees.
- To organize their repatriation or their allocation to various countries which might be able to receive them and to find means for work for them and
- To undertake relief work amongst them with the aid of philanthropic societies.

Despite the great efforts made by League of Nations the international law relating to refugee problem could not gain much impetus beyond the rudimentary stage. When the United Nations was established in 1945 it recognized from the outset that the task of caring for refugees was a matter of international concern. Therefore, the General Assembly of the United Nations in the year 1946 had adopted a resolution that laid the foundations for United Nations activities in favour of refugees. It has established the International Refugee Organisation (IRO). It had a mandate to protect those refugee groups that has been recognized by the League of Nations. UNHCR's mandate has gradually been expanded to include protecting and providing humanitarian assistance to what it describes as other persons "of concern", including internally-displaced persons (IDPs) who would fit the legal definition of a refugee under the 1951 Refugee Convention and 1967 Protocol, the 1969 Organization for African Unity Convention, or some other treaty if they left their country, but who presently remain in their country of origin. UNHCR thus has missions in Colombia, Democratic Republic of the Congo, Serbia and Montenegro and Côte d'Ivoire to assist and provide services to IDPs.

The Human Rights International Law: The following Declarations and Convention guarantee the Human Rights of Refugees:

- The Universal Declaration of Human Rights.

- The Convention Relating to the Status of Refugees.
- The Convention Against Torture and other Cruel, Inhuman or Degrading Treatment of Punishment.
- The Geneva Convention Relative to the Protection of Civilian Persons in Time of War.
- The Protocol Additional to the Geneva Conventions of 12 August, 1949 and relating to the Protection of victims of International Armed Conflicts, the convention relating to the Status of Stateless Persons.
- The Convention on the reduction of Statelessness.
- The Convention on the Prevention and Punishment of the Crime of Genocide.
- The International Convenant on Civil and Political Rights.
- The International Convenant on Economic, Social and Cultural Rights.
- The Convention on the Elimination of All Forms of Racial Discrimination.
- The Convention on the Elimination of All Forms of Discrimination Against Women.
- The Convention on the Rights of the Child.

According to the Universal Declaration of Human Rights, Articles 9, 13, 14 and 15 "No one shall be subject to arbitrary arrest, detention or exile.......Everyone has the right to freedom of movement and residence within the borders of each State. Everyone has the right to leave any country, including his own, and to return to his country.....Everyone has the right to seek and to enjoy in other countries asylum from persecution.....Everyone has the right to a nationality......" According to The Convention Relating to the Status of Refugees, Articles 3, 4, 21, 22, 23, 24, 26, 33 and 34" the Contracting States shall apply the provisions of this Convention to refugees without discrimination as to race, religion or country of origin.....The.....States shall accord to refugees within their territories treatment at least as favourable as that accorded to their nationals with respect to freedom to practice their religion…….As regards housing , the……States…..shall accord to refugees…..treatment…..not less favourable than that accorded to aliens generally in the same circumstances….. The …..States shall accord to refugees the same treatment as is accorded to nationals with respect to education….the same treatment with respect to public relief and assistance……the same treatment…..in respect of……..remuneration, hours of work,…..minimum age of work,…..social security…..Each….State shall accord to refugees……the right to choose their place of residence and to move freely within its territory subject to….regulations applicable to aliens generally…….No……State shall expel or return a refugee in any manner whatsoever to the frontiers of territories where his life or freedom would be threatened on account of his race, religion, nationality, membership of a particular social group or political opinion….The……States shall…..facilitate the assimilation and naturalization of refugees…..” According to the Convention Against Torture and Other Cruel, Inhuman, or Degrading Treatment of Punishment, Article 3 “No State Party shall expel, return or extradite a person to another State where there are substantial grounds for believing that he would be in danger of being subjected to torture.” According to the Geneva Convention Relative to the Protection of Civilian Persons in Time of War, Article 44 “the Detaining Power shall not treat as enemy aliens exclusively on the basis of their nationality…..of an enemy State, refugees who do not, in fact, enjoy the protection of any government.” According to the Protocol Additional to the Geneva Conventions of 12 August, 1949 and Relating to the Protection of Victims of International Armed Conflicts, Article 73 “Persons who, before the beginning of hostilities, were considered as stateless persons or refugees…….shall be protected persons….., in all circumstances and without any adverse distinction.”

According to the Convention relating to the Status of Stateless Persons, Articles 4, 16, 17, 21, 22, 23, 24, 26, and 31. “The ….States shall accord to stateless persons within their territories treatment at least as favourable as that accorded to.......nationals with respect to freedom to practice their religion.....A stateless person shall have......the same treatment as a national in matters pertaining to access to the courts.....;....treatment.....not less favourable than that accorded to aliens generally.....as regards...employment...As regards housing.... treatment...not less favourable than that accorded to aliens generally......The.....States shall accord to stateless persons the same treatment.........accorded to nationals with respect to elementary education....;....the same treatment with respect to public relief and assistance....;...the same treatment....in respect of ......remuneration,...hours of work,.....minimum age of employment ..,and the enjoyment of ......collective bargaining; Social security (legal provisions in respect of employment injury, occupational diseases, maternity, sickness, disability, old age,.......unemployment, family responsibilities.....Each.....State shall accord to stateless persons....the right to choose their place of residence and to move freely within its territory..... The.....States shall not expel a stateless person lawfully in their territory save on grounds of national security or public order. The expulsion of such a stateless person shall be only....in accordance with due process of law." According to the Convention on the Reduction of Statelessness, Articles 1, 4, 8, and 9" A....State shall grant its nationality to a person born in its territory who would otherwise be stateless, if the nationality to a person, not born in the territory.....who would otherwise be stateless, if the nationality of one of his parents...... was that of that State.....A......State shall not deprive a person of his nationality if such deprivation would render him stateless.....A...State may not deprive any person or group of persons of their nationality on racial, ethnic, religious or political grounds." According to the Convention on the Prevention and Punishment of the Crime of Genocide, Article 1 "The.....Parties confirm that genocide.....is a crime under international law which they undertake to prevent and to punish." According to the International Covenant on Civil and Political Rights, Articles 2, 12, 13, 14, and 26 "Each State Party......undertakes to respect and to ensure to all individuals within its territory.....rights......without distinction of any kind, such as race, colour, sex, language, religion, political or other opinion, national or social origin, property, birth or other status. ...Everyone lawfully within the territory of a State shall...have the right to liberty of movement and freedom to choose his residence. Everyone shall be free to leave any country, including his own.......No one shall be arbitrarily deprived of the right to enter his own country. An alien lawfully in the territory of a State Party......may be expelled....only...in accordance with law and shall....be allowed to submit the reasons against his expulsion and to have his case reviewed by ...the competent authority......All persons shall be equal before the courts and tribunals...All persons are equal before the law and are entitled without any discrimination to the equal protection of the law..." According to the International Covenant on Economic, Social and Cultural Rights, Articles 11, 12, and 13. "The States Parties....recognize the right of everyone to an adequate standard of living for himself and his family, including adequate food, clothing and housing.....;....recognize the right of everyone to the....highest attainable standard of physical and mental health....; the right of everyone to education....Primary education shall be compulsory and available free to all......"

According to the Convention on the Elimination of All Forms of Racial Discrimination, Articles 2, 5, and 6 "States Parties condemn racial discrimination and undertake to pursue .....a policy of eliminating racial discrimination in all its forms........Each State Party undertakes to engage in no act......of racial discrimination...; Each State Party undertakes to engage in no act....of racial discrimination.....; Each State Party shall prohibit and bring to an end......racial discrimination by any persons, group or organization...States Parties undertake to prohibit and to eliminate racial discrimination in all its forms and to guarantee the right of everyone, without distinction as to race, colour, national or ethnic origin, to equality before the law, notably in the enjoyment of...political rights...civil rights...economic, social and cultural rights...States Parties shall assure....effective protection and remedies......against any acts of racial discrimination....." According to the Convention on the Elimination of All Forms of Discrimination Against Women, Article 9 "States Parties shall grant women equal rights with men to acquire, change or retain their nationality......equal rights with men with respect to the nationality of their children."

According to the Convention on the Rights of the Child, Articles 7 and 22. "The child shall be registered immediately after birth and shall have the right to a name,....a nationality......States Parties shall take appropriate measures to ensure that a child who is seeking refugee status or who is considered a refugee.......shall......receive appropriate protection and humanitarian assistance in the enjoyment of...rights.....States Parties shall provide... cooperation in....effort...to protect and assist such a child and to trace the parents or other members of the family of any refugee child....for reunification with his or her family. In cases where no parents or other members of the family can be found, the child shall be accorded the same protection as any other child.....deprived of his or her family environment....." Bengali Refugees in India in 1971: As a result of the Bangladesh Liberation War, on 27 March 1971, Prime Minister of India, Indira Gandhi, expressed full support of her Government to the Bangladeshi struggle for freedom. The Bangladesh-India border was opened to allow the tortured and panic-stricken Bengalis safe shelter in India. The governments of West Bengal, Bihar, Assam, Meghalaya and Tripura established refugee camps along the border. Exiled Bangladeshi army officers and voluntary workers from India immediately started using these camps for recruitment and training of freedom fighters (members of Mukti Bahini). As the massacres in East Pakistan escalated an estimated 10 million refugees fled to India causing financial hardship and instability in that country.

RIGHTS GUARANTEED UNDER THE REFUGEE CONVENTION 1951

The Convention sets the minimum standards of treatment of refugees, including the basic rights to which they are entitled.

It also establishes the juridical status of refugees and contains provisions on their rights to gainful employment and welfare, on the issue of identity papers and travel documents, on the applicability of fiscal charges, and on their right to transfer their assets to another country where they have been admitted for the purposes of resettlement.

The Convention prohibits the expulsion or forcible return of persons having refugee status. Its article 33 stipulates that "no Contracting State shall expel or return (refouler) a refugee in any manner whatsoever to the frontiers of territories where his life or freedom would be threatened on account of his race, religion, nationality, membership of a particular social group or political opinion". Article 34 concerns the naturalization and assimilation of refugees. Other provisions deal with such rights as access to courts, education, social security, housing and freedom of movement. Let us examine the provisions in detail.

Article 1 Refugee means any person who owing to well founded fear of being persecuted for reasons of race, religion, nationality, membership of a particular social group or political opinion, is outside the country of his nationality and is unable, or owing to such fear, is unwilling to avail himself of the protection of that country, or who not having a nationality and being outside the country of his former habitual residence as a result of such events, is unable or, owing to such fear, is unwilling to return to it.

Article 2 Every refugee has duties towards the country in which he finds himself.

Article 3 No discrimination on the basis of race, religion, or country of origin.

Article 4 Right to freedom to practice their religion and freedom as regards the religious education of their children.

Article 7 Right to equality of treatment.

Article 8 Right to nationality.

Article Right to acquire movable and immovable property.

Article Right to association, non-political and non-profit making associations.

A refugee shall have free access to the Courts of law and shall receive the treatment as a national in matters pertaining to access to the Courts Right to engage in wage earning employment.

Article 18 Right to self employment, the right to engage on his own account in agriculture, industry, handicrafts, and commerce and to establish commercial and industrial companies.

Article 19 Right to practice a liberal profession.

Article 20 Right for rationing system for the general distribution of produces wherever the population is large and food in short supply.

Article 21 Right to housing.

Article 22 Right to elementary education, access to studies, the recognition of foreign school certificates, etc.

Article 23 Right to public relief and assistance wherever it is accorded to the nationals.

Article 24 Right to enjoy the fruits of legislations such as remuneration, hours of work, overtime arrangements, holidays with pay, restriction on home work, minimum age of employment, apprentice ship and training, women's work and the work of young persons and employment of the benefits of collective bargaining. Social security in matters relating to employment, injury, occupational disease, maternity, sickness, disability, old age, death, unemployment, family responsibilities, etc.

Article 26	Right to freedom of movement.
Article 30	Right to transfer the assets which they have brought into its territory to another country where they have been admitted for the purpose of resettlement.
Article 31	Right against imposition of penalties on account of their illegal entry or presence on refugees who comes directly from a territory where their life or freedom was threatened.
Article 32	The receiving country shall not expel a refugee on grounds of national security or public order.
Article 33	The receiving country shall not expel or return a refugee to the frontiers where his life or freedom would be threatened on account of his race, religion, nationality, membership.
Article 34	The Contracting, States shall as far as possible facilitate the assimilation and naturalization of refugees. They shall in particular make every effort to expedite naturalization proceedings and to reduce as far as possible the charges and costs of such proceedings.
Article 35	Co-operation of the national authorities with the United Nations.
Article 36	Information on national legislation.
Article 37	Relation to previous conventions.
Article 38	Settlement of disputes.
Article 39	Signature, ratification and accession.
Article 40	Territorial application clause.
Article 41	Federal clause.
Article 42	Reservations.
Article 43	Entry into force.
Article 44	Denunciation.
Article 46	Article 46. Notifications.

CONCLUSIONS

The problem of refugees continues to challenge the international community. While refugee-receiving States should maintain their condiment to the protection of refugees and encourage tolerance towards diversity, refugee-producing States have the duty to prevent acts that produce mass exoduses of their populations. The world needs to reach an agreement on how best to prevent new flows of refugees. The root causes of these situations should be further studied and rectified. If poverty is the major cause of refugee flows, some solutions could be found in development aid or technical assistance. If human rights violations are the principal causes of mass exoduses, solutions may lie in continuous monitoring by United Nations human rights bodies, condemnation of violations by the international community and the appointment of Special Rapporteurs to study specific situations and to make suggestions. If violent conflicts are the causes of flows, solutions may be found in preventive diplomacy, in the promotion of mediation as the means to conflict resolution and in respect for provisions of humanitarian law. At all times, however, the international community should be prepared to meet demands in cases of emergency. In this respect, the early warning system set up by the United Nations Secretary-General could be of immense value. It could play an important role in predicting which situations are likely to generate large numbers of refugees. A coordinated and system-wide response will always be the most effective way of dealing with emergencies. Another new challenge is posed by the internally displaced, those who are unable to cross borders and reach a territory in which they could receive the protection and assistance which they desperately need. It is estimated that there are over 24 million internally displaced person in the world. The situation of many of them is excruciating, as they are often forced to remain within combat zones are undernourished and have no access to clean water or medical supplies. The internally displaced will perhaps constitute the greatest challenge for the international community in coming years.

REFERENCES

Dr. S. K. Kapoor (2000), *International Law*, Central Law Agency, Allahabad.

External Reference Group on People Smuggling, *External Reference Group on People Smuggling,* Canberra, 1999.

Goodwin-Gill, Guy (1996), *The Refugee in International Law,* Clarenden Press, Oxford.

Jopke, Christian (1999), *Immigration and the Nation State: US, Germany & Great Britain,* OUP, Oxford.

Loescher, Gill, *Refugees and the Asylum Dilemma in the West,* Pennsylvania State Uni Press, Pennsylvania

UNHCR *The State of the World's Refugees: In Search of Solutions,* OUT, Oxford, 1995.

Principle of Non Refoulement and Refugees Under International Perspective

MARUTHI T. R.*

INTRODUCTION

The most difficult problem faced by the international community today is a problem of refugees; in fact it has turn out to be a global issue. Refugees being deprived from their rights are pushed out from their own country carrying untold miseries and a plight of fear in their eye. Often these are the group of people who witness the massive violence against them, at the time of war, famine choate conditions and wide spread displacement generally arises out of ethnic, tribal and religious conflict. International refugee law is articulated primarily to define the status of those who are forced to flee across boundaries in search of safety and security, and to regulate the rights and obligations of states in the provision of protection and assistance for them.

It occupies a set of complex crossing points between humanitarian assistance, state sovereignty, international relations, cultural and legal specificity, migration control, individual or collective human rights, and international criminal law. Every year the world witnesses the migration of certain group-seeking refugee in other country. The natural and human condition in fact have contributed for increase in

* Lecturer in Law, Dos in Law, University of Mysore, Mysore, Karnataka.

migration for about 700, people a day have been forced to leave their own country and takes shelter elsewhere. Millions of people are today forced to flee their homes as a result of conflict, systematic discrimination, or other forms of persecution. The core instruments on which they must rely to secure international protection are the 1951 Convention Relating to the Status of Refugees and its 1967 Protocol.[1] To cote the instance Sri Lankan refugee, refugees from Bangladesh and the refugees from Burma have found a shelter in Indian Territory. 21st Century is fundamentally era of political economical changes in international system which intern resulted in large-scale movement of people. With respect to this, issue calls for attentions are? Whether refugee movement had to do anything with respect to political and security repercussions for both the sending and receiving stages?

Are they the people with absolutely no right? Whether receiving states own on obligation toward them? Whether international community has adopted any reciprocal expression of responsibility toward them if so, what could be the limitation of these obligations? These issues have raised humanitarian concern and have demanded humanitarian responses. Having therefore concluded that we have a customary rule, we must be able to state clearly and in a way that can be practicably applied, what the rule requires. This is where the international community is currently running into problems. Previously, when the refugee numbers were fairly low and situations of mass influx less common,[2] there was less pressure on states to press the limits of the rule. Today, however, with domestic and foreign policy factors forcing states to re-evaluate their asylum laws, the principle of non-refoulement[3] is finding itself being reviewed and in some circumstances, eroded. This paper examines in detail the principle of non-refoulement, which protects refugees from being returned to places where their lives or freedoms could be threatened. It looks in detail at the principle itself, its status at international law and in what circumstances it applies. The paper also considers ways in which the current system could be changed in order to protect the non-refoulement principle, while still catering to the need of states.

ORGANIZED INTERNATIONAL EFFORT FOR PROTECTION OF REFUGEE

Organized international effort for refugees began in 1921 when League of Nations appointed the first High Commission for Refugees. Over the next few year scope and function of assistance programme gradually expanded since 1951 international institution for protection of refugee region composed of United Nation High Commissioner for Refugees and have being doing a commendable jobs, National Government, Non Governmental Organization have developed a response of strategy and permitted some refugee in their country of first asylum and enable the other to settle in 3rd world country. States of refugees are defined under various international instruments right from 1920 to 1951. Refugee law is a dynamic body of law, informed by the broad object and purpose of the 1951 Refugee Convention and its 1967 Protocol, as well as by development in related areas of international law, such as human rights law[4] and international humanitarian law.

These are definitely not the concept of customary international law and the law does not define them, they are invariably subject to several treaties and agreement; contracting states in this way own an obligation of care toward the group of people and hence in their context. The concept of non-refoulement of the refugees has been developed. The achievements of the Convention and UNHCR have been enormous and should be recognized. In the 1951 Convention, the international community enshrines the protection principle and the principle of non-refoulement and created for the first time a functioning system to tackle the protection needs of those who flee persecution. What was designed as a measure to deal with the refugee crisis arising from World War II has proved enduring.

Development of international protection of refugee in turn endowed responsibility between the contracting state not to expel or return a refugee to the frontier territory where his or her life or freedom would be threatened on account of his race, religion and nationality. States have failed to develop a co-operative system of sharing responsibility for fulfilling their obligations under international refugee law, and refugee law does not contain clear provisions identifying the individual State responsible for granting durable protection. Refugees are thereby trapped in a system where States' responsibilities for providing protection are not clearly defined. The attribution to the State of conduct amounting to refoulement is determined by the principles of the law on State responsibility. The international legal responsibility to act in conformity with international obligations wherever they may arise is the overriding consideration.[5] So, the principle of non-refoulement prescribes that non refugee should be returned to a country where he/she is likely to face persecution or torture application of this principle would be inconvenient. Sometime to these contracting states, reference to the scope & application of this principle to certain categories of asylum seeker, exception to its application both on territorial & extra territorial limits can be made.

EVOLUTION OF THE TERM

To look back, no law of a country made any reference to the right of refugee except the Aliens Act 1905 of U.K. the Act stood as a seen of need to protect the persecuted. Section 1 of 1905 made exception to refusal of entry for want of means in respect of there seeking to avoid prosecution or punishment on religious or political ground. Non-refoulement is a principle of customary international law. The principle of non-refoulement of refugees can be regarded as embodied in customary international law on the basis of the general practice of States supported by a strong *opinion juris.* The telling point is that, in the last half-century, no State has expelled or returned a refugee to the frontiers of a country where his life or freedom would be in danger-on account of his race, religion, nationality, membership of a particular social group or political opinion-using the argument that refoulement is permissible under contemporary international law. Prior to the 1930s this principle did not exist at international law. In order to understand the principle it will be useful to look at the circumstances and reasons surrounding its development. During the first half of this century the idea that it was fundamentally wrong to return refugees to places where they would clearly be in danger was mentioned occasionally by states in agreements or statutes, or was evident in the practice of some states.

International practice of the principal in fact begin after the first world war, only in 1933 does the first reference to the principle of non return of refugee under international instrument appears. A prerequisite for individuals to claim their rights is a domestic institutional system through which this can be done, but which refugees have lost. Their basic right to belong to a political community is at stake and must be redressed by the international community.

The term non-refoulement is derived from the word refouller a French term which mean drive back or repel any who fails to breach once defense. Being more or less a term of art covering in particular; when distinguished refoulment from expulsion or deportation later would more be a formal process were by lawfully resident also may be required to leave state, or forcibly removed.

It would hence be right to say that only in mid 19th century the concept of asylum and the principle of non-extradition of political offender began. In 1940 UN expressly accepted that refugee or displaced person, who have valid objection to return to their country of origin should not be compelled to do so. International institution established in the same year was charged with the responsibility of resolving the problem of displacement left out due to war; in the same year around 1,620,000 refugees were assisted with resettlement from Eastern Europe to Western Countries.

The matter of refugees right which was having only abstract aspect of identity got a real status of international concern when ECOSOC one of the Wing of UN undertook the task of preparing a revised & consolidated Convention.

1949 being a landmark year were discussion was taken by the member country, a desirable course to draft the text of such Convention. In 1950 Ad hoc Committee under ECOSOC twice met in New York in Jan, Feb & Aug of 1950 whereby the contracting states undertook the responsibility not to expel or return refugee in any manner to the frontier with respect to this Universal Declaration of Human Rights 1948 had also highlighted the rights of refugee. Protection against refoulement has also come to be recognized in human rights law. The obligation to protect individuals against torture an other severe ill treatment has developed into a prohibition on States removing persons to a territory in which a real risk of such ill treatment exists. Non-refoulement is a very important legal and humanitarian principles of international law. This principle is normatively established both in treaty and in custom, and thus it constitutes an integral part of customary international law. It may be regarded as the cornerstone of international refugee law.

NATURE, SCOPE & EXTENT OF APPLICABILITY OF THE PRINCIPLE

The principle of non-refoulment cannot be absolute to say, the application of this principle was objected by the state at the early. States had resisted exclusion of such right to the asylum both in 1948 & 1951 Convention.[6] Art. 33 of 1951 Convention could not be claimed by the refugees against whom there are reasonable ground for regarding danger to the security of the country in which he or she have been convicted by a final judgement of a particular crime. The principle of non-refoulement further raises the question as to its personal scope and relation to the issue of admission and non-rejection at the frontier, though its rule is designed to benefit the refugees. Principle again is jeopardized when issue concerning definition of refugee arouses .Recognition of refugees' status under International law is essentially declaratory in nature.

Obligation to protect the individual arises as soon as the individual or groups concerned satisfy the criteria of refugee. States have contended that granting of protection to the refugees being their obligation was only humanitarian and not legal.

The most accurate assessment to the scope of this principle is that there is no uniformity in its application. International practice to its application differed from country to country for instance Swiss & Dutch interpreted that their obligation was merely restrictive on plenipotentiary Conference of 1951. Interpretation of non refoulement in their personal law was limited were it was specified that the principle would be applied only among those refugees who already existed in their state territory and nothing about non applicability of Article 33 of 1951 Convention outside the context. The Dutch considers that word returned related only to refugees already within the territory and mass migration was not covered. On other hand narrow interpretation of the principle did not fully square with the meaning of refoulment in European Immigration Law.

Intention seems to be very clear that state parties were new prepared to include any article of entry in this convention as an admission of the refugees. It could well be assumed that 1951 convention was sole binding on the parties to the convention. The 1951 Convention has made a major contribution to general international law and human rights law principles. Provisions such as the definition of the term 'refugee' and the guarantee against forcible return to territories where persecution is feared (non-refoulement) have become principles of public international law.

WIDER PERSPECTIVE OF INTERPRETATION

In order to shape up the principle of non refoulement last not least obligation of the state was conducting the 1967 Protocol which in turn amended the existing 1951 Convention thus non refoulement was powerfully expressed in Art 3 of 1984 UN Convention. From the past 45 years, the concept has been given a wider scope. Today the concept of non-refoulement is embodied in regional instrument also for instance Art 22 (8) of 1969 American Convention Human Rights included a central feature of non-refoulement. In America the regional protection of asylees goes back to 1889 Montevideo Treaty or International Peace Law article 16 proclaims that political refugees shall be accorded inviolable asylum.

1951 Convention amended by 1967 Protocol have endowed binding obligation on state parties, Prohibition of refoulement is set out in Art 33(1) of 1951, convention[7] as follow:

No contracting state shall expel or return refugee in any manner whatsoever to the frontier of territory was his life or freedom would be threatened. 1967 Protocol does not bring any change to the status of refugees but specified the status of the contracting states as having a binded obligation to be undertaken to protect the right of Refugee as such by operation of 1951 Convention it refers to all states party of 1967 protocol with or not they are party to 1951 Convention.

Art 33 of the Refugee Convention protects refugees from being returned either directly or indirectly to places where they may be persecuted. It is clear therefore, that the safe third country principle is doing much to undermine non-refoulement .Even if states are not seen as directly violating non-refoulement, the safe third country rule provides a way to circumvent international law.[8]

Referring to the language of Art. 1 (2) 1967 Protocol it seems that protection is accorded to the refugees, as mentioned earlier the term refugees is not taken in restrictive sense and as such it would include any person who owing to well founded fear of being persecuted for reason of race, religion, and nationality of particular social group is outside the country of his nationality and is unable or unwilling to avail himself of the protection of that country accordance. The non-refoulement principle has clearly undergone substantial development since its emergence as a vague morality-based rule. Not only is it described as the foundation of the foremost international legal instrument relating to refugees, but it has also been transplanted into other treaties. Although this indicates the importance of non-refoulement internationally, its expression in so many different ways and in so many different instruments, also serves to undermine its effectiveness.

Henceforth argument that non refoulment only avails to those who have been formally recognized as refugee under municipal law no longer holds good because Art. 1(2) of 1951 Convention does not define refugee as being person who have for many recognize as refugee under municipal law. It simply provides that the term shall apply to any person who owing to well founded fear of being persecuted. So as per 1951 Convention a person who satisfy the condition under Art. 1 (2) as refugee?

EXCEPTIONS TO THE PRINCIPLE

As already highlighted that the concept of non-refoulement is not absolute guarantee of protection, nationality, security and public order can be a justification for derogation to this extend criminals have to be excluded from the status of refugees. Art 33 (2) expressly provides that the benefit of non-refoulment may not be claimed by a refugee "whom they are contracting state have reasonable ground for regarding as danger to the security of the country or who have been convicted by the final judgment of particular serious crime. The decision to be taken is left out to the descrisonery any pairs of state authority regarding the identity and status of the individual who claim himself to be a refugee. "Hats off" to the British representative who made such proposal in 1951 Conference and asked for inclusion of Art. 33 (2), probably the issue of national security is supported both by Art. 33(2) of 1951 convention and the immigration law and practice in general.

Extraterritoriality, the safe third country principle, temporary protection systems and justifications and exceptions are only examples of the need to define the parameters of non-refoulement.

To what extend one is convicted of particularly serious crime must also be shown to constitute danger is yet to be clear, for sure the principle of serious crime is not a term of art but principle of natural justice. For temporary residence purpose in due course of pending resettlement provision is made under 1969 Organization of African Union, which is without exception. The absence of any formal exception could be remarkable an appreciable in the view of dimension of the refugee problem, which has been faced by individual African states. State could further deny admission of certain category of asylum seekers such as Stowaway's and other refugee who rescue at the sea may be refoulded or returned back refugee boats may be towed back to transit or sale third countries. Here again state authorities induce expulsion through various form of threat and coercion.

IN BRIEF

Stowaway's refugees are group of people trying to seek entry through seaway at the coastal zone of the country. If a Stowaway's asylum seeker tried entry in the country may ask the shipmaster to keep the Stowaway's on board and travel onto the next part of call and in due course of their act state would not be breaching the principal of non-refoulement. Ten Executive Committee working group first briefly examined this issue of asylum seeker during a rescue at sea meeting in Geneva in July 1928. The executive committee analyzed the problem with respect to stowaway refugee and conducted that no kind of discrimination should be made against them. This asylum seeker should be allowed on entry and the state are ought to abide to the principal of non-refoulment. In reality but, practice of state treatment to stowaway asylum seeker differ.

However recommendation were made by the Executive Committee of 1982 not to send back the Stowaway refugees to a nation were there would be threat to their personal limb or life.

Rescue at sees, seems to be a recent practice and again these group are left out helplessly recent example are Cubans,

Haitians & Indo Chinese provide a shelter to this group have been firmly clear in both treaties and international law. The problem was recognized at early 1975 and in the same you're the executive committee stressed obligation of shipmaster and state under the 1910 Brussels and 1958 Geneva Convention and called for grant of first asylum. Several countries supported U.K. step for rescuing the refugees at 1980s Executive Committee meeting. In nevertheless the obligation of the state to abide by this responsibility is yet in question; because attitude of the state differed as per the situation and circumstance.

Often state has witnessed entry of illegal entries such as in care with USA were they have objected the entry of Asylum seek by boat. Sovereign state has do have ultimate right to decide the entry of sail of ship in territorial sea, of course high sea are not subject to the excessive of sovereignty by any state. Only in exceptional cases are the ships on high sea boarded namely suspicion of piracy or slave trading. If ship has no nationality or has the same nationality as the worship purported; Again here stowaway refugee or those rescuing at sea by boat their right for settlement in any coastal zone of neighboring country is very much governed by bilateral agreement.

OBLIGATION AND ENFORCEMENT

The concept of non refoulement endowers a great responsibility of abiding and casting obligation on the state to allow own refugees to entry the land of contracting country state; the question next arise of enforcement in case of breach. To, cote here simple denial of entry of ship to territorial water cannot be equated with breach of principal of non-refoulement; the ad hoc committee in its comment in 1950 draft convention observed. The obligation not to return refugee to a country where he was persecuted did not imply an obligation to admit him to the country were he seeks refugee for the return of refugee ship for example to the high sea cannot be constructed as a violation of obligation.

The nature of obligation and its observation is definitely a normative attitude the enforceability of denial action of any state cannot be determined in practice. International perspective of the refugees right though may be descriptively determined the right of the refugee in country were they seek asylum or shelter is definitely a concept to be determined by the municipal law of land and sweet will of the attitude adopted by the internal govt. Internal and international attitude developed by the countries to rescue the refugee are in fact respected by most state as a general rule of customary international law, though several commentator be repeatedly said that this principle holds. The status of *jus cogens* to put in other word non-refoulement was a rule of *jus cogens*. It is clearly of grave importance to prove that non-refoulement has gained the status of custom. If we can show we have a customary rule then the problems caused by inconsistent implementation of this principle become less significant. Numerous commentators have examined the principle of non-refoulement to establish whether it is now custom.

RELATIONSHIP OF NON REFOULEMENT WITH EXTRADITION & ILLEGAL ENTRY

Extradition is a lawful act of one contracting state with another contracting state were the later will have all legal right over the individual to be extradited from the former country 1951. Convention have said nothing about extradition of refugees; Further Art 33 of 1956 did not prejudice the extradition principal and held that serious criminal will be excluded from the benefit of refugee status.

Extradition of refugee cannot be on any other ground to support this view 1957 European Convention on Extradition for example, prohibited extradition if requested party has substantial ground for believing that a request for extradition for any ordinary criminal offence had been made for the purpose of prosecuting or punishing a person on account of his race, religion nationality or political opinion. Judicial decisions from different countries support that a serious risk of prejudice can be considered in justify protection of extradition refugee cases. In Fernandez V/s. Govt. of Singapore court in other country have consolidate the basic principle of protection against extradition in favour of refugee.

Illegal entry of individual shall as generally deny by any state. International law's view of normative quality of non–refoulment about legal states of refugees is irrelevant state seeking to avoid responsibility will often clarify them as illegal emigrant .Immigration formalities are to be fulfilled by the individual to seek asylum in any country in case with refugee this was not formally required. At 1951 Conference several representative considered the undertaking not to impose penalties on refugees on account of illegal entry.

SUGGESTIONS

The principle of non-refoulment is core one based on *jus cogens,* hence a precise balance between the national interest and interest of human rights has to be observed.

International obligation of states to abide to this principle though has less legal status of enforceability; it should be abided as a rule of customary international law. There must be review to the 1951 Convention thoroughly. If it is not possible let there be convening new Convention on Refugee status. Furthermore there ought to be mutual co-existence, good order, and reciprocity among the states without which it would virtually impossible to create harmony among the states.

Individual right of a refugee under international sphere could only be understood by international community, when there will be a mutual undertaking of shared responsibility to provide shelter. The fundamental humanitarian principle of non-refoulement has found expression in various international instruments adopted at the universal and regional levels and should be accepted by States. Today India need a proper mechanism to regulate the problems of refugee indeed it would be a necessity for an Indian govt. to establish a permanent mechanism and procedure for handling the refugee crises in India. The fundamental importance of the observance of the principle of non-refoulement both at the border and within the territory of a State of persona who may be subjected to persecution if returned to their country of origin irrespective of whether or not they have been formally recognized refugees.

Unless there is no regional law on refugee it would be hard enough to identify who is refugee and their right simply would be put into hardship by not providing humanitarian treatment that he or she is entitled to.

CONCLUSIONS

To conclude in context of refugee situation, the concept of non-refoulemnt is very important. Since no refugee or asylum seeker should be driven back from the country of refugee; character of non-refoulment differ from expulsion and deportation usually occurs when foreigner is found to be guilty of doing something against the interest of state. Several convention and declaration has amply provided to be fruitful. Since over the last 50 years broader and liberal interpretation of non-refoulment principle has been developed through state practice, state has allowed large number of refugee not only to cross their territories but also remain in their country. Individual practice of state international organization has further elaborated the principle. The current principle embodies both non-return and non-rejection of refugees.

This principle has consolidate to be bedrock in promotion and protection of human rights with no discrimination this principle is applicable to every one who has well founded fear of persecution or has such ground to believe that person would be in danger of personal security or life, if he satisfy the criteria of refugee. The problem of refugee is definitely one concerning to the human rights. Since protection of human right is no more a matter of domestic concern and has become international concern.

The principle of non-refoulement in respect of refugees or asylum seekers constitutes bedrock in promotion and protection of human rights. The principle is applicable to every one who has a well-founded fear of persecution or whether there are substantial grounds for believing that the person would be in danger of personal security or life. In the context of refugee situation, the concept of non-refoulement is very important because no refugee or asylum seeker should be driven back from the country of refuge or asylum to any country where he/she is likely to face persecution or personal danger to life or security or torture. Non-refoulement is a very important legal and humanitarian principle of international law. This principle is normatively established both in treaty and in custom, and thus it constitutes an integral part of customary international law. It may be regarded as the cornerstone of international refugee law.

NOTES AND REFERENCES

1. Chimni, B. S. (1993), "The Meaning of words and Role of UNHCR in Voluntary Repatriation", *International Journal of Refugee Law,* Vol. 5.
2. Garvey Jack (1985), "Towards a Reformulation of International Refugee Law", *Harvard International Law Journal,* Vol. 26.
3. Saxena J. M. (1986), "Legal Status of Refugees: Indian Position", *Indian Journal on International Law.*
4. Garcia Mora M. (1956), *International Law and Asylum as a Human Rights,* Washington DC Publications.
5. Enka Tirk Feller Nichoilson (2003), *Refugee Protection in I L UNHCR Global Consultations on International Protection,* University of Cambridge UK.
6. See 1951 Refugee Status Convention.
7. *Ibid*, Article 33 (1).
8. See Universal Declaration on Human Rights 1948.

Refugees and Human Rights: A Study of Sri Lankan Tamil Refugees

Y. GURAPPA NAIDU*

The twentieth century had been marked by a number of mass flights of people fleeing their mother lands, seeking a new life in other countries. Today, the world is witnessing wars and armed conflicts in a number of countries around the global and violating the human rights of people very oftenly even though the existence of international humanitarian laws. Each armed conflict has created refugees and many people to be homeless in their own country, in a foreign land and running hither and thither to protect their lives. Like other refugee communities in India, the Sri Lankan Tamils are considered as refugees in political sense. Their freedom of movement drastically curtailed and they were treated with some degree of suspicion. Many of the Tamil refugees living in welfare camps were not interested to returning home is due to landlessness, concern about children's safety, not interested to leave behind family and friends, lack of educational facilities in return areas, health problems and disabilities, houses and other property occupied by the army or police or located with high security and lack of employment opportunities in return areas. Improving infrastructure, raising the quality of education, increasing access of the poor

* Associate Professor, Department of Political Science & Public Administration, Sri Venkateswara University, Tirupati-517502, A.P.

to social services, rebuilding of the conflict areas and reintegrating them into the national economy is the need of the hour. These measures certainly help to delink contact with LTTE terrorist protection of human rights and extending humanitarian assistance if it is undertaken in collaboration with UNHCR, NGOs and such other national and international organizations. All these initiations help for the protection and promotion of the human rights of refugees both in camps and in repatriation.

The 20th century was referred by many as the century of the up-rooted and the homeless men. It had been marked by a number of mass flights of people fleeing their native lands, seeking a new life in other countries. Human rights, violations are a major factor in causing the flight of refugees as well as an obstacle to their safe and voluntary return home.[1]

Since all aspects of human life needed protection, the rights are given to each individual to express and to protect his personality and to safeguard his singularity in a multitude of social pressures and forces. But it does not mean that rights are independent of society. However, a society can be transformed, improved upon and be better administered. At the same time there is no justification for its distribution and also the destruction of the institutions it had created.[2]

In 1990, there were about 15 million refugees in the world over and at the end of 2000, there were more than 22 million and the number has been going fast.[3] According to UNHCR–2005 statistics, by the end of 2004, number of refugees in the globe was estimated to be 9.2 million persons showing a net decrease of approximately 3,56,000 refugees from 9.6 million refugees recorded in the beginning of 2004.[4] The world today is witnessing wars or armed conflicts in a number of countries around the globe. What so ever may be the reasons, wars and armed conflicts violate the human rights of people-the right to life, education, health and nutrition, etc. Inspite of the existence of international humanitarian laws, the human rights violations are very often taking place. Each armed conflict has created refugees, many people to be homeless in their own country, homeless in a foreign land and running hither and thither to protect their lives. Fear and many more causes have created a situation and normal life is disturbed, the situations defy a definition and a justification of the denial of the basic right to live.[5]

CONVENTION ON THE STATUS OF REFUGEES

The people become homeless on account of a number of reasons. The homeless persons can be the refugees, the returnees, the asylum seekers and internally displaced persons. Under international law, a refugee is a person, who is outside his country and cannot return because of a well-founded fear of persecution, for any one or more of the five reasons: religion, race, membership of a particular social group and because of that fear cannot return to his or her country; or has fled because of war and civil conflict. In the broad context, race comprises of all ethnic groups. Discriminations meted out to the ethnic groups to the extent that it becomes difficult for these groups to enjoy basic human rights, would provide a ground for the refugee status.[6]

Circumstances have changed during these fifty years and above and even though wars have been checked by "International organizations" efforts, treaties and conventions, however the problems of refugees have not come to an end. Refugees are still being created due to circumstances other than wars. The terrorist anti-human organizations have been still creating the refugees problems. In Kashmir valley, the Kashmiri pandits have been compelled to take shelter in the other parts of their own country due to atrocities and genocide committed by some terrorist organizations.[7] hence, it may be noted that one of the important achievements of the UN has been the creation of consciousness of human rights by world community and its people. The result was that the question of human rights, which was properly considered as a matter falling exclusively within the domestic jurisdiction of states has obtained an international character by virtue of the provision of the UN charter.[8]

DISPLACED PERSONS AND THE ASYLUM SEEKERS

There is one question more related to the persons who constitute more than 6 millions in different regions of the world. They are the persons or communities who have left their home province or federated state and to take shelter in the other part of the same federation or union. They have not to cross any border of a country, nor they demand shelter or refuge in another country. Do such persons or communities fall under the definition of refugees? Certainly not, but they are in legal language only displaced persons.[9]

Another category, the asylum seekers are those people who have left their country of origin and who have applied for refugee status and their applications are still pending. They wish to get better job opportunities and better economic status, but not recognized as a reason for becoming a refugee.[10] Ultimately the refugees may be defined as persons who have left their homeland or place of residence due to unavoidable and oppressive circumstances and are not prepared now to go back to their homeland or original place of residence. During 2004, a total number of 6,76,000 applications for asylum or refugee status were submitted to governments or UNHCR officer in 143 countries. The number of applications during 2004 decreased by 19 per cent compared to 2003 where 8,30,300 applications were lodged globally. The largest number of new and appeal asylum claims were filed by nationals from the Russian Federation (35,200), Serbia and Montenegro (30,900), China (29,000) the Democratic Republic of the Congo (28,700), Turkey (27,000), Iraq (23,500), Somalia (22,900), the Islamic Republic of Iran (15,500), India (15,300) and Pakistan (15,300). The category of asylum- seekers in the total population of concern to UNHCR consists of those asylum-seekers whose claim has not yet been decided or who are otherwise registered as asylum-seekers. The number of undecided asylum cases, both at the first instance and on appeal decreased by 16 per cent to reach 839,000 by the end of the 2004.[11]

THE UNITED NATIONS HIGH COMMISSIONER FOR REFUGEES (UNHCR)

The office of the UNHCR was established on January 1951, by the General Assembly of UNO in the place of the short-lived International Refugee Organisation. The International Community of Nations has tried to evolve mechanisms to deal with the problem of refugees. The functions of the High Commissioner are to provide international protection to refugees who fall within the scope of his statue[12] and may be broadly divided into nine categories: (a) promotion or grant of asylum, (b) reunion of families, (c) application of doctrine of non-refoulement, (d) maintenance and material assistance, (e) assimilation or resettlement, (f) supervision, (g) coordination, and (h) public relations. The UNHCR has become the focal point for maintenance of and material assistance to refugees. In 1971, UNHCR was requested to act as a focal point for coordination of assistance from the UN system to millions of Bengalis who had fled to India. UNHCR also assisted in the return of these people to their homeland in 1972 and again in 1973, following Delhi agreement, UNHCR oranised a massive airlift between Pakistan and Bangladesh for the return of Bengalis and Pakistanis to their respective homelands. More recently, UNHCR was called upon to undertake a large programme of humanitarian assistance in Zaira for the benefit of about 10,00,000 refugees who are the victims of genocide and massive human rights violations in Rwanda. Another large scale humanitarian assistance programme was done by the UNHCR in Iraq in 1991-92 where 4 million people were displaced in the 12 months after the Iraqi's invasion of Kuwait during August 1990. Relief was provided by international agencies and also by the 13-nation coalition force, around 30 bilateral donors and about 50 NGO's. The crisis also resulted in an enhanced appreciation of the importance of early warning mechanism and emerging response capacity in tackling major humanitarian crisis.[13]

Sadhana Sharma (2002) remarked that the total number of people concern to the UNHCR have increased from 17 million in 1991 to 27 million in 1995. The UNHCR statistics show a drop of about 4-7 million between 1995 and 1998. These include refugees, returnees and persons displaced within their own countries. The total population concern to UNHCR increased from 17.0 million persons at the end of the 2003 to 19.2 million by the end of 2004. Refugees constitute 48 per cent of the total population of concern to UNHCR, who were 56 per cent during 2003 about half (54 per cent) of all refugees have benefited from UNHCR assistance programmes. The number of refugees directly assisted through UNHCR were reduced to 5.0 million refugees by the end of the year 2004.[14]

SRI LANKAN TAMIL REFUGEES–A STUDY

Historical Perspective

India was severely affected by the influx of thousands of Tamil Refugees from Sri Lanka in 1983, when violence broke out in their country between the majority Sinhalese and the minority Tamil militant group, the Liberation Tiger of Tamil Eslam (LTTE). Four years prior to the 1987 Indo-Sri Lanka Accord, an estimated 1,35,000 Sri Lankan Tamils sought refugee in India. Again between August 1989 and February 1991, nearly 12, 200 Tamil refugees took shelter in various refugee camps in India. Like other refugee communities in India, the Sri Lankan Tamils are considered as refugees in political sense and granted as asylum by the Government of India.[15] Although many of the refugees have been repatriated to Sri Lanka over the years, about 61,000 Sri Lankan Tamils were living in 103 government run camps during 2004 in Tamil Nadu. An additional 20,000 refugees were living out side the camps and about 1,22,074 persons were granted Indian citizenship. Agricultural loans were provided, ranging from Rs. 300 to Rs. 4300. People with background in trade and commerce were given loans upto Rs. 5000 per family.[16]

The Tamil United Liberation Front (TULF) coming into prominence in 1970's for the first time spoke of a separate home land or Eelam for the Tamils. The TULF got widespread support after measures such as Tamil standardization rules were passed which restricted entry of Tamil students into Ceylonese Universities despite their getting higher marks than the Sinhalese. Due to split in the TULF, more radical group that younger elements drifted towards armed groups–TELO, the EPRLF, PLOTE and of course, the LTTE and thus lead to armed struggle for Eelam, a struggle that rages in the hapless Island to this day. However, by 1983, the situation had changed radically and officials, overtely aided or abetted anti-Tamil violence. Tamil homes and business establishments in Colombo were systematically destroyed. Then violence spread to the northern and eastern provinces of Sri Lanka. The military action of Sri Lankan Government against the Tamil insurgents is resulting in mass killing and torture and fleeing of Tamils in general to India for safety. More than 1,25,000 people have crossed over to India since July 1983 and they have been 'granted refugee status'.[17]

From 1983 onwards the Sri Lankan Tamils, began crossing to India fleeing the action of the Sri Lankan security forces. The reactions in India, particularly in Tamil Nadu, naturally caused deep concern from the aspect of human rights. Then Indira Gandhi deputed G. Parthasarathi to visit Sri Lanka and to offer India's good offices in seeking a solution to the problem. Meanwhile, the Tamil extremists intensified their fight, as did the Sri Lankan armed forces to overcome the Tamils. Mr. JR. Jayewardene approached the USA and Britain for military assistance but they have not responded. Then only he turned to India which swallowed the bait to prove its ascendancy in the region.[18] On July 29, 1987 Jayewardene and Rajiv Gandhi signed the 'India-Sri Lanka Accord', acknowledging the legitimacy of India's security concerns in the region and consequently jointly seeking to implement a solution to the ethnic problem. However the 'accord' remains on paper. The violence committed by the LTTE has left India cold. Whatever sympathy was there, it has been squeezed out by Rajiv Gandhi's assassination in 1991. A limited stir was already visible in a few coastal areas of Tamil Nadu. The Pattali Makkal Katchi (PMK) led by S. Ramadoss has been able to evoke a favourable response on the banning of LTTE in India. The then Tamil Nadu Chief Minister, Mr. K. Karunanidhi, expressed the feelings of a large number of Tamils when he said, "we have no sympathy for the militants, but this does not mean that we have no sympathy for the Sri Lankan Tamils".[19]

ASSISTANCE PROGRAMMES

During July 1983 and November 1987, a total of 1,34,053 Tamil refugees were reported to have come to India. Of them only 17,000 were registered and the rest stayed with their relatives. As a result of the Indo-Sri Lankan Accord in 1987; 25,885 Tamil refugees left India during 1987 and 1989. Due to the escalated violence in Sri Lanka 1,22,241 Tamil refugees were reported to have come to India during 1989 and 1991. The Indian authorities had classified them on the basis of primary enquiry into (1) ordinary refugees–1,10,552 ordinary refugees were kept in 186 camps in 19 districts of Tamil Nadu and 218 in Orissa and (2) 2,239 refugees, who are suspected to have links with militants, are kept in separate camps along with 763 refugees who have violated the rules relating to Registration under Foreign Act. These refugees also have strict restrictions on their freedom of movement drastically curtailed and were treated with some degree of suspicion by the Indian government. The refugees who were lodged in special camps strongly guarded by the security forces.[20] The scale of relief assistance extended to a person of Indian origin coming from Sri Lanka in the form of cash was ranging from Rs. 150 for a family with one member to Rs. 502.50 for a family with five members. In addition to that, food, coffee/ milk, meals, subsidized ration, medical free hospitals, cremation and sradh grant, additional relief assistance were provided for those who have arrived in destitute condition from the riot affected areas of Sri Lanka. Travel concessions were also provided to the repatriates from Sri Lanka. The repatriates were also made eligible for journey allowance as a grant of free travel facility.

Most of the assistance activities focus on UNHCR's protection role. The office implements and supports initiatives at the local level to address concerns over human rights abuse, minority rights, statelessness and property and land restitution. The office also implements some assistance activities to provide immediate humanitarian need of spontaneous returnees and IDPs. Those interventions entail assistance in the form of community development and basic household support, which include monitoring of their general well-being. Interventions also support initiatives by the government of Sri Lanka to find relocation or local integration alternatives for those who were still displaced.

ORGANISATION AND IMPLEMENTATION

The management structure of the UNHCR in Sri Lanka in the later part of 2005 operate with a total of 115 staff members, 35 international including three IPDs and 15 international UNVs and 80 nationals including nine national UNVs. The UNHCR representation in Colombo is responsible for the overall management of the programme and for liaison with government, embassies and NGOs. To ensure adequate presence in the field UNHCR maintenance of offices in six locations, the sub-office in Vayuniya covers field offices in Mannar, Trincomalee and Batticaloa, with sub-office at Jaffna covering field-office at Killinochchi. The total budget of $8,870,031 was earmarked during 2005 for programme support, $1,750,669 for various activities and other services, $7,119,362 for protection, monitoring and coordination, community services, domestic needs, legal assistance, operational, support to agencies and transport/logistics.[21]

POSITION OF THE REFUGEES

Following the assassination of former Prime Minister Rajiv Gandhi in 1991 by a suspected member of the LTTE, the refugee camps were moved away from coastal areas to isolated interior regions of Tamil Nadu so as to prevent contact amongst the refugees belonging to different camps. The movement of refugees out side the camps were restricted and the camps had morning and evening curfews. Families were often shifted from one camp to another as a security precaution. The Indian government did not permit International NGOs and Aid Agencies, including UNHCR to have access to the camps. Refugees who disobey the rules may have their monthly stipend and rations cut off as punishment. Some of the refugees describe (as per the observations of the many researchers) the camps as being nothing more than jails. Many of these restrictions seem arbitrary given that the 20,000 refugees out side the camp have no limitations on their movements, although they do not receive aid from the Indian Government.[22]

Udayakumar (2002) in his paper on "India: Tamil Refugees Hope Talks Will Get Them Home" observed that the Sri Lankan Refugees were optimistic of the peace talks in Thailand as the one chance that they may yet see the homeland in Jafna that they fled 20 years ago, they are hopeful, for the first time that both sides (the government and the tigers) have to give and take and that alone will bring lasting peace to the country. While India as a whole and ethnic Tamils in Southern Tamil Nadu have only a general interest in the Thailand talks, the Sri Lankan inmates of this camp are eager to return to their country and resume their lives as teachers, clerks and officials. For the Sri Lankan Refugees, India is safe but in India they are nothing but coolies (daily wagers working as labourers). Further, Udaya Kumar remarked that the Pzhazilai refugee camp is one of the four in Kanyakumari district on the southern tip of India has housed some 80 families from Sri Lanka since 1990. Some families took their chances and returned to Sri Lanka in 1992 and 1995, but at last 65 families have continued living in Pazhavilai over the years, they have held uncertain hopes of returning to their homes in places like Mannar, Vayuniya and Trincomalee, areas made famous for the fierce but inconclusive war between the Sri Lankan Army and the LTTE, which has been fighting for a separate Tamil homeland for the last 23 years.

The feelings of the Sri Lankan refugees from Vayuniya camp are that the current talks would succeed because both sides are sick and tired of the violence and destruction. Udayakumar also noted that most of the men and women in the refugee camps think that their lives might change in the next few months. However they do not have any concrete plans about their return trip to Sri Lanka, they do foster that hope fondly in their hearts. In another refugee camp by name Kottaram near to Kanyakumari, the refugees say that they cannot wait to go back to their country. They also expressed that in their country, they can buy a piece of land, or build a house, or do anything that pleases them if there is peace around them. Living as a refugee make them feel wasted.[23]

However, the camp based refugees were grateful to the Indian government for permitting them to stay in India and making educational and health facilities available to their children. In particular, the Sri Lankan refugees were pleased with the opportunities they had for the education of their children in India, although a quota is imposed on Sri Lankan refugees attending universities. Life in the camps, however, has been far from easy for the refugees. They receive a small stipend each month and a few basic supplies from the Indian government, which are inadequate for survival. The refugees do whatever day jobs they can find, such as construction work or house painting. Since more than a thousand people have been living in one camp for a decade in crowded warehouses where each family lives in a 10 feet by 10 feet partitioned area. In other camps, refugees are living in temporary shelters, which were built prior to the refugee influx as short-term housing and are now falling apart. Basic facilities in the camps, such as toilets and water pumps, constructed by Indian authorities in the early 1990s, broke down long ago and have not been repaired. Sanitary problems in the camps, were cited by many as a serious problem.

The refugees who had been in India since 1995 and most since 1990 had very few options to live in the camps, especially as returning to their homes in Sri Lanka was not feasible in the past due to the ongoing war between the LTTE and the Government. With the cease-fire agreement between the Sri Lankan Government and the LTTE in early 2002, the security situation has improved significantly in Sri Lanka. Several thousand of refugees have returned to Sri Lanka. None of these refugees alleged that the Government of India is pressuring them to go home, although they fear that pressure may come in the future. In addition to the concerns about security in their homeland, an obstacle to return was that refugees want to take back with them the meager belongings they have acquired during their stay in the camps. If they return with UNHCR assistance by air, they can take back not more than 20 kg's of their belongings. Therefore, many proposed that UNHCR arrange their transport by ship and they can take all of their belongings, which consist usually of a few sticks of furniture, blankets and cooking pots.[24]

Some of the refugees who come to India have had children born to them in exile. Those children speak the local dialects and appear comfortable with their meager surroundings. They attend local schools and even excel in their studies in a district that has the distinction of having the best rural schools in the whole of India, but have no idea about their country of origin or the deadly conflict that has ravaged the lives of their parents.[25] The other refugees are hesitant to return to Sri Lanka at this point because their homes lie in high security zones, occupied by the Sri Lankan army from where all residents have been displaced. These refugees only want to return when they were able to go back to their original homes. A reason also mentioned by the refugees for not returning was the fear that their children will be recruited by the LTTE. The other cause affecting return was the standard of educational facilities in parts of Sri Lanka which was not as high as the standard in India. Many Sri Lankan Tamils prefer that the education of their children should be completed in India.

REPATRIATION OF LANKAN TAMIL REFUGEES

Between 1983 and 2001, the conflict produced over a million refugees and IDPs. The repatriation of refugees from Tamil Nadu in Southern India to Sri Lanka has been the largest organized exercise of its kind done in collaboration with the UNHCR. In the first phase between 1987 and 1990 nearly 42000 Sri Lankan Tamils returned. Of them two thirds were parts of the organized repatriation involving the UNHCR. A second phase of the repatriation of Sri Lankan refugees from India commenced in early 1992 under the bilateral agreement between the Government of India and Sri Lanka. In July 1992, the Government of India and UNHCR reached an agreement on UNHCR verification of the voluntary nature of the repatriation. Some 29000 refugees returned during 1992, leaving about 80,000 in 131 camps and an estimated 30,000 outside the camps in Tamil Nadu, according to an official government figures. In January 1993, UNHCR offered to finance the rental of a flat-bottomed boat for the Voyage from Rameswaram to Talaimannar and an ocean going vessel from Madras to Trincomalee to transport another 7000 refugees. Again in February 1994, another 36,000 were repatriated to Manner Island from Rameswaram. However, the process of repatriation was suspended in February 1994 and had resumed again in September 1994. When 1054 refugees left Madras for Trincomalee in eastern Sri Lanka by the ship M.V. Nicabar and completed this phase of repatriation on October, 1994.[26]

At the time of the ceasefire agreement in 2002, there were about 84000 Sri Lankan refugees in Tamil Nadu. There was a greater focus on the needs of those who cannot or do not want to return to their places of origin for lack of security or reasons of ethnicity, political opinion or vulnerability. In 2005, a steady stream of refugees has spontaneously returned to Sri Lanka from India. Since February 2002, 9496 refugees from camps in Tamil Nadu have returned across the Palk Strait and UNHCR has facilitated the priority return of 2345 refugees by air. However, 57,000 Sri Lankan refugees remained in camps in Tamil Nadu have returned across the Palkl Strait and UNHCR has facilitated the priority return of 2345 refugees by air. However, 57,000 Sri Lankan refugees remained in camps in Tamil Nadu as on June 2004. UNHCR will continue to work closely with the Government of Sri Lanka and India to facilitate the repatriation of priority cases and prepare for organized voluntary repatriation. This approach was sustained until the Sri Lanka environment becomes conductive to large-scale organized voluntary returns.[27]

HUMAN RIGHTS VIOLATION AND PROBLEMS OF REFUGEES

Sadhna Sharma, in his paper on "Refugees" (2002) states that: the refugees can pose a number of stresses and stains on the receiving state and difficult to any country to carry on its normal economic functioning with a 10 per cent increase of refugees. The social effects can be quite frustrating. This can lead to xenophobic reactions from the receiving populations. The warning groups, when they take refuge in another country, can strain relations between the sending and the receiving state. Certain groups from among the refugee population may exploit the situation and turn to banditry and looting, etc., to fulfill the basic requirements. The terrorist groups can operate from the refugee camps masquerading as refugees. This can become a serious problem for the law enforcement agencies. However, the foreign policy constraints between the sending the receiving state can stand in the way of humanitarian concern.[28]

The UNHCR Global Appeal on "Sri Lanka", (2005) made an effort to explain that: in order to achieve lasting peace the fundamental issues such as human security and minority rights need to be addressed .The general human rights situation in Sri Lanka has improved since the ceasefire. However, violations of human rights continue especially, but not exclusively, in areas controlled by the LTTE. Such violations include forced recruitment, including child soldiers, hostage-taking in retaliation for desertion by cadres, extortion and results and killing of political opponents. While instances of inter-ethnic conflict are decreasing, deep mistrust and apprehension continues to linger in some communities and there is a risk of occasional localized violence. UNHCR has thus supported various community based monitoring, intervention and capacity building mechanisms. Although the ceasefire in Sri Lanka held, violations of human rights and other protection problems continued to a general climate of fear especially in the east. The forced recruitment of children and adults by the LTTE remains key interntional concern, as more than 4000 have reportedly been abducted and forcibly recruited since the ceasefire. All these concerns impacted heavily on the IDP population in Sri Lanka. Respect for human dignity and defence of human life and liberty bring the two branches of the world legal order together. That is the reason why the thrust of the refugee law is to define and to protect the rights of the refugees. UNHCR took the view that the conditions in the country still did not favour any large scale organized voluntary return operation.[29]

Sadhna Sharma (2002) observed that: A crucial aspect of the refugee issue has been overlooked till recently. The environmental degradation, felling of millions of trees to be sued as fire wood in the refugee camps; killing of the wild life animals and running of the flora and fauna of the refugee site and destruction of the eco-system and the economic infrastructures. Many related problems have emanated from these issue. Further, he concluded that the international community of the nations has a challenging responsibility in regard to the issue of refugees and requires, a new perspective to balance the legal, political, social, economic, environmental, cultural, humanitarian and human rights aspects with the state security issues.[30]

Udayakumar (2002) in his paper "India: Tamil Refugees Hope Talks Will Get Them Home" collected the views of the refugees in Kottaram camp near Kanyakumari. He was informed that the Government of Tamil Nadu out five dollars to the head of each family every month and three dollars to other adults and a dollar and fifty cents to each child. But this was barely sufficient to keep them going. However, they are grateful for measures taken like supply of rice and electricity and drinking water in the camps, but the future is bleak. Many have died in the harsh living conditions on the sea front. The able-bodies men and women are allowed to leave the camps for manual labour in and around the refugee camps. But jobs are very few and sporadic. Most men who work in the banana plantations around Pazhavilai may be restricted to the camp when dignitaries visit the area or when the political times are hard in India or Sri Lanka. Every now then, following each upsurge in the fighting between the LTTE and the army, the refugees ranks have swelled. The last time that happened was after the deadly attack on Colombo airport by the Tiger rebels. The refugees are also helpless when the authorities decide to break up families for administrative reasons. The living conditions can be described as abysmal. Most of the refugees are crowded into hovels, some of which have the luxury of an asbestos sheet for roofing and the others are thatched huts that leak when it rains.[31] Thus the feelings of some refugees can be quoted that "where is the place where the voice of the refugees can be heard? And also refugees the so called homeless, hopeless, stateless and what else if the medium of being themselves is aimless" they are now in a desperate situation. They have lost hope of returning to their homes with dignity. Avenues for getting scholarships for higher education beyond 12th standard have been closed, since the refugees come under neither category and higher education was denied to them. This has created a major social problem and there was a case for India to relax the rules and admit them with scholarships .This was a humanitarian problem and not a political or ethnic one and Sri Lankan government is not going to object either. The frustrated young jobless refugees with no avenues open were likely to pour into India and create social instability. India would not like the issue to get internationalized either. It is within India's competence to mediate and solve the issue once for all. India has a moral responsibility and earlier it gets involved better it would be for refugees who are looking up to India as the last resort.[32]

CONCLUSION

Though Tamil Nadu hosted several thousands of Sri Lankan Tamil refugees as well as militant groups since 1983, the situation was changed in 1987 when Indian troops were sent to Sri Lanka to bring peace ended up in fighting the LTTE. About 56000 Tamil Sri Lankan refugees were housed in 101 refugee camps. When conditions became more favourable for refugees returning to Sri Lanka, in collaboration with the Government of Sri Lanka and India, the UNHCR need to play an effective role by providing an alternative means of transportation so that refugees have the option of returning by boat with all their belongings.

It is also observed that many of Tamil refugees living in welfare centres/camps were not interested to returning home. The main reasons are landlessness, concern about children's safety, not interested to leave behind family and friends, lack of educational facilities in return areas, old age, health problems and disabilities, houses and other property occupied by the army or police or located with high security and lack of employment opportunities in return areas. It is in this context suggested that, improving infrastructure, raising the quality of education, increasing access of the poor to social services, rebuilding of the conflict areas and reintegrating them into the national economy, removing legislative and regulatory barriers to private investments and promoting enhanced rural livelihoods and commercialization. All these initiations help to promote the refugees and human rights in home country and create confidence among refugees to return home land.

Although, the Tamil Nadu Government was kind enough in receiving the Sri Lankan Tamil refugees with the help of Indian Government, the Tamil Nadu Government has been facing lot of problems in maintaining the refugee camps, such as security, education, employment, financial problems, environmental pollution problems, arranging facilities for their return journey, to delink contracts with LTTE terrorists, protection of human rights and extending humanitarian assistance in collaboration with UNHCR, NGO's and such other National and International organizations. It is suggested that a fixed term of 5 to 10 years depending on the intensity of the crisis need to prescribed at he International level by UN. If within the stipulated period the refugees are unable to leave the receiving country to their mother land the entire expenditure for the maintenance of the refugee camps and other financial commitments need to bared by the refugee home government. These measures help to reduce the burden of on the part of receiving country and enhance the commitment on the part of the refugee home land. All these steps eliminate conflicts between the receiving country and refugee mother country. This also leads to provide assistance programme effectively and protection and promotion of the human rights of refugees.

It is necessary that protection sensibilities must be better integrated in the programme work of UNHCR. A comprehensive planning process and involvement of the Division of International Protection in formulating responses to emergencies would be crucial. New training programmes should be established for protection of officers on human rights and humanitarian law and institutions. In this regard, there should be collaboration among other UN agencies and sections, including the departments of peace-keeping operations, the humanitarian affairs and the centre for human rights. Specialized agencies such as the UN Relief and Works Administration, and NGOs such as the International Committee of the Red Cross and others should also be involved to over see the issue of violation of the human rights of the refugees both in the camps and in repatriation.

NOTES AND REFERENCES

1. Manik Chakrabarty (1998), "*Human Rights and Refugees–Problems, Laws and Practices*", Deep and Deep Publications, New Delhi, p. IX.

2. Sadhna Sharma (2002), "Refugees", Third Concept, November, p. 17.
3. Manik Chakrabarty, *Op.cit.*, p. XII.
4. ———(2004), Global Refugee Trends UNHCR, Geneva, June 2005, p. 2, *in http:/www.unhcr,org/statistics.*
5. Sadhna Sharma, *Op.cit.*, p. 17.
6. *Ibid.* p. 18.
7. Anand, V. K. (2001), "Human Rights", Allahabad Law Agency, Faridabad, p. 253.
8. Naorem Sanajaoba (1994), *Human Rights: Principles, Practices and Abuses*, Omsons Publications, New Delhi, p. 196.
9. Anand, V. K., "Human Rights", *Op. cit,* p. 253.
10. Sadhna Sharma, "Refugees", *Op.cit.*, pp. 18-19.
11. ———(2004), Global Refugee Trends, UNHCR, *Op.cit.,* p. 6.
12. Bajwa, G. S. (1995), *Human Rights in India: Implementation and Violations,* Annual Publications Pvt. Ltd., New Delhi, pp. 75-76.
13. Manik Chakrabarty, *Op.cit.,* pp. 10-11.
14. ———(2004), Global Refugee Trends, UNHCR, *Op. cit.*, pp. 2-5.
15. Manik Chakrabarty, *Op. cit.,* p. 16.
16. In *http://www.refugeesinternational, org/content/article/detail/933/.*
17. Bernard Laviric (1985), "Sri Lankans in Tamil Nadu", Refugees, No. 24, December, p. 11. Quoted by Manik Chakrabarty, *Op.cit.*, pp. 161-163.
18. Kuldip Nayar (1992), "No Decision Yet on Lanka Tamils", The Statesman, 6th Oct. p. 8, Quoted by Manik Chakrabarty, *Op. cit.,* p. 163.
19. Manik Chakrabarty, *Op. cit.,* pp. 163-164.
20. *Ibid,* p. 164.
21. UNHCR–Global Appeal on Sri Lanka, 2005, pp. 250-251.
22. *http://www.refugeesinternational.org/content/article/detail/933/.*
23. Udayakumar, S. P., "India: Tamil Refugees Hope Talks Will Get Them Home", in *http://www.ipsnews.net/srilanka/inida 1609.shtml.*

24. In *http://refugeesinternational,org/content/article/detail/933/.*

25. Udayakumar, S.P., "India: Tamil Refugees Hope Talks Will Get Them Home. *http://www.ipsnews,net/srilanka/inida 1609.shtml.*

26. Manik Chakrabarty, *Op.cit.,* pp. 168-169.

27. UNHCR–Global Appeal on Sri Lanka–2005, pp. 148-150.

28. Sadhna Shama, "Refugees", *Op. cit.,* p. 20.

29. UNHCR-Global Report on South Asia, 2004, p. 368.

30. Sadhna Sharma, Refugees, *Op.cit.*, p. 21.

31. Udayakumar, S. P., "India: Tamil Refugees Hope Talks Will Get Them Home", *http://www.ipsnews.net/srilanka/inida 1609.shtml.*

32. Chandrasekharan, "Bhutan: Bhutanese Refugees: Repatriation Chances Look Bleak" in *http://www.saag.org/notes3/note 212.html.*

Obscuring the Asylum-Seeker in the Refugee: A Note on the Ambit of Non-refoulement in Refugee Law

RENUKA DHINAKARAN* & VYDYANATHAN LAKSHMANAN**

The problem of mass exodus of refugees and their influx into a nation have put international refugee law at a crossroads time and again. Questions such as whether the principle of non-refoulement is applicable to situations of mass exodus have also been under consideration of the international community for over a long period of time–in an effort spasmodically pursued by state behaviour and consistently contentious with the global refugee program administrator, the UNHCR. Further, the supposed territoriality application of this principle and the competing considerations of national security and humanitarianism have clouded this field of international law with sufficient doubts. This paper seeks to evaluate the existing literature and the development of the law, as evidenced by contemporary state practice on the subject and seeks to make an argument for the pre-eminence of the principle of non-refoulement even in cases where states have attempted to put forth exceptions to the rule by citing security reasons and instances of mass exodus.

Under Article 33 of the Convention Relating to the Status of Refugees, 1951, the Contracting States are prohibited from returning a refugee in *any manner whatsoever* to the frontiers

* The School of Excellence in Law, The Tamil Nadu Dr. Ambedkar Law University, Chennai, India.

** The School of Excellence in Law, The Tamil Nadu Dr. Ambedkar Law University, Chennai, India.

of territories where he would be subjected to persecution.[1] This is known as the principle of non-refoulement, with the state so sending back referred to by the French word *refouler*. However, certain nations have issued declarations under various circumstances that 'asylum-seekers', especially those who come through boats, can be interdicted and ordered to leave the territorial waters of such nations, even if it meant forcibly sending them back. The question whether such mass repatriation of 'asylum-seeker' amounts to a violation of the principle of non-refoulement has been answered both the affirmative and negative by the domestic courts of these nations and by the international community.

The fact that the term 'asylum-seeker(s)' is being put forth for the purposes of this argument is creating fundamental nomenclature problems. The distinction that states strike here is that one who lawfully pleads entry is an asylum-seeker while one, by whatever means, has some how found his presence in the territory of another state becomes a refugee. However, this distinction is artificial and rather perverse; for a person illegally entering might have to show greater than the one standing at the borders than he does not attract any of the exception clauses in Article 33(2). It appears that the purpose of conferring this uneasy legal status to a person as an 'asylum-seeker', not being a 'refugee' under the Convention, but one still satisfying the substantive requirements there under, enables states to evade the exacting pressures of the Refugee Convention. This is rightly so because if these persons were to be termed 'refugees', it would amount to doing two things with legal repercussions: firstly, the state so saying might be forced to agree that the persons in question are indeed refugees under international law; secondly, there is the problem of automatic application of the caveat in Article 33 that prohibits, in *any manner whatsoever,* the return of these persons and thus rendering, even the interdiction of these people for the purpose of forcing them to leave by coercion, illegal. We argue that regardless of this distinction between refugees and asylum-seekers, if at all one exists, the prohibition in Article 33 is wide enough to cover all those who are on the verge of a border or have entered a border, subject to the only condition that the person so entering fears one or more of the kinds of persecutions that the Convention lists.[2]

The preceding paragraph does not, however, seek to cast doubts on the prevalence of the term 'asylum-seekers' in international law before the 1951 Convention. In fact, the law on seeking and providing what has been referred to as 'diplomatic asylum' was considered by the ICJ in the *Asylum* case,[3] in 1950, before the Convention came into being.[4] The term 'asylum' can be categorically traced back to the UDHR,[5] which provides, in very generic terms, that a person fleeing persecution has the right to seek and to enjoy *asylum* in other countries. Introspection shows that this provision was neither intended at that time to create legal consequences for states,[6] nor was it envisaged then that an exclusive convention on refugees under the UN aegis would be born. Thus, the right to *asylum* was used in a normative sense and on somewhat comparable lines to what is today the legal doctrine of non-refoulement. This was potentially a nascent move towards according legal status to the rule which was suddenly heightened by the fact that the Refugee Convention did not use the word 'asylum-seeker' but consistently adhered the 'refugee' terminology.[7] It is doubtful if it was predicted then that the term refugee–naturally implied to include and subsume within it all its nomenclatural synonyms and variations, a fact well evidenced by the wide definition in Article 1 (A)–would create problems like the ones we are witnessing now, a distinction between a refugee and an asylum-seeker.

However, there has come to be a view that the principle of *non-refoulement* embodied in Article 33 of the Refugee Convention is applicable only to those who have gained admission to the territory, even if illegally, but not to those who seek asylum at the frontiers.[8] Apart from the theoretical distinction that we seek to thwart between refugees and asylum-seekers, there has been this self-legitimized follow-up action that states have taken on the basis of this distinction.

It is put forth by these states that since asylum-seekers have not entered borders, including territorial waters, the states would have a right to refoul them outside their borders since the Convention is territorially operative and cannot apply to or control state parties' activities outside their borders. Supporters of this view resort to the *travaux* pre'paratoires of the Convention where, they argue evidence can be found that the participants in the Conference took pains to record the same. However, the deliberations show the contrary.[9] Some states even went further to stress that Article 33 did not cover cases of mass migration.[10] Judge Edwars, in *Haitian Refugee Center* v. *Gracery*[11], observed "that 'expulsion' would refer to a 'refugee already admitted into a country' and that 'return' would refer to a 'refugee already within the territory but not yet resident there'."[12] Thus, it is argued that the Convention was not intended to govern parties' conduct outside their national borders. This view has found recognition and approval within the academic community as being correct.[13]. These scholars argue that even the UNHCR has implicitly acknowledged that the Convention has no extraterritorial application,[14] though the validity of this argument is yet to be tested.[15]

It is also argued that state practice in this area has been consistent with this provision. Commentators point out instances such as these, in *Sale v. Haitian Centers Council, Inc.,* where the US Supreme Court upheld the order of President Bush declaring the immediate return of all passengers in the Haitian boats seeking asylum to Port-Au-Prince without any screening as valid on the ground that the Refugee Convention does not apply outside the territory of a state party.[16] Various other states in applying the principle of non-refoulement with regard to return of asylum-seekers at the frontiers have followed this precedent.[17] Thus, it is believed by these commentators that a categorical refusal to allow disembarkation cannot be equated with breach of the principle of non-refoulement, even though it may result in serious consequences for asylum-seekers.[18] Even if such a refusal amounted to a breach, it has been observed that the silence maintained by the international community during the mass repatriations concerning the Rwandan and Kosovo refugees, suggests that the principle can be violated with no adverse consequences.[19]

Further, there is no doubting that terrorists are far more likely to pursue illegal migration channels to infiltrate a state than to use asylum procedures as, according to normal procedure, asylum-seekers are subject to rigorous identity and security checks, document verification, administrative, scrutiny, suspicion of credibility, and, in some states, mandatory administrative detention.[20] The nations which support this theory resort to Security Council Resolution 1373 (2001)[21] which has declared that all member countries shall ensure, in conformity with international law, that refugee status is not abused by the perpetrators, organizers or facilitators of terrorist acts. Also, under customary international law, in order to safeguard the population (i.e., of the state in which asylum is sought), as in the case of mass influx of persons, refugees may be rejected at the frontier,[22] more so, when there is a possibility of entry of terrorists in the guise of asylum-seekers. The General Assembly Declaration on Territorial Asylum provided that exception may be made to the principle of non-refoulement for national security reasons in order to safeguard the population, as in the case of a mass influx of persons.[23]

However, we submit that the acceptance of this principle as a rule of international law would undermine the very existence of refugee law. The Security Council and the General Assembly Resolutions in this context cannot be seen as clarifying or substantially qualifying what is in quite unequivocal terms in the Convention. The binding nature of Security Council Resolutions under Article 25 of the Charter read with Article 103, as one even above any other treaty obligation–to the extent of modification of those obligation – has not been that easy a conclusion and the scholarly community has quite consistently cautioned that the Security Council is incompetent to alter or modify treaty obligations.[24]

The position of law should be assumed to be expressly clarified by the General Assembly in a later resolution, where the Assembly, while condemning terrorist activities, "Stressed the importance of full compliance by States with their obligations under the provisions of the 1951 Convention and the 1967 Protocol relating to the Status of Refugees, including the principle of non-refoulemnt of refugees to places where their life or freedom would be threatened on account of their race, religion, nationality, membership in a particular social group or political opinion, and *affirming that the present Declaration does not affect the protection afforded under the terms of the Convention and Protocol and other provisions of international law.*"[25]

Rightly, the UNHCR has declared that the principle of non-refoulement applies to asylum-seekers both at the borders and within the territory.[26] In fact, in the light of state practice[27] since 1951, a strong case can be made that non-refoulement now includes non-rejection at the frontiers, and further that non-refoulement of refugees has crystallized as a rule of customary international law binding on all States.[28]

With respect to mass influx, it has very weakly and very rarely been asserted that the non-refoulement rule ceases to apply in such situations. On the contrary the Executive Committee of the UNHCR has expressly stated that in such cases "the fundamental principle of non-refoulement......must be scrupulously observed."[29] It has also reaffirmed the fundamental importance of the observance of the principle of non-refoulement at the border and within the territory of a state, of persons who may be subjected to persecution if returned to their country of origin irrespective of whether or not they have been formally recognized as refugees.[30]

In the situations of large-scale influx, the so-called asylum-seekers should be admitted to the State in which they first seek refuge and if that State is unable to admit them on a durable basis, it should always admit them at least on a temporary basis and provide them with protection.[31] However, during a mass exodus, it may not be possible to carry out individual screening or RSD procedures by the High Commission. In such circumstances, particular when civilians are fleeing for similar reasons, it may be appropriate to declare 'group' determination of refugee status, whereby each civilian is considered a refugee, *prima facie*–in other words, in the absence of evidence to the contrary.[32]

Regardless of any other consideration, if a person is fleeing persecution, armed conflict, threats to life or object poverty, that person is entitled to minimum human rights and minimum standards of treatment.[33] Even in situations of mass influx, where other priorities like national security may prevail, the emphasis on individual procedural rights may be replaced by a group or categories approach.[34]

It also appears that the principle of non-refoulement cannot be violated on the ground that persecution has not emanated from the state. Persecution may also emanate from entities for which no link with the state can be established and which the state is unable to control.[35] Persecution that does not involve state complicity is still, nonetheless, persecution.[36] Perhaps, an analogous phenomenon in the law can be seen here as useful to construct this argument. When states traditionally do bear international responsibility for the wrongful acts committed by private actors on its territory, with certain qualifications though, it can be seen that when a state is unable to prevent violence against its own people, it has failed in its paramount duty to protect the life and property of its citizens, thus subjecting them to persecution indirectly. The normative underpinnings behind the rule against refoulement have been taken to the level of arguing that a State, which returns a refugee, causes persecution akin to an accomplice of the persecutor.[37] Furthermore, the UNHCR believes that non-refoulement has gained customary status[38]. and even *ius cogens.*[39]

It is true that under Article 33 (2) of the Refugee Convention, if there are reasonable grounds for regarding a refugee as a danger to the national security of the country of refuge, the protection against refoulement under Article 33 (1) cannot be availed of. This rule needs to be interpreted restrictively and the assessment of the danger needs to be individual and *ex futuro.*[40] Thus, *refoulement* may be done only if a provable danger to the national security or community of the country of refuge exits,[41] which is possible only when refugees are given an opportunity to establish their refugee status. International law, in keeping with its high human rights standard and the object of the Convention, should be assumed to have relinquished this discretion to states in the strictest manner.[42] Indeed, while this being apart, it has even been suggested that the substantive issue relating to what is actually 'persecution', should be considered from a perspective that would underline the subjective nature of the issue, providing for refugee status on *prima facie* proof.[43] If an issue, important as proof of persecution itself could take a beneficial meaning, it needs to be asked why the technicalities of Article 33 should not give way to the object and purpose of the Convention. A fair, efficient and expeditious procedure for the determination of refugee status even in situations involving large numbers is definitely obligatory under international law.[44]

As might be seen, this paper seeks no modification or rewriting of the international refugee law regime. It rather carves an argument in favour of removing the practices that have been plaguing the issue by trying to state what would be the right interpretation of the Convention. The paper sees a merely corrective role for states and the UNHCR through an effective clarificatory process.

NOTES

1. Article 33(1) runs: "No Contracting State shall expel or return ("refouler") a refugee in any account of his race, religion, nationality, membership of a particular social group or political opinion."
2. The precondition of fear of persecution has consistently been held to be a *sine qua non* requirement for the application of refugee status, see, *Lluvia v. Lluvia, 23* ILR 388, *Yugoslav Refugee (Germany) case,* 26 ILR (1958-II) 496, *Determination of Refugee Status (Germany) case,* 32 ILR 227, *Asylum (Algerian*

Refugee) case, 32 ILR 230 and *Polish Refugee (Germany) Case,* 38 ILR 146.

3. *Columbia v. Peru,* ICJ Reports, 1950, p. 226.

4. For a historical evolution of the law on refugees, see, Rodger, Jessica, 'Defining the Parameters of the Non-refoulement Principle', LL.M. Research Paper, International Law (Laws 509), Faculty of Law, Victoria University of Wellington, 2001, para 8, available at *http://www.refugee.org.nz/JessicaR.htm. [Last visited 11.01.2007].*

5. Article 14 (1).

6. The legal status of UDHR as an instrument, at the time of adoption, was not binding, though it has achieved customary status today.

7. Note that the term 'asylum' is used only once in the Convention, in the Preamble.

8. Guy & Goodwin-Gill, *The Refugee in International Law,* 74, Oxford (1983), there was a second edition of the book in 1996.

9. The Swiss delegate expressed this opinion according to which States were not compelled to allow large groups of persons claiming refugee status of cross its frontiers, which was recalled by the Netherlands delegate. The President *ruled* that the interpretation of the Netherlands representative should be placed on record, see, *Conference of Plenipotentiaries on the Status of Refugees and Stateless Persons,* Summary Record of the Thirty-fifth Meeting, UN Doc. A/CONF.2/SR.35, at pp. 21-22 (July 25, 1951); thus, it is quite clear that the Swiss delegate neither wanted to suggest terminological differences between refugees and asylum-seekers, nor argue on the territoriality of the Convention, but rather conveyed a fear premised on the specific issue of mass exodus, which now ultimately stands accounted for by the mechanisms in Article 33(2). See also Blackmun J, *infra* note 15 (internal citations omitted), where he argues that the *travaux* is of no importance here since Article 33 is plan and clear and as a matter of treaty interpretation, the *travaux* ought not to be looked at for any help.

10. See Robinson, N, 'Convention Relating to the Status of Refugees: Its History, Contents, and Interpretation: A Commentary', Institute of Jewish Affairs, New York (1953): UNHCR Reprint, 1997.

11. 257 US App. DC 413:809, F. 2d 840.

12. See a similar reasoning of the US Supreme Court on Article 33, in *Sale v. Haitian Centre's Council Inc., infra.*

13. See, Robinson, N, *op.cit.*, pp. 162-163 (*The Study on Statelessness* [UN Dept. of Social Affairs 60 (1949)] ("Art. 33 concerns refugees who have gained entry into the territory of a Contracting State, legally or illegally, but not to refugees who seek entrance into [the] territory"); note here that the term 'asylum-seekers' has been conspicuously avoided; Grahl-Madsen, *The Status of Refugees in International Law,* Leiden, Sijthoff, 94, (1972) ("Article 33 only prohibits the expulsion or return (refoulement) of refugees to territories where they are likely to suffer persecution; it does not obligate the Contracting State to admit any person who has not already set foot on their respective territories").

14. Officer of the UN High Commissioner for Refugees, Handbook on Procedures and Criteria for Determining Refugee Status, 46 (Geneva, Sept. 1979) (Quoting Official Records of the General Assembly, Thirty second Session, Supplement No. 12 (A/32/12/ Add.1), paragraph 53 (6) (e)).

15. Blackmun J, in his dissenting opinion in *Sale* v. *Haitian Centers Council, Inc.,* 113 S.Ct. 2549 (June 21, 1993) (internal citations omitted), points out that it was consistent American position that the Convention even applied to the high seas, citing, 5 Op. Off. Legal Counsel 242, 248 (1981) (under proposed interdiction of Haitian flag vessels, "[i] individuals who claim that they will be persecuted.....must be given an opportunity to substantiate their claims" under the Convention); United States as a Country of Mass First Asylum; Hearing Before the Subcommittee on Immigration and Refugee Policy of the Senate Committee on the Judiciary, 97th Cong., 1st Sess., 208-209 (1981) (letter from Office of Attorney General stating: "Aliens who have not reached our borders (such as those on board interdicted vessels) are ....by the UN Convention and Protocol).

16. See, *supra* note, Blackmum J dissented that the process of arrival at this construction negates the cardinal rule of plain reading of something that is clearly worked, thus making the majority interpretation a "puzzling progression", going "astray" (internal citations omitted).

17. The Tanzanian Government, in 1995, closed its broders to a group of more than 50,000 Rwandan refugees who were fleeing renewed violence. Similarly 500,000 refugees were returned to Rwandan from Zaire in late 1996. Furthermore, the UNHCR, actually assisted the return of refugees from Tanzania.
18. Guy & Goodwin-Gill, *op.cit.,* p. 87 (1983).
19. Howland, Todd, 'Refoulement of Refugees: the UNHCR's Lost Opportunity to Ground Temporary Refuge in Human Rights Law', 4 U.C. Davis, *J. Int'l L & Pol'y*, 73, 85 (1998).
20. Australia detains all asylum seekers arriving in Australia without permission: Crock & Saul, *Future Seekers: Refugees and the Law in Australia,* Federation Press, Sydney, pp. 75-98 (2002).
21. SC Resolution 1373, dated 28.09.2001 (Press Release SC/7158), available at *http://www.un.org/News/Press/docs/2001/sc7158.doc.htm (last visited on 11.01.2007).*
22. Acknowledged in Article 3 (2) of the Declaration on Territorial Asylum 1967.
23. GA Res. 2312 (XXII) (Dec. 14, 1967).
24. The need to stress the same arose in the specific context of the Security Council's intervention in the working of the ICC, through a series of resolutions that either abused the powers of the Council under Article 16 of the Rome Statute or provided absolute immunity to non-nationals of contributing states who are in the territory of a state party.
25. GA Res. 51/210, 88th Plenary Meeting (17 Dec. 1996), Annexure on Declaration to Supplement the 1994 Declaration on Measures to Eliminate International Terrorism, pp. 5-7.
26. See for example, UNHCR Executive Committee Report, 1977; available at, *http://www.unhcr.ch/refworld/unhcr/excom/xconc/excom6.htm* (last visited 11.01.2007).
27. The principle of non-refoulement applies to persons within the State's territory as well as to persons seeking admission at the border, Comment by the European Council on Refugees and Exiles (ECRE) on the Right to Asylum in the Draft Charter on Fundamental Rights of the European Union, May 2000, paras. 7, 8.
28. Guy, Goodwin-Gill, *op.cit..,* pp. 97-100 (1983), The question of persistent objection might not arise here fore two reasons, one

being that the issue would never pertain to treaties and secondly since a misinterpretation cannot be put on a Convention for a state to relinquish its otherwise applicable obligation.

29. UNHCR Executive Committee Conclusion 22, *http://www.unhcr.ch/cgibin/texis/vtx/home/opendoc.htm* (last visited 11.01.2007).
30. UNHCR Executive Committee Conclusion No. 6 (XXVIII)–1977, Conclusion endorsed upon the recommended of the Sub-Committee on International Protection of Refugees.
31. Conclusion No. 22, Report of the 32nd Session, UN Doc. A/AC.96/601, para 57(2).
32. *Ibid.*
33. Rodger, Jessica, *op.cit.*
34. See generally, Jones, David Thomas, 'Sale v. Haitian Centre's Council, Inc.', 88 AJIL 114 (1994).
35. *Zachariah v. Republic of Cyprus (1962)* 2 All ER 438; *McMullen v. Immigration and Naturalization Service* 79 ILR 602; the danger of persecution which is a requirement for refugee status, has been held to include persecution at the hands of private persons or non-governmental groups, now clubbed under the banner of 'non-state actors' in the context of human rights and state responsibility law.
36. UN High Commissioner for Refugees, Information Note on Article 1 of the 1951 Convention, Geneva, March 1995, p. 5, Also see UNHCR Handbook on Protecting Refugees, available at, *http/www.unhcr.ch/* (last visited on 11.01.2007)
37. *Travaux Préparatoires,* Commentary on Article 31, para 3, note 1: "The turning back of the refugee to the frontiers of the country where his life or liberty is threatened on account of his race, religion, nationality or political opinions........would be tantamount to delivering him into the hand of his persecutors."
38. See, Summary Conclusions on The Principle of Non-refoulement, UNHCR & Lauterpacht Research Centre for International Law (in collaboration), Global Consultations on International Protection, Cambridge Roundtable, 2001, available at *http://www.unhcr,bg/globalconsult/principe non refoulement en. pdf* [hereinafter 'Cambridge Roundtable'].

39. Newmark, L Robert, 'Non-Refoulement Run Afoul: The Questionable Legality of Extraterritorial Repatriation Programs', 71 Wash. U.L.Q. 833, 845; however, regardless of the question as to the existence of *ius cogens* as superior norms (a question in dispute today), the elevation of the non-refoulement rule on refugees to a peremptory status is marred by divergent state practice. This is so, for, however stupendous the UNHCR might stick to these practices, it is only states that can, if at all, create *ius cogens* norms. We would however willingly concede a *lex ferenda* status to the question. More uniform and rigid adherence to the principle in our times should make a case for qualification of the norm as peremptory in the future.

40. Bruin, Rene & Wouters, Kees, 'Terrorism and the Non-derogability of Non-refoulement', 15 *Int'I Journal of Refugee Law,* 5 (2003).

41. *Ibid.*

42. See Cambridge Roundtable, *op. cit.*

43. Aleinikoff, T Alexander, 'The Meaning of Persecution in United States Asylum Law', 3 *Int'1 Journal of Refugee Law,* 5 (1991).

44. See however, Kagan, Michael, 'The Beleaguered Gatekeeper', 18 *Int'I Journal of Refugee Law,* 19 (2006), on the sad state of Refugee Status Determination (RSD) conducted by the UNHCR, archiving the particular instances where states and the High Commission have relinquished the responsibility to each other.

Development of International Standards on Rights of Disabled Person

B. S. Patil*

INTRODUCTION

The state has two major duties towards man, a duty to provide for the fundamental needs and the duty to protect a person against harm that can be caused by illegal acts.

The role of the state as a protector can be scrutinized regularly and effectively. With the advent of 24 hour news channels and much improved communication technology, the performance of the State can be monitored constantly[1]. But in reality it is the role of the states as a provider that plays a major role in the progress report of the ruling party. But the assessment of the performance is a difficult task. The State formulates various policies and schemes and constitutes authorities; in which it makes huge investments. But the end result of the scheme will not be available immediately. This difficult task of assessment can be answered by keeping International norms and standards as a yardstick. The state may or may not be party to such International Conventions or Declarations, but it serves as a guideline for the assessment.

This article is an attempt to consolidate the International Conventions, Declarations and Norms dealing with Human Rights as a whole and Right of Disabled Persons in particular.

* Lecturer in Law, V.M. Salgaocar College of Law, Miramar, Panaji, Goa.

The International law relating to human rights and dignity can be classified into two categories, the Human Rights Law and the Humanitarian Law. The Human Rights Law deals with the rights of human beings in all the aspects of the life and it is the law which operates during peace time. This category of law imposes both positive and negative obligations on the state to protect the human rights. The positive obligation is of taking actions and actively involving in protecting human rights[2]. And negative obligation of state is to abstain itself from violating the human rights[3]. On the other hand humanitarian law comes into operation and gains recognition during wartime. These laws protect the civilians during combats, provide special protection to the women and children not involved with the war, and safeguard the combatants captured by the enemy troops[4].

The human rights became part of the international law and could be developed to this stage due to United Nations Organisation. The development of Human Right is a recent phenomenon, and United Nations Organization has made it an international obligation. It began as a declaration and has graduated itself to the level of imposing obligations on the state. The development is to such an extent that a sovereign state is under the duty to submit report to the International Monitoring Committee. This development is a result of acceptance of Human Rights as an international phenomenon.

EVOLUTION OF HUMAN RIGHTS

Human Rights Law Development is primarily based on international treaties, rather than customary sources of international law. The major contributor for the development of International Human Rights Law has been United Nations Organization.[5] The other major source of development of human rights law has been treaties of Regional Bodies[6], Bilateral Treaties and International Non Governmental Organizations[7].

The Human Rights Law can be classified into three categories viz the first generation, the second generation and third generation of human rights law. The first generation of Human Rights essentially deals with liberty of individual and participation in political life. They are fundamentally of a civil and political nature, and serve to protect the individual from excesses of the state[8]. The second generation human rights mainly relate to equality and began to be recognized by governments after World War I. They are fundamentally social, economic and cultural in nature. They ensure to the members of the citizenry equal environment and treatment[9]. The third generation of human rights is those rights which go beyond mere civil and social rights as expressed in various Human Rights progressive documents. These rights include group rights, right to self determination, right to environment and natural resources[10].

The human rights law can be classified as soft law and hard law. The general declaration and recognition of rights by international community or organization is considered to be a 'soft law'. Under the soft law the signatory nation will be recognizing them as a group of rights. But the state is under no obligation to take steps to protect them. Further the international community will not be in a position to demand enforcement of the soft law. On the other hand the 'hard law' not only declares rights but also the law takes steps to enforce the recognized rights by establishing Independent Monitoring Authority. The authority established under the hard law, is empowered to visit, inspect and also demand the submission of report[11]. Under this category of law the signatory nation recognizes the group of rights and is under the international obligation to implement those recognized rights.

The contribution of international community in development of 'hard human rights law' is remarkable. There are seven Conventions which stand out as notable contributions. These seven Conventions create seven supervisory authorities to oversee the performance of the state in protecting and promoting the rights enshrined in the Convention. These Conventions generally deal with the human rights issue, and cover the general needs of the Human

Being. But these instruments fail to create proper platform for the special needs of the special groups, like indigenous groups, disabled groups, etc.

INTERNATIONAL CONVENANT ON CIVIL AND POLITICAL RIGHTS[12]

This Convention is supported by two optional protocols. This Covenant is applicable generally to all the humans. It is developed to protect the Civil and Political rights of the individual in particular and of the society in general. These rights are important to establish a 'people centric' and 'people responsive' government[13].

The Covenant considers the principles proclaimed in the Charter of the United Nations and declares that 'to lay down the foundation of freedom, justice and peace in the world it is necessary to recognize the inherent dignity and equal and inalienable rights of all members of the human family. The covenant considers these civil and political rights as derived from the inherent dignity of the human person[14].

The ICCPR imposes a duty on the States Parties, including those having responsibility for the administration of Non-Self-Governing and Trust Territories, that they shall promote the realization of the right of self-determination[15]. India became signatory to the Covenant on the 10th of July 1979, but in the capacity of a conditional signatory.

INTERNATIONAL COVENANT ON ECONOMIC, SOCIAL AND CULTURAL RIGHTS[16]

This covenant is applicable to all human in common. This covenant has been enforced to protect the human's enjoyment of freedom from fear of want. This objective could be achieved only by providing and protecting the conditions whereby everyone may enjoy his economic, social and cultural rights, as well as his civil and political rights. The duty of enforcing or respecting these rights is on state and also on the fellow citizens. All the individuals are under the obligation to promote and observe the rights recognized under the

Convenant[17]. India became a conditional signatory to the Convenant on the 10th of July 1979.

INTERNATIONAL CONVENTION ON THE ELIMINATION OF ALL FORMS OF RACIAL DISCRIMINATION[18]

This convention was passed in consideration of Charter of United Nation, where the dignity and equality to all human is protected irrespective of its race, sex, language and religion. Further considering the Universal Declaration of Human Rights, which provides for equality before law and equal protection of law without discrimination, and also considering the basic concept that all human are born free, equal in dignity and rights. Based on the above principles the Conventions affirmed to eliminate all forms of racial discrimination. On the 4th of January 1969, India became signatory to the covenant.

CONVENTION ON THE ELIMINATION OF ALL FORMS OF DISCRIMINATION AGAINST WOMEN[19]

This Convention defines discrimination against women as any distinction, exclusion or restriction made on the basis of sex, which has the effect or purpose of impairing or nullifying the recognition, enjoyment or exercise by women, on a basis of equality of men and women, of human rights and fundamental freedoms in the political, economic, social, cultural, civil or any other field[20]. To this Convention too India became a conditional signatory on the 8th of August 1993.

CONVENTION AGAINST TORTURE AND OTHER FORMS OF CRUEL, INHUMAN OR DEGRADING TREATMENT OR PUNISHMENT[21]

The convention was signed by India on the 14th of Oct. 1997, but the same has not yet been ratified. This convention is brought into force exclusively to fight against cruel, inhuman and degrading forms of punishments.

THE CONVENTION ON THE RIGHTS OF THE CHILD[22]

This Convention addresses the need of the protecting the rights of the child. As the family is the fundamental group of social, and the natural environment for the growth and well-being of all its members and particularly children needs necessary protection and assistance so that the child can fully assume its responsibilities within the community[23]. This Convention was signed by India on the 11th of January, 1993 and the Convention recognizes the child's need for the full and harmonious development of his or her personality, and he/she should grow up in a family environment, in an atmosphere of happiness, love and understanding.

INTERNATIONAL CONVENTION ON THE PROTECTION OF RIGHTS OF ALL MIGRANTS AND MEMBERS OF THEIR FAMILIES

In December 1990, the General Assembly adopted the Convention. The Convention opened a new chapter in the history of efforts to establish the rights of migrant workers and to ensure that those rights are protected and respected. It is a comprehensive international treaty, inspired by existing legally binding agreements, by United Nations human rights studies, by the conclusions and recommendations of meetings of experts, and by the debates and resolutions on the migrant worker question in United Nations bodies over the past two decades[24]. Presently India is not party to the Convention.

Further the International Human Rights Law can be classified in to Main stream Instruments, which apply to all humans, and Group-Specific Instruments, which provide special protection to persons with special needs[25]. This phenomenon of Group Centric Instruments is a recent development in the area of Human Rights. The need arose, when Main Stream Instruments were not sufficiently competent to provide justice to the requirements of the special groups. These Group Specific Instruments reiterate rights in the similar path of main stream instruments. But these instruments address the special needs, which was not possible in main stream instruments.

EVOLUTION OF INTERNATIONAL CONCERN ON RIGHTS OF DISABLED PERSONS

The UNO's early approach was to promote rights of disabled persons by formulating projects and creating bodies to implement these projects. This approach of UN did not help in recognizing the rights of disabled persons. As the general Human Rights Instruments were not capable of broad interpretations to provide shelter to the rights of disabled persons, this approach had charity aspect inbuilt. Further the UN considered only physical disability as criteria to be eligible under the project. This insensitive approach has to be condoned as the rights of disabled were still in nascent stage.

The first decade of functioning of the United Nations Organistion (1945-1955) created two principal bodies, the United Nations Secretariat and the Economic and Social Council, to deal with the disability issues. Their focus was on promoting the rights of persons with physical disabilities, such as blindness and deafness. The Projects concentrated on disability prevention and rehabilitation. In the year 1946 a special body called Social Commission was established to specifically look into the issues relating the disability[26].

In the year 1950, in the sixth session, the Social Commission took two reports for consideration: 'The Social Rehabilitation of the Handicapped' and "The Social Rehabilitation of the Blind". The problems faced by the disabled and rehabilitation of disabled were discussed at the Geneva Conference. This Conference has a unique achievement of giving rights of disabled a comprehensive approach by involving all UN bodies. The conference was attended by the Secretariat, the International Labour Organization (ILO), the World Health Organization (WHO), the United Nations Educational, Scientific and Cultural Organization (UNESCO), the International Refugee Organization, (IRO) and the United Nations International Children's Fund'. The outcome of the session was an agreement on the need to establish international standards for the education, treatment, training and placement of disabled persons, with particular attention to be given to the blind in underdeveloped countries. The Economic and Social Council also recommended the States to consider measures to help the handicapped persons[27].

In 1957, during eights session, the Social Commission discussed international rehabilitation for the physically disabled. The UNO made an attempt to raise awareness on the disability issue and emphasized the need for rehabilitation programmes throughout the world[28]. Programmes approved by the United Nations, ILO, WHO, UNESCO, UNICEF and IRO fall under different headings: viz.

- A new approach to disability,
- The education of public opinion,
- A complete rehabilitation programme,
- Developing rehabilitation services,
- Training rehabilitation personnel,
- Organizing and financing rehabilitation services,
- The contribution of the United Nations and the specialized agencies,
- The contribution of non-governmental organizations,
- And methods of coordinaton[29]

The Social Commission had done major progress in the area of rehabilitation of disabled. But even in these sessions, the approach was to create awareness, and provide special emphasis on rehabilitation, etc. But lately the UN has gradually changed its approach by making attempts to read the needs of the disabled person as rights under the established International Instruments.

In the year 1969, the General Assembly adopted the Declaration on Social Progress and Development, which affirms, the fundamental freedoms and principles of peace articulated in the Charter of the United Nations, which addresses the provision of health, social security, and social welfare services for all persons, aiming at the rehabilitation of the mentally and physically disabled so as to facilitate their integration into society.

On 20th December 1971, the General Assembly proclaimed the Declaration on the Rights of Mentally Retarded Persons and made a call for national and international action to ensure that it becomes the accepted basis and frame of reference for protecting the rights of the disabled.

At its twenty-fourth session in the year 1975, the Commission for Social Development recommended elimination of physical and architectural barriers that prevent the full social integration of disabled persons. On the 6th of May 1975, the Economic and Social Council adopted Resolution 1921 (LVIII), dealing with disability, prevention and rehabilitation of the disabled[30]. In the month of December of the same year, the General Assembly adopted the Declaration on the Rights of Disabled Persons, which states that all persons with disabilities are entitled to the rights stipulated, without discriminating as to race, colour, sex, language, religion, political or other opinions, national or social origin, state of wealth, birth or any other situation.

In 1976, the General Assembly recommended to all the Member States to take into account the recommendations outlined in the Declaration on the Rights of Disabled Persons while formulating policies, plans and programmes. It also proclaimed '1981' as International Year for Disabled Persona, stressing that, the Year should be devoted to fully integrating the disabled persons into society and encouraging relevant study and research projects to educate the public on the rights of the disabled persons. A trust fund for Member States' contributions to the International Year was established by the Secretary-General. In the year 1978, the Secretary-General established the Intergovernmental Advisory Committee for the International Year of Disabled Persons. International Non-Governmental Organizations participated in the International Year and established First Founding Congress of Disabled Peoples International, in Singapore.

The General Assembly adopted the World Programme of Action concerning Disabled Persons in the year 1982. The disability policy was completely restructured and it is now structured in three main areas: prevention; rehabilitation; and equalization of opportunities[31].

In 1988, the General Assembly called upon Member States to place special emphasis on the equalization of opportunities for disabled persons.

In 1989, the Secretary-General was requested by the General Assembly to bring the attention of Member States to the Tallinn Guidelines for Action on Human Resources Development in the Field of Disability[32]. The Guidelines recognize disabled persons as agents of their own destiny rather than as dependent objects of governments and seek to realize the full potential and capabilities of each individual. Employment is seen as a means for disabled persons to exercise effectively their full rights as citizens. The Guidelines state that disabled persons should be trained and employed in the work force on an equal basis with other members of society.

In 1991, the Rapporteur submitted the report to the Sub-Commission biannually on the Human Rights situation of the disabled. In the last report in 1991; the Rapporteur recommended the establishment of an international ombudsman. Later the General Assembly adopted the Principles for the Protection of Persons with Mental Illness and for the Improvement of Mental Health Care[33]. The General Assembly adopted Twenty-five principles to define the fundamental freedoms and basic rights of persons with mental illness.

The end of the Decade of Disabled Persons was marked by the General Assembly with the Declaration of 3 December as the International Day of Disabled Persons. The General Assembly also summarized the United Nations' goals in the field of disability, emphasizing once again the importance of the full integration of disabled persons into society and encouraging future United Nations Conferences to include discussion on disability issues. The Economic and Social Council welcomed the proclamation by establishing the Economic and Social Commission for Asia and the Pacific of the Asian and Pacific Decade of Disabled Persons, 1993-2002.

In 1993, the Standard Rules for the Equalization of Opportunities for Persons with Disabilities was adopted by the General Assembly. The Rules summarizes the message of the World Programme of Action and state preconditions for equal opportunity. They also target areas of equal participation and promote implementation measures and monitoring mechanisms.

The World Conference on Human Rights reconsidered the universally recognized Human Rights Instruments in light of contemporary issues and adopted the Vienna Declaration and Programme of Action. The Conference recognized all human rights and fundamental freedoms as universal, and thus to unreservedly include persons with disabilities.

The International Conference on Population and Development was held in Cairo in 1994. It recognized the importance of equalizing opportunities for people with disabilities.

The Preparatory Committee for the United Nations Conference on Human Settlements, held in Istanbul, Turkey, in June 1996, issued a draft statement of principles and commitments and a global plan of action, which pay particular attention to persons with disabilities deserving affirmative governmental action.

The UNO initiated an endeavor to pass an exclusive convention on the rights of disabled persons. As an outcome of the idea mooted in the late 90's, the Convention on the Rights of Persons with Disabilities and its Optional Protocol were adopted by the United Nations General Assembly on 13 December, 2006 and opened for signature on 30 March, 2007[34].

On the same day, 81 Member States and the European Community signed the Convention, the highest number of signatures of any human rights convention on its opening day.

44 Member States signed the Optional Protocol, and 1 Member State ratified the Convention[35].

The Convention was negotiated during eight sessions of an Ad Hoc Committee of the General Assembly from 2002 to 2006, making it the fastest negotiated human rights treaty. The Convention aims to ensure that persons with disabilities enjoy human rights on an equal basis with others.[36].

CONCLUSION

The United Nation Organization has been in forefront in development of international concern for disabled. The drafting of the convention[37], on the basic principles of inherent dignity, individual autonomy including the freedom to make one's own choices and independence of persons has been latest attempt by the United Nations Organization. The convention has been ratified by over 100 countries and UN is hopeful of bringing it into action in the year 2008.

The International Human Rights Law has developed in the form of series of conventions to provide benefit for groups with special needs. The evolution of law has reached its pinnacle from mere recognizing the needs of disabled, to declaration of rights of disabled and finally enforcing the rights of disabled in the form of conventions.

This evolution of International recognition of rights of persons with disabilities has created pressure groups in the form of NGO's and other associations, empowered by the International Conventions these pressure groups were able to sensitize the national legislature and lobbied to implement legislations protecting the rights of disabled. These conventions also created pressure groups in the form of international community and United Nations monitoring authorities. These attempts have helped in implementing internationally recognized rights. The state has also developed many indigenous policies to protect the rights of the disabled and provide effective participation and inclusion in society. The attempts of the state and empowering of the organizations are result of international concerns.

NOTES

1. The recent events, like 2008, New Year celebration incident of women molestation at Mumbai and 5th Jan. 2008 incident of road rash by unruly bikers at Faridabad, stands out as proof of regular scrutiny of state performance.
2. Duty of the state to safeguard economic, social and cultural rights of socially backward groups, minority groups, etc.
3. Duty not to violate freedom of speech and expression, freedom of assembly, etc.
4. Geneva Conventions and Geneva Protocols and additional Protocols.
5. For the contribution of United Nation Organization refer to the basic Human Rights Instruments.
6. African Union, European Union, Council of Europe and Organization of American States, etc.
7. The major contributor for the development of Humanitarian law has been International Committee of the Red Cross (ICRC). See M.K. Balchander and Rose Verghese 'Introduction to *International Humanitarian Law*'. Indian Centre for Humanitarian Law and Research, ICRC, New Delhi.
8. First generation human rights include freedom of speech, right to a fair trial, freedom of religion and voting rights.
9. Second generation human rights essentially includes right to employment, right to housing and health care etc.
10. *http://en.wikipedia.org/wiki/Three_generations_of_human_rights*
11. The role and authority of international monitoring authority differs from one convention to other. All the authorities mentioned may not be enjoyed the single authority.
12. The convenant was adopted and opened for signature in the year 1966, and the covenant was ratified and accessed by General Assembly resolution 2200A (XXI) of 16 December 1966 *entry into force* 23 March 1976, in accordance with Article 49.
13. *http://www.unhcr.ch/html/menu3/b/a_ccpr.htm*
14. See preamble of the International Covenant on Civil and Political Rights.
15. Article 5 of International Covenant on Civil and Political Rights.

16. *http://www.unhcr.ch/html/menu3/b/a_cescr.htm.* The covenant was adopted and opened for signature in 1966, and the covenant was ratifiedand accessed by General Assembly resolution 2200A (XXI) of 16 December 1966
17. See preamble of the International Covenant on Economic, Social and Cultural Rights.
18. *http://www.unhcr.ch/html/menu3/b/d_icerd.htm.* The covenant was adopted and opened for signature and ratification by General Assembly resolution 2106 (XX) of 21 December 1965 *entry.*
19. This international convention was adopted in 1979 by the United Nations General Assembly. Described as an international bill of rights for women, it came into force on 3 September 1981.
20. *http://www.un.org/womenwatch/daw/cedaw/*
21. The text of the Convention was adopted by the United Nations General Assembly on 10 December, 1984 and , it came into force on 26 June, 1987; 26.
22. Adopted and opened for signature, ratification and accession by General Assembly resolution 44/25 of 20 November 1989.
23. *http://www.unhchr.ch/html/menu3/b/k2crc.htm*
24. *http://www.unhchr.ch/html/menu6/2/fs24.htm*
25. Disability Manual, 2005, National Human Rights Commission, New Delhi, 2005 at p. 40.
26. Disability *http://www.un.org/esa/socdev/enable/dis50y00.*
27. Disability *http://www.un.org/esa/socdev/enable/dis50y00.*
28. The attempt was made in the year 1956 and UNO created a fund in the name of International Social Service Review.
29. Disability *http://www.un.org/esa/socdev/enable/dis50y00.*
30. Disability *http://www.un.org/esa/socdev/enable//dis50y00*
31. *http://www.un.org/esa/socdev/enable/documents/a62-157e.doc*
32. The International Meeting on Human Resources in the Field of Disability, convened at Tallinn, Union of Soviet Socialist Republics, from 14 to 22 August 1989, having considered the situation of human resources development in the field of disability, the recommendations were made for development in the field of disability.

33. Adopted by General Assembly resolution 46/119 of 17 December 1991, for list of principles refer http: / /*www.unhchr.ch / html / menu3 / b / 68.htm*
34. *http: / / www.un.org / esa / socdev / enable / rights / convtexte.htm*
35. *http: / / www.un.org / disabilities /*
36. *Ibid.*
37. Convention on the Rights of Persons with Disabilities was adopted on 13 December, 2006.

Remedies Under International Law to Victims of Human Rights Violations

KULJIT KAUR*

INTRODUCTION

Today, the protection of human rights is generally recognized to be a fundamental aim of modern international law. In recent decades, almost every international organization-regional and global-has adopted human rights norms and responded to human rights violations by opening avenues of redress for individuals against oppressive action by member states. Consideration of human rights issues has reached into all organs and bodies of the United Nations, including the Security Council, which has identified serious human rights violations as threats to the peace. As a result, international human rights law has reduced the content of the reserved domain of state sovereignty. No state can credibly claim that its treatment of those within its territory or jurisdiction is a matter solely of domestic jurisdiction.

For all its revolutionary advances, however, human rights law has yet to develop a coherent theory or consistent practice of remedies for victims of human rights violations. While many groups have pressed for effective avenues of redress, others have claimed priority for "reconciliation" following periods of oppression or insisted on amnesty for violators. International

* Reader and Head, Department of Laws, Guru Nanak Dev University, Amritsar-143 005.

human rights bodies that have jurisdiction to hear complaints often limit themselves to declaring findings of fact and law, sometimes recommending compensation of an unspecified amount be paid to the victims of violations[1].

The innovative nature of human rights litigation may account for the incoherence and inconsistency. Many human rights tribunals have been unsure about the extent of their power to afford remedies and have tended to focus on cessation of violation rather than redress for the victims. Another factor may be the lack of national judicial experience of most members of international tribunals. The most likely reasons, however, are the sudden development and unprecedented nature of international human rights law. Having emerged hesitatingly following the Second World War and then expanded rapidly in recent years, it displays an uneven proliferation of international complaints mechanisms and techniques that has created a mixture of remedies drawn from the traditional law of state responsibility, domestic legal systems, and the different views of judges about the role of tribunals in affording relief to victims of state abuse.

The remedial task is to convert law into results, to deter violations and restore the moral balance when wrongs are committed. The Latin maxim *ubi jus ibi remedium* (for the violation of every right, there must be a remedy) is not, and perhaps cannot be, strictly observed in practice. Rights have gone unremedied in the past and are likely to go unremedied in the future. Yet, in the literature, many scholars include the element of enforceability in their definition of legal rights, because a right entails a correlative duty to act or refrain from acting for the benefit of another person. Unless this duty is somehow enforced or enforceable, it is only a voluntary obligation that can be fulfilled or ignored at will. The aim of remedies, to vindicate interests that have been injured, thus requires that human rights law, representing fundamental interests, develop not only a primary theory of what duties are owed, but a secondary theory of what duties exist when a primary duty is violated[2].

In practice, the human rights litigant typically seeks to have government conduct declared wrongful and to have a remedy imposed against the state, even where the act or omission is based on the will of the majority expressed in legislation. The range of remedies could proceed from relatively no intrusive remedies, such as declaratory judgments and monetary damages, to injunctions, prohibitions and affirmative orders. The declaratory judgement merely pronounces a particular practice or condition to be illegal, leaving officials free to choose if and how to remedy the situation. The damage award assesses the harm that the misconduct has caused and imposes the cost upon wrongdoer. In general, tribunals should seek to create a hypothetical by aiming to produce the situation that would have existed if the wrongdoer had not violated the rights of the victim.

THE DUTY OF STATES TO AFFORD REMEDIES

There are close to one hundred human rights treaties adopted globally and regionally. Nearly all states are parties to some of them and several human rights norms have become part of customary international law. Yet, like all law, human rights law is violated. It has not ended governmental oppression and by itself cannot prevent or remedy all human rights abuses. Appropriate remedies can have a dissuasive effect on those who would commit violations, as well as serving to redress the wrongs done to victims. Remedies are thus a significant aspect of ensuring the rule of law.

The right to a remedy when rights are violated is itself a right expressly guaranteed by global and regional human rights instruments. Most texts guarantee both the procedural right of effective access to a fair hearing and the substantive right to a remedy[3]. Some international agreements explicitly call for the development of judicial remedies for the rights they guarantee, although effective remedies could be supplied by non-judicial bodies[4]. The role of international tribunals is subsidiary and only becomes necessary and possible when the state has failed to afford the required relief.

THE COMPETENCE OF HUMAN RIGHTS TRIBUNALS TO AFFORD REMEDIES

There are two sources of authority for human rights bodies to afford remedies when the state has failed to do so. The first is the express power granted by the instrument creating the institution. The second is the inherent power of any judicial or quasi-judicial body to redress the wrongs litigated before it.

Express Authority to Provide Redress

Close to a dozen international procedures allow victims to denounce violations of their human rights by a state party to the relevant treaty. Public and private procedures created by the UN Human Rights Commission address gross and systematic violations of internationally-recognized human rights, while working groups accept complaints or information about violations of specific human rights. Within the larger.

United Nations systems, the International Labor Organization and UNESCO have developed human rights complaint procedures for violations of rights within their mandate. Human rights treaty bodies established pursuant to the International Covenant on Civil and Political Rights, the Convention on the Elimination of All Forms of Racial Discrimination, and the Convention against Torture may receive petitions within their specific jurisdictional limits.

None of the permanent United Nations treaty or internal bodies has express legal competence to order compensation or other remedies[5]. The Human Rights Committee, the Committee on the Elimination of Racial Discrimination, and other bodies that accept individual communications may make recommendations or express views to the state concerned. The recommendations sometimes call on the state to pay compensation or afford other remedies, but until recently they did not specify amounts that may be due or indicate other forms of redress.

In addition to institutions with general human rights jurisdiction, other permanent international tribunals are competent to adjudicate specific human rights matters. The Administrative Tribunals of international organizations hear cases involving workers' rights, discrimination and sexual harassment. These tribunals have considerable remedial competence. The International Criminal Court may allow victims of international crimes to file claims for redress following prosecution of the accused and the court may order remedies directly against the person convicted or compensation to be paid from an international Trust Fund.

Inherent Powers

Inherent judicial powers to afford remedies have long been recognized in international jurisprudence and derive from the law of state responsibility, which requires a state to make reparations when it fails to comply, through an act or omission attributable to it with an obligation under international law[6]. The well-known ICJ formulation of the obligation to redress harm is stated in the *Chorzow Factory* case:

> "Reparation must, as far as possible, wipe out all consequences of the illegal act and reestablish the situation which would, in all probability have existed if that act had not been committed. Restitution in kind, or, if this is not possible payment of a sum corresponding to the value which a restitution would bear; the award, if need be, of damages for loss sustained which would not be covered by restitution in kind or payment in place of it–such are the principles which should serve to determine the amount of compensation due for an act contrary to international law[7]."

Notably, the ICJ indicated that the basic principle of reparation articulated in the *Chorzow Factory* case applies to reparation for injury to individuals, even when the statute of a tribunal contains a specific jurisdictional provision on reparation[8].

TYPES OF REMEDIES

In the jurisprudence of the UN Human Rights Committee to date, the specified remedies have included one or more of the following:

(a) public investigation to establish facts,

(b) bringing to justice the perpetrators,

(c) compensation,

(d) ensuring non-repetition of the violation,

(e) amending the law,

(f) providing restitution of liberty, employment or property,

(g) providing medical care and treatment,

(h) permitting the victim to leave the country,

(i) enjoining an imminent violation.

Guarantees of non-repetition are an important aspect of the Committee's approach to remedies. If frequently calls upon states parties to take steps to ensure that similar violations do not occur in the future. It also has stressed repeatedly that states parties are under an obligation to take immediate steps to ensure strict observance of the provisions of the Covenant.

PROBLEMS IN THE LAW OF REMEDIES

As human rights tribunals have been increasing asked to afford remedies for human rights violations, various difficult issues have arisen concerning matters such as who is entitled to remedy, how should compensation be calculated, should the degree of misconduct by the state be taken into account in determining the type or quantum of the remedies afforded, and how should mass violations be handled?

Who is Entitled to a Remedy?

The Human Rights Committee has indicated that family members may be considered victims of violations perpetrated on one of their relatives. The Committee has on several occasions demanded that compensation be paid to the families of deceased victims of torture or disappearance for mistreatment of the victim prior to death[9]. Cases have been brought by a brother, wife, daughter, niece or grandchild. In this case of a disappearance, the Committee found that the mother of the disappeared was a victim entitled to reparations.

Calculation of Damages, Including Aggravated Violations

A declaration that the responding state has or has not violated a guaranteed right or rights of the victim forms the heart of the judgement in all international human rights complaint procedures. United Nations organs and the regional Commissions issue such a declaration as the basis for recommending measures that the state should take to remedy the wrong. The recommendations can be very general or may be more detailed as to the nature and scope of redress that should be afforded.

There are three kings of compensatory damages: nominal (a small sum of money awarded to symbolize the vindication of rights and make the judgement a matter of record); pecuniary damages (intended to represent the closest possible financial equivalent of the monetary loss or harm suffered); and moral damages (compensation for dignitary violations, including fear, humiliation, mental distress). Compensatory damages generally provide for:

1. past physical and mental suffering,
2. future physical and mental suffering,
3. medical expenses,
4. loss of earnings and earning capacity,
5. incidental out of pocket expenses, including e.g. travel, nursing care,
6. property injury or loss, and
7. permanent disability and disfigurement[10].

The problem of calculating damages is complex. A court considering the case of a victim who suffers a permanent disability as a result of official torture can calculate the costs already incurred, such as past medical expenses, therapy charges, damage to property and lost earnings prior to judgement. Justice also demands, however, that the court consider lost future earnings and opportunities, and other losses which require prediction of future events, including loss in enjoyment of life. Reduced life expectancy may be claimed, although national jurisdictions are split on whether this is recoverable[11].

Loss of life produces several kinds of injury. The victim and her or his successors are deprived of the income the victim would have earned during the remainder of the victim's working life. In addition, each member of a family contributes personal services and emotional support and these are lost at death. Last but not least, the victim also has been deprived of the intangible but most valuable enjoyment of life.

Lost wages frequently are included as an element of compensatory damages where death, injury or any other consequence of the violation limits or precludes future employment. To calculate a future earnings award, the court must predict what the victim world have earned during her or his lifetime, including all prospects for advancement. This requires consideration of the victim's personal characteristics: age, occupation, education and projected lifespan, issues of fact that are case-specific. It is important to consider life cycle variations in income. A maturing worker becomes more proficient, acquires new skills and generally progresses to more responsible jobs. After a certain age, the important slows and abilities may diminish, leading to decreased wages. Occupation wage profiles in the relevant country can assist in determining the appropriate amount of earnings using actuarial figures. In death cases, mortality tables published by insurance actuaries are accepted as accurate by many courts in determining life expectancy. If the victim is unemployed or without any fixed wage recovery should be had for impairment of his earning capacity. On the other hand, if the victim is in business and his or her efforts are the predominant factor in business earnings, this loss should be claimed as well.

CONCLUSIONS

As compensation is the most common remedy provided for human rights violations, every legal system should strive for certainty in calculating damages to avoid under or over-compensating a victim. Uncertainty and arbitrariness in awards undermines respect for the law. Indeed, legal certainty represents one of modern jurisprudence's central concerns, as the law searches for order and predictability. The rule of law implies that society administers justice by fixing standards that individuals may know and understand prior to controversy and that reasonably guarantee all individuals like treatment. Accurate assessment also is necessary because inadequate or excessive awards frustrate the compensatory, retributive and deterrent functions of the law.

The prevalence of compensation as a remedy should not diminish consideration of the need for other kinds of redress. When rights are infringed, someone has been victimized because of an unwarranted act of interference and can therefore justifiable reclaim his or her prior position. This focus on the victim demands provision of something equivalent in value to that which was lost or restoring precisely that which was removed. The primary goal of human rights remedies thus should be rectification or restitution rather than compensation. When rights are violated, the ability of the victim to pursue self-determination is impaired and it is not justifiable generally to assume that compensation restores the moral balance *ex ante.* A morally adequate response addresses itself in the first instance to restoring what was taken.

NOTES AND REFERENCES

1. Mrs. Dinah Shellon, Professor at Washington University, *'The Jurisprudence of Human Rights Tribunals on Separations'*, at 37th Annual Study Session, July 2006, Strasbourg.

2. See M. Ginsberg, On Justice in Society (1965), 74; I. Jenkins, Social Order and the Limits of Law (1980), 247.
3. On access to justice, see Jeremy McBride, 'Access to Justice and Human Rights Treaties', (1998) 17 Civil Justice Q. 235.
4. International Covenant on Civil and Political Rights, Article 2 (3) (b).
5. The United Nations Compensation Commission was established to provide remedies to victims of the Iraqi invasion of Kuwait, but it is an ad hoc body and has jurisdiction over more than human rights violations. See U.N. Security Council Resolution 687 (1991) of 3 April 1991, U.N. Doc. S/RES/687 (1991), (1991) 30 I.L.M. 852 (1991) and Security Council Resolution 692 (1991) of 20 May 20 1991, (1991) 30 I.L.M. 864) (compensation is due for 'any direct loss, damage, including environmental damage and the depletion of natural resources, on injury to foreign Governments, nationals and corporations, as a result of Iraq's unlawful invasion and occupation of Kuwait'; para 16).
6. Cheng relies on legal reasoning in claiming that reparation is due for any legal wrong: 'It is a logical consequence flowing from the very nature of law and is an integral part of every legal order': B. Cheng, General Principles of Law as Applied by International Courts and Tribunals (1953), 170.
7. Factory at Chorzow Case, PCIJ (1928) Series A, No. 17 page 29 *supra note* 4, at 47.
8. Application for Review of Judgemet No. 158 of the UNAT, Advisory Opinion, 1973 ICJ Rep. 197-198 (July 12), citing Case Conserning the Factory at Chorzow (Merits) (Ger. V. Poland), 1928 PCIJ, ser. A, No. 17 (Sept. 13).
9. See Bleier v. Uruguay, Comm, No. 30/1978, Human Rights Commission, 37th Session, UN GAOR Sup. No. 40 at 130, UN Doc. A/37/40, Annex X (1982). The Committee has formulated the obligation to pay compensation in various ways:
   (a) Compensation to the victim (the disappeared person) and family for 'any injury which he has suffered' (Comm. No. 30/1978, Bleier v. Uruguay);
   (b) Compensation to the husband for the death of his wife (No. 45/1979, Suarez de Guerrero v. Colombia);
   (c) 'Appropriate' compensation to the family of a person killed (No. 84/1981, Dermit Barbato v. Uruguay) or to the

'surviving family' (No. 146/1983 and 148-154/1983 Baboeram *et al.* v. Suriname);

(d) Compensation 'for the wrongs suffered' (No. 107/1981, Quinteros v. Uruguay);

(e) Compensation for physical and mental injury and suffering caused to the victim by the inhuman treatment to which he was subjected (No. 110/1981, Antonio Viana Acosta v. Uruguay).

10. Berry v. City of Muskogee, 900 F. 2d 1989 (10th Cir. 1990): 'In an action involving death, appropriate compensatory damages would include medical and burial expenses, pain and suffering before death, loss of earnings based upon the probable duration of the victim's life had the injury not occurred, the victim's loss of consortium, and other damages recognized in common law tort actions'.

11. See J. Fleming, 'The Lost Years: A Problem in the Computation and Distribution of Damages', (1962) 50 Cql. L. Rev. 598.

Human Rights of Children

S. N. YOGISH*

INTRODUCTION

Human Rights are essentially a product of democracy. Man's struggle against tyranny has been long and sustained. Tyranny has from time to time, surfaced in different forms and modes. Human being has always tried to assert their right, more often than not successfully. Sometimes there has been a dismal failure, onslaught on human rights continues. So does man's struggle against tyranny.

Human rights are the basic and absolute rights that every person has because he or she is a human being. They recognize the vulnerability of the human being in civil, political, economical, social and cultural processes and provide protection.

Every human being has these rights although the extent to which they can be enforced in practice varied from country to country. Having rights comes with having duties and responsibilities. In preserving the freedom, rights and justice for all, everyone has a responsibility to abide by the law and everyone has duties in the community. In exercising freedoms and rights, everyone must also respect the rights and freedoms of others.

At the international level most of these basic human rights have been described in the United Nations (UN), Universal

---

* Lecturer, DOS in Economics, Kuvempu University, Jnana Sahyadri, Shankaraghatta–577 451.

declaration of Human Rights 1948). Some of the basic human rights include.

- The right to equal treatment and non-discrimination.
- The right to nationality.
- The right to own property.
- The right to education.
- The right to work and to just and favourable conditions of works.
- The right to freedom from slavery and forced labour.
- The right to freedom of movement.
- The right to equal assess to public service in the country.
- The right to freedom of through, opinion and expression.
- The right to freedom of association.

The fundamental human rights are often described in each country's contribution which guarantees the fundamental rights of its citizens, regardless of their sex, race, ethnicity, class or caste, religion or other statuses. National legal rights are those rights which are defined by national laws in each country, usually consisting of constitutional rights and specific rights laid down in national legislation such as the penal code, the labour code and the civil code and rules such as government regulations.

While there is considerable variations in national legislation between countries most constitutions world wide state that everyone is equal before the law and that each person us entitled to equal protection under the law without discrimination. If person is entitled to seek justice and to just and fair judicial process.

In 1998 ILO member states adopted the declaration of fundamental principles and rights at work which sets out the core labour principles that are fundamental to the rights of the human beings at work, irrespective of the level of development of countries. The core labour principles endorsed by the international community over four main areas:

- The elimination of all forms of forced and compulsory labour.
- The abolition of child labour.
- The elimination of description on respect of employment and occupation.
- Freedom of association and the recognition of the right to collective bargaining.

ABOUT CHILD RIGHTS

A century that began with children virtually no rights in ending with children having the most powerful legal instrument that not only recognizes but protects their human rights. Carol Bellany-UNICEF Executive Director.

Since, child rights adoption in 1989 after more than 60 years of advocacy, the conversion on the right of child has been ratified more quickly and by more governments than any other human rights instrument. Its basic premise is that children with fundamental freedom and inherit rights of all human beings.

Many governments have even further enacting legislation, creating mechanism and putting into place a range of creative measures to ensure protection and realization of the rights of those under the age of 18.

Nevertheless as UN Secretary General Kofi Anan said "The Principle of all children, all rights is still much too far from being a reality".

The rights of the child as defined by the convention on the right of child include four core principles as follows.

EQUALITY

Like adults, children can be just to discrimination which has a negative impact on a child's opportunities and conditions in life. Therefore all children are entitled to equal rights and governments have an obligation to uphold these. For example:

- Right to birth registration.
- Right to protection from all forms of abuse, neglect, discrimination and exploitation.

RIGHT TO SURVIVAL AND HEALTHY DEVELOPMENT

Every child has a right to develop to develop his/her fullest potential and is entitled to:

- Right to basic needs, including food, shelter and access to health care.
- Right to free primary education
- Right to childhood-to rest and play and to have friends
- Right to protection from economic exploitation or any work that interferes with education or that is hazardous and harmful to health, physical, mental and social development.
- Right to assistance for children with special needs: for example: child refugees displaced children, child victims for abuse and disabled children.

PARTICIPATION

All boys and girls, according to their age and maturity, have the right to affect them. Boys and girls should be encouraged to take part in decision making at home, in school and in their own community. Key participation rights are:

- Right to express views and opinions
- Right to receive and give information in an accessible and understandable form
- Right to be an active member of community to enjoy own culture, to practice own religion and to use own language
- Right to be a member of a group.

BEST INTEREST OF THE CHILD

The two notions of children a competent human beings on the one hand and as children who are vulnerable and need protection on the other hand may confliction deciding what is best for the child. This principle provides the solution to this problem: all decisions that affect boys and girls must give primary consideration to them. In determining what is best for them, it is important to seek the views of the affected girls and boys.

CHILD LABOUR

Work is not always bad for children and can be healthy but it can also seriously hamper children's development. In order to decide whether children's economic activities are healthy or harmful the international community has set the following yard sticks.

CHILD WORK

- Light work (less than 14 hours/week) for 12-17 year olds.
- Not harmful to child's health and development.
- Not obstructing schooling or vocational training.
- Not hazardous in nature.

CHILD LABOUR

- Regular work (14-43 hours/week).
- Causes physical or psychological damage.
- Hinders educational and mental and or physical development.
- Child under minimum age set by ILO Convention No 138.
- Hazardous was defined by provisions of ILO Convention No. 182.

THE WORST FORMS OF CHILD LABOUR

- All forms of slavery or practices similar to slavery, such as sale and trafficking of children, debt bondage and seldom and forced or compulsory recruitment of children for use in armed conflict.

- The use, procuring or offering of a child for prostitution of pornography and for pornographic performances.
- The use, procuring or offering of a child for illicit activities, in particular for the production and trafficking of drugs.

Child Labour Statistics

Age group and sex	*Economically active children*	*Child labour*	*Children hazardous*	*Definitions of child labour based on ILO conventions Nos. 138 and 182*
5-11	109.7	109.7	60.5	In ages 5-11 = all children
Boys	56.3	56.3	30.7	economically active activities
Girls	53.4	53.4	29.8	
12-14	101.1	76.6	50.8	In ages 12-14 = all children in
Boys	52.7	41.5	30.6	economically activities
Girls	48.4	35.1	20.2	excepts those in light work
15-17	140.9	59.2	59.2	In ages 15-17 = all children in
Boys	75.7	34.4	34.4	hazardous work and other
Girls	65.8	24.8	24.8	work forms of child labour.
Total (5-17)	351.7	245.5	170.5	Statistics does not include
Boys	184.1	132.2	95.7	children engaged in work that
Girls	167.6	113.3	74.8	is not considered economic activities such as domestic work where girls are after found.

Children in the Worst Forms of Child Labour

Worst forms of Child Labour	*Global Estimates*	*Estimates in Asia-Pacific*
Forced and bonded labour	5.7	5.5
Forced recruitment into armed conflict	0.3	0.12
Prostitution and pornography	1.8	0.59
Helicit activities	0.6	0.22
Trafficked children	1.2	0.25
Subtotal	8.4	6.43
Children in hazardous work	170.5	104
Total	178.9	110.5

According to ILO report every child counts new global estimates on child labour;

- 70% of child workers are in agriculture, fishing, hunting and forestry.
- 9% of child workers are in manufacturing.
- 9% of child workers are in whole sale, retail trade, restaurants and hotels.
- 6% of child workers are in community, social and personal services.
- 4% of child workers are in transport, storage and communication.
- 4% of child workers are in construction, mining and quarrying.

At the start of the new millennium about 18% boys and girls up to the age of 14 were economically active. In other words, were working for money and other compensation. In 2002, 211 million children aged 5-1 years and economically active. Sixty per cent (127 million) were found in Asia, and the Pacific. One of every five children in this age grow-up was working in this region.

In sub-saharan Africa there were 48 million children working. One of every three children in this age group was working in this region. Just over 6% (13.4 million) were found in North Africa and the Middle East and 8% (17.4 million) in Lating America and the Caribbean.

Following the ILO definitions of child labour, as many as 246 million children aged from 5-17 are in child labour. Of this group, 110 million are younger than 12 of all child labour as many as 170.5 million are found in hazardous work and 6.05 million in this category are younger than 12.

Statistically should be considered critically because by nature child labour exploitation is hidden and getting accurate information is difficult. The number of working girls is underestimated by statistical surveys which do not generally account for unpaid economic activities such as domestic work or hidden activities such as prostitution, the type of work in which more girls are involved.

One of the most wide spread forms of labour exploitation of children is domestic work. Traditionally, domestic work is seen as an easy and safe work for children especially for girls. However, it has been proven recently that domestic work can be among the dangerous work for children and has been recognized as a worst form of child labor. While, domestic work with good employers can offer children in poverty chance to develop, a good education and earn a living, domestic work in most countries has a very low status and is among the lowest paid and many CDW's end up being exploited. Because most CDWs live in and have little freedom, their life and safety after depends on the mercy of the employers. An overwhelming majority of CDWs are girls and many face physical, emotional or sexual abuses.

There are an estimated 1.2 millions children being trafficking for labour and sexual exploitation worldwide, about 250000 in Asia and Pacific. However, estimates of the number of children being trafficked often vary widely, depending on the source. For example, numbers of children trafficked for prostitution in India range between 25,000 and 50,000 respectively. Therefore estimates should be considered with caution. Despite difficulty in determining the exact number of trafficked children, there is a clear trend that it is rising worldwide particularly for sexual exploitation. In South and South east Asia, the overwhelming number of child victims of trafficking are girls with the exception of Sri Lanka and to a lesser extent Pakistan, where boys are also found to be trafficked for commercial sexual exploitation.

TRAFFICKING AND PROSTITUTION

Human trafficking affects a considerable number of indigenous peoples. This has been particularly documented in South and South east Asia. In Nepal, an IPEC Rapid Assessment of trafficking in girls, with specific references to prostitution, shows the presence of several different ethnic groups. Trafficking of indigenous girls is also being documented in Thailand, Burma, Indonesia and Cambodia.

In India, abduction, trafficking of Adivasi girls linked to brothers, forced concubinage and the overall inadequacy of legal protection available to Adivasi women at risk of rape or trafficking requires urgent action. B. Janardhan quoting M.Devi from 1984, notes that traffickers still continue to purchase Adivasi children and women openly, often at a prie cheaper than that paid to purchase animals. A whole network of slaves exists stretching from the Adivasi villages to centers as far away as Ludhiana, Jalandar, Amritsar and Hoshiarpur Districts in Punjab. A large proportion of migrant workers are women and face sexual exploitation at all stops in that belt. A group do contractors recruit these Adivasi women through older women who themselves have been victims of these practices. After receiving the recruits the contractors transport the human cargo to states such as Punjab. The recipients of the Human cargo auction the Adivasi girls in the open market. These slaves are paid roughly Rs. 15 a day or Rs. 1000 on an average.

Similar processes have been described in Taiwan, China where high numbers of indigenous girls have been trafficked top work in the sex industry. While indigenous peoples account for only 1.6 per cent of the Taiwanese population estimates of the percentage of indigenous women involved in the sex industry range from 20% to 60%. Moreover, the presence of minor and debt bondage is considerable.

Known as sold daughter prostitution girls are contracted for a period of years or even for life against an initial payment to her parents, with or without her informed consent. The girls are usually minors and find themselves in the low price brothels, where conditions are worst.

There is little information regarding trafficking and prostitution among indigenous peoples in Africa. However, abduction raids taking place in Sudan during the last 15 years of civil war are known to have particularly focused on one conflict zone. Bahr and Ghazal, and have many affected Dinka children. Often put to work to look after cattle for Arab Baggara pastoralist groups from North Sudan.

The total number of children involved ranges from 5000 to 14000. In many cases children who have been forced into labour have also been forced to forget their own language and identity.

As noted in a recent IPEC rapid assessment on trafficking in children in the Thailand, Laos, and Myanmar border areas, surveys may not necessarily succeed in identifying trafficking among indigenous communities. It may exist but the hidden away by already stigmatized communities.

CONVENTION ON THE RIGHT OF CHILD

The human rights of children and the standards to which all government must aspire in realizing these rights for all children are most concisely and fully articulated in one international human right treaty, the convention on the right of the child. The convention is the most universally accepted human rights instrument in history it has been ratified by every country in the world except two and therefore uniquely places children center stage in the quest for universal application of human rights. By ratifying this instrument national government have committed themselves to protecting and ensuring children rights and they have agreed to hold themselves accountable for the commitment before the international community.

The optional protocol on the involvement of children in armed conflict entered into force in February 12th 2002. On that date becoming a binding instruments for states having ratified it.

To date 117 countries have signed and 88 have ratified this protocol.

Optical protocol on the sale of children and child prostitution and pornography.

1. It entered into force on 18th January 2002. On that date becoming a binding instrument for states having ratified it.

2. To date 110 countries have signed and 87 have ratified this protocol.

But on varied legal systems and cultural traditions, the conventions ofth right on the child is a universally agreed set on non-negotiable standards and obligations. It spells out the basic human rights that children every where without discrimination have the right to survival to develop the fullest to protect from harmful influence, abuse and exploitation and to participate fully in family, cultural and social life. Every right spelled out in conversion is inherent the human dignity and harmonious development of every child. The conversion protects children rights by setting standards in health care, educational and legal civil and social services. The standards are bench marks against which progress can be accessed.

States that are partly to the convention are obliged to develop and undertake all actions and policies in the light of the best interests of the child.

The conversion on the right of the child is first legally binding instrument to incorporate the full range of human rights and 4 civil, political and economical, social, cultural and 4 rights. Two optional protocols on the involvement of children in armed conflict and on the sale of children, child prostitution, pornography we adopted to strengthen the provision of the conversion in these areas. They entered into force respectively on 12th January and 18th January 2002.

PROVIDING QUALITY EDUCATION

Education is a human right and key factor to reducing poverty and child labour and promoting democracy, peace and tolerance and development. Yet more than 100 million children of primary school age, the majority of the girls are not enrolled in school. Millions more are taught by untrained and underpaid teachers in over crowded, unhealthy and poorly equipped classrooms and 1/3rd of children do not complete five years of schooling the minimum required for basic literacy.

As agreed at the world education forum in Darkar which reconfirmed the mandated role of the United Nations

Educational Scientific and Cultural Organization in coordinating education for all partners and maintaining their collective momentum within the processes securing education we will accord high priority to ensuring by 2015 that all children have access to and complete primary education that is free, compulsory and of good quality. We will also aim at progressive of secondary education.

As a step forwards these goals, we resolve to achieve the following targets.

1. Expand and improve comprehensive early childhood, care and education, for girls and boys especially for the most vulnerable and disadvantaged children.
2. Reduce the number of primary school age children who are out of school by 50% and increase net primary enrollment or participation in alternative, good quality primary education programmes to at least 90% by 2010.
3. Eliminate gender disparities in primary and secondary education and achieve gender equality in education by 2015, with a focus on ensuring girls full and equal access to and achievement in basic education of good quality.
4. Improve all aspects of the quality of education so that children and young people achieve recognized and measurable learning outcomes especially innumeracy, literacy and essential life skills.
5. Ensure that the learning needs of all young people are met through access to appropriate learning and life skill programmes.
6. Achieve a 50% improvement in levels of adult literacy by 2015, especially for women.

To achieve these goals and targets we will implement the following strategies and actions.

1. Develop and implement special strategies to ensure that schooling is readily accessible to all children and

adolescent and that basic education is affordable for all families.

2. Promote innovative programmes that encourage schools and communities to search more actively for children who have dropped out or are excluded from school and from learning, especially girls and working children, children with special needs and children with disabilities and help them enroll, attend and successfully complete their education, involving governments as well as families, communities and non governmental organizations as partners in the educational process. Special measures should be put into place top prevent and reduce drop out due to inter alia, entry into employment.
3. Ensure that all basic education programmes are accessible, inclusive and responsive to children with special learning needs and for children with various forms of disabilities.
4. Develop and implement special strategies for improving the quality of education and meeting the learning needs of all.
5. Provide education and training opportunities to adolescent to help them acquire sustainable livelihood.
6. Develop strategies to mitigate the impact of HIV/AIDS on education systems and schools students and learning.

ARMED CONFLICT

Two million children have been killed in armed conflict in the last decade. Three times as many have been seriously injured or permanently disabled. Millions of others have been forced to take part in or witness horrifying acts of violence. Increasingly children are targets not identical casualties, a devasting carriage that reflect a wide trend in recent decade, a rise in proportion of war victims who are civilians from 5% over 9%.

In countless cases, the impact of armed conflict in children themselves may be removed form the public in institutions, prostitution. Those who have lost parents often experience humiliation, rejection and discrimination, suffering in silence as their self esteem crumbled. Their insecurity and fear cannot be measured.

CONCLUSION

Human rights are the basic and absolute rights that every person has because he or she is human being. All human rights apply to all boys and girls. While, societies may vary in their ideas on childhood and child development. One thing that all can agree on, is the importance of the well being of the children.

However, over the past few years, the stories of child abuse has grabbed the attention of the international community, provoking world wise discussion of this issue child labour remains a major cause of child exploitation and abuse in the world depriving millions of children world wide of adequate education and good health. Many of these children are the victims of the worst forms of child labour, which include slavery, bonded labour drug trafficking, commercial, sexual exploitation, domestic labour, armed conflict and all other physically and morally hazardous types of the work.

Today, it is well recognized everywhere that children need special care and protection for healthy development b'coz of their special needs and vulnerability. Numerous international organizations, government in both developing and industrialized countries and advocacy groups are creating and implementing strategies and initiatives the address the issues of child rights violations. Special instruments have been drawn up to safeguard and enforce child rights. The recognized standard is the UN convention on the right of the child (CRC), which was drawn up in 1989 and has been ratified by all most all countries in the world. The convention gives guiding principles to protect child rights. It is intended to make people aware of the importance of protecting human rights of children.

We make this solemn pledge secure in the knowledge that in giving high priority to the rights of the children to their protection and development and ensure the well being all children in all societies.

REFERENCES

Van. G. Bueren, *The International Law on the Rights of the Child.* Martinus Nijhoff Publishers, pp. 22-30.

Parker S., *The Best Interests of the Child. International Journal of Law,* pp. 1-10.

Jyotsna Tiwari, *Child Abuse and Human Rights,* pp. 1-25.

Paras Diwan and Peeyushi Diwan, *Human Rights and the Law,* pp. 18-22.

David Son S., *Human Rights,* pp. 5-10.

Chiranjeevi S., *Human Rights in India,* pp. 4-50.

Child Health and Nutrition in India—Plight and Right

V. Basil Hans*

'Of the estimated more than 20 million low-weight births each year in the developing world, more than half occur in South Asia and more than one third in India'. (UNICEF, 2006)

INTRODUCTION

There is a consensus among development thinkers and policy-makers that the objective of development is not merely to ensure that children 'survive' but that they 'live'[1]. It is for this very reason that a development strategy solely directed to ensure 'child survival' will not be adequate to ensure a satisfactory state of health and nutrition among children" (Gopalan, 1984). Global concern about the health of women and children of the developing countries has drawn greater attention during the recent past (Neeraja, 2003). Along with continued efforts at protecting the life of children from all possible threats to life, the civil society needs to address the plight of children the world over deprived of their right to develop physically, mentally and socially on account of poverty, disease, illiteracy, malnutrition and other symptoms of under-development. Therefore, we are justified in using a rights-based perspective that also underlines the role of development in the promotion of human rights in general and the rights of children in particular. This is the image is

* Head, Arts Department, St. Aloysius Evening College, Mangalore—575 003, D.K. District, Karnataka, INDIA.

presently much-appreciated in the developing world." (Singh, 1998).

The plight of children in the developing countries is bewildering. Everyone one seems to know what is needed for their healthy growth but no one is sure as to whether is right to make their future bright. Health situation of millions of children at homes, or elsewhere is still an ill-managed condition. This does not augur well for a nation where commitment to the cause of children is as old as its civilization and a time honoured belief in the culture is that the child is a gift of the Gods. Over the years, however, due to various kinds of neglect, deprivation and abuse the lot of the children plummeted into a disadvantaged group. This has also made interventions–by state and private organizations–necessary for child protection and care. Laws, institutions and schemes not withstanding there is at present an unscathed indifference regarding child health as a right and an integral part of social justice.

Health of today's children would determine the wealth of tomorrow in a large measure. Therefore, it is essential to periodically gauge the condition of health and nutrition of our children, to take every step necessary for the betterment of the condition and above all treat child healthcare as a concomitant of citizenship-rights and duties included.

RIGHT TO HEALTH OF THE CHILD–THE RATIONALE

In a civic society it is a healthy feature if human rights include the right to health of children both in letter and spirit. One of the societal considerations has been that children are property of the parents and it is they who can decide and do whatever they felt right with them. The need for extending care to the child was stated in the Geneva Declaration of the Rights of the Child[2] adopted by the League of Nation General Assembly in 1924 (Subramanian, 1997; wikipedia, 2007). Among other things the Geneva Declaration stated that "The child that is hungry must be fed, the child that is sick must be nursed, the child that is backward must be helped. The delinquent child must be reclaimed, and the orphan and the waif must be sheltered and succoured".

Even with the advent of the era of human rights after World War II, the assumption was that all human rights applied automatically to children. But not much was seen in practice as far as protection and promotion of child health was concerned. While in every other respect–education included–some progress was made with serious efforts in the domain of children, particular needs of health and nutrition were neither specifically nor adequately addressed in the rights-based instruments and interventions. Children continued to be vulnerable and victims of abuse, exploitation, under-nourishment, disease and even deaths due more to neglect than natural reasons. Recognising this state of affairs, the UN Convention on the Rights of the Child (CRC) brought forth a pervasive document which subsequently ratified by many of the member states of the UNO.

A unique feature of this endeavour was that for the first time we have in one document a Statement of the Rights of the Child, so far fragmented in many an instrument. The focus now was on issues of justice and prevention of exploitation of children. The needs and aspirations of the child put at higher plane both on the national and international agenda .The 1948 UN Universal Declaration of Human Rights proclaimed that,

> "*Everyone* has the right to a standard of living adequate for the health and well-being of himself and of his family, including food, clothing, housing and medical care and necessary social services, and the *right* to security.... Motherhood and childhood are entitled to special care and assistance (Article 25)".[3]

On 20 November 1959, the General Assembly of the UN adopted a Declaration of the Rights of the Child which paved the way for a broader perspective of child rights–economic, social and cultural and the role of specialized agencies and international organizations concerned with the welfare of children. It indicated that, "the *child,* by reason of his/her physical and mental immaturity, needs special safeguards and care, including appropriate legal protection, before and after birth".[4]

In 1989, there was another CRC. The Preamble of The Convention itself stated that children should receive necessary protection and assistance for their growth and well-being from the family and the community; and they should be provided an atmosphere of love, happiness and understanding for their full and harmonious development of their personality. It emphasized three things:

- need for special consideration for children living in exceptionally different conditions in all countries of the world.
- accepting the importance of the traditions and cultural value of each society for the protection and development of children.
- recognizing the importance of international co-operation in child welfare.

The Convention incorporated various Articles (about 54 of them) ranging from defining the child-age to preservation of identity, prevention of abuse and serving the best interests of children, including parentless children and disabled children.[5] Article 24 dealt with health of the child (see Box 1 for details). Articles 25, 26 and 27 dealth with periodic review of placed children, social security of children, and standard of living of children, respectively.

The Vienna Declaration of Human Rights 1993 also urged nations to tackle the problems of exploitation and abuse of children by addressing their root causes. Need for sensitization through awareness and information was felt. It is befitting therefore, that the international human rights regime found it necessary to engender access to information as a key component of all rights to ensure the all round development of the individual. One of the general comments of the Committee on Economic, Social and Cultural Rights is that,

BOX 1

RIGHT TO HEALTH

- States Parties recognise the right of the child to the enjoyment of the highest attainable standard of health and to facilities for the treatment of illness and rehabilitation of health. States Parties shall strive to ensure that no child is deprived of his or her right of access to such health care services.
- States Parties shall pursue full implementation of this right and, in particular, shall take appropriate measures:
  - (a) to diminish infant and child mortality,
  - (b) to ensure the provision of necessary medical assistance and health care to all children with emphasis on the development of primary health care,
  - (c) to combat disease and malnutrition including within the framework of primary health care, through *inter alia* the application of readily available technology and through the provision of adequate nutritious foods and clean drinking water, taking into consideration the dangers and risks of environments pollution
  - (d) to ensure appropriate pre-and post-natal health care for mothers,
  - (e) to ensure that all segments of society, In particular, parents and children are informed have access to education and are supported in the use of basic knowledge of child health and nutrition, the advantages of breast-feeding, hygiene and environmental sanitation and the prevention of accidents, and
  - (f) to develop preventive health care, guidance for parents, and family planning education and services.
- States Parties shall take all effective and appropriate measures with a view to abolishing traditional practices prejudicial to the health of children.
- States Parties undertake to promote and encourage international cooperation with a view to achieving the full reaslisation of the right recognized in this article. In this regard, account shall be taken of the needs of the developing countries.

"Accessibility to the highest attainable standard of health includes information accessibility i.e. to seek, and impart information concerning health issues subject to confidentiality of information about public health... Right to maternal [,] child and reproductive health includes access to information" (Nayak, 2006).

For a welfare state like India that seeks the well-being of all, a concern and treats children as "God's greatest gift to man' a commitment for ensuring the best of health and nutrition for children would not be out of place.

New economic reforms and hightech advances in India and elsewhere has not in a single bit reduced the rightful place of children in society. Far from it, a civil society is expected to pass the test of 'inclusive development' if it has to justify 'modernisation'. Modernisation has no meaning when the voiceless and vulnerable remain marginalized and these include the children too. Rightly therefore, child health and nutritional aspects are in the realm of human rights and social justice.

THE INDIAN SCENE

India has a strong base in its Constitution for evolving a child rights structure with adequate provisions for their health and nutrition. Article 24 of the Constitution prohibits the employment of children below 14 years in any factory or mine or in any other hazardous occupation. Article 39 provides a policy direction towards securing health and strength of children of the tender age–physical, mental and moral. Among other things it states:

(i) that the health and strength of workers, men and women, and the tender age children are not abused and that citizens are not forced by economic necessity to avocations unsuited to their age or strength: and

(ii) that children are giving opportunities and facilities to develop in a healthy manner and in conditions of freedom and dignity and childhood and youth are protected against moral and material abandonment.

This article embodies the welfare and justice precepts of health. Besides these provisions, a number of Acts such as the Juvenile Act, Child Marriage Restraint Act, Child Labour (Prohibition Act) and so on. We are only near to treating right to health as a fundamental right. In the meanwhile social maladies including sidelining of issues related to child health continue.

India was one of the signatories in 1978 of the Alma Ata Declaration of Health For All (HFA) by 2000. Our country's working group on Health had recommended the goal of reduction in IMR from 125 to below 60 by 2000 AD (Hans, 1997). The HFA strategy transformed the traditional concept of health as one of mere removal of a disease to the promotion of health. Conceived in this sense any improvement in health needs contribution not only from the medical sector but also from the areas of agriculture, food and nutrition, etc.

In 1992, India ratified the UN Convention on Rights of the Child. The Charter of Child Rights (CRC) is built on the principle that "*all* children are born with fundamental freedoms and *all* human beings have some inherent rights". The Charter confers four basic rights on all children across the world, viz, the right to survival (to life, health, nutrition, name and nationality), the right to development (to education, care, leisure, recreation), the right to protection (from exploitation, abuse, neglect), and the right to participation–to expression, information, through and religion "(CRY, 2006). It is therefore in the realm of human rights and social justice.

Modern India's achievements in science and technology and their application in agriculture, industry, communication, media and entertainment and to a considerable extent in medicine and surgery is something to be genuine proud of all. But mere growth of hitech hospitals and pharmaceutical industries cannot be construed as endured health security for all. Despite overall gains in health since independence, the low and nutritional status as also disparities in accessibility of health services between the rich children and the poor children still exists. The progress made in health and nutrition in independent India should be gauged in the backdrop of the success in other fields.

India has reduced absolute poverty by more than half. It has dramatically improved literacy. It has become one of the world's fastest growing economics with average growth rates of 8 per cent over the past three years. It has emerged as a global player in information technology, business process outsourcing, telecommunications, and pharmaceuticals. It is now the world's fourth largest economy in purchasing power parity terms .It is the world's largest producer of milk, and the second largest producer of fruits and vegetables. But despite a long history of state intervention, the morbidity and mortality among children continue to be a major cause of concern (see Box 2 for some features). Werner Schultink the nutrition and child development chief for UNICEF in India feels that this situation is both disappointing and worrying. At the same time this is also a challenge for a country that provides software to the world (Zaheer, 2007). Low health and nutritional status of children in India is in fact a sad part of the story of the country's socio-economic development.

Not only the state of health of the children but also the health structure and spending in India leaves much to be desired. Of every 100 Rupee allocated by the government, only three rupees and seventy-seven paise is being allocated for children. The share of child budget in Union Budget is low at present (see Table 1). In the Union Budget 2006-2007 the share of child health in total resources of budget was low at 0.556 per cent compared to child education's 3.487 per cent.

The government has not doubt recognized the importance of early care for the health and growth of children. Therefore, it has launched a number of schemes such as Crèche/Day Care scheme for Working and Ailing Mothers; National Fund for Child Care Services; Integrated Child Development Services (ICDS); Balwadi Nutrition Programme; Early Childhood Education through assistance to Voluntary Agencies, etc. Similarly we have some organizations that can uphold and protect the physical and social health rights of the children

BOX 2

CHILD HEALTH, HYGIENE AND NUTRITION IN INDIA

- India's child population is 375 million, more than any country in the world.
- There are not enough beds to accommodate 25 million annual births.
- More than 2 million children in India die before their first birthday.
- As far as India is concerned it is sad fact that more than half of the child population[1] in India is malnourished.
- Out of the 300 million children in India, a lot live in an economic and social environment which could impede the child's physical and mental development.
- It is estimated that there are 314,700 street children in Bomnay, Calcutta, Madras, Kanpur, Bangalore and Hyderabad combined and about 100,000 in Delhi.
- Less than 50 per cent of girl child births are being registered by parents because of gender bias!
- India's mortality rate for infants up to four years old is 68 deaths per 1,000 live births, according to the National Population Policy 2000 and to be achieve by 2010.
- More than half of all children under the age of four are malnourished and 30 per cent of newborns are significantly underweight.
- India has 25 million disabled children. 75 per cent of the disability is preventable.
- Every year 7-8 lakh children die from preventable disease like diarrhea.
- Only 44 per cent of children have received immunization schedule; 14 per cent have not received a single vaccine.
- IMR (per 1000) was 63 in 2004.
- There are about 127 million children below the age of 6 in India, out of which 60 million live below the poverty line.
- India has the largest number of working children in the world.

viz. National Institute for Hearing Handicapped, National Institute for Multiple Handicapped, Rehabilitation Council of India, National Handicapped Finance and Development Corporation, Ministry of Social Justice and Empowerment, Ministry of Health and Family Welfare Ministry of Human Resource Development, Department of Women and Child Development and so on. The policies and legislative measures taken by the government since 1991 include Infant Milk Substitute, Feeding Bottles and Infant Foods (Regulation of Production, Supply and Distribution) Act 1992, National Nutritional Policy 1993, National Charter for Children 2004 and National Plan of Action for Children 2005.

Table 1
Child Budget in India

Year	*Total Union Budget (BE) (Rs. Cr.)*	*Total Child Budget (BE) (Rs. Cr.)*	*Percentage Share of Child Budget in Union Budget*
1	*2*	*3*	*4*
2004-05	477829.04	11695.72	2.45
2005-06	514343.82	19841.01	3.86
2005-06	563991.13	27674.58	4.91

Source: GOI Expenditure Budgets 2004-2005, 2005-2006, and "What does Union Budget 2006-07 have for children?", Haq Centre for Child Rights, Delhi, reproduced from *Integrated Child Protection Scheme* (ICPS), Draft, 17th August 2006, Chapter-I. Conceptual Background of the Scheme.

LINKS BETWEEN FOOD, NUTRITION AND HEALTH–FINDINGS FROM STUDIES

Analysis of linkages between food, nutrition and health is important in the context of studies on poverty, food security as well as on child health and welfare. Experts in health economics and human development such as Panchamukhi and Laxmi Devi feel that issues related to measurement of under nourishment and the effects of nutritional status on (human) capital formation are vital aspects in the field of nutrition economics and the discussions of new paradigm of development and in the context of "human security".[8]

Good Nutrition is a multidisciplinary effort and multistage phenomena. Since it is linked very closely to education, it is required that nutritional planning be an integral part of educational programmes in nutrition within schools.[9] Sukhatme has analysed the significance of "calorie-intake norms" of nutrition under the Integrated Child Development Scheme (ICDS). His study reveals that despite increasing amounts being spent on providing nutritious foods to children there was no substantial impact on their actual weight .One reason for this emanated form indifference to the interaction between child and his/her suroundeings.[10]

Low intakes of food, diminished health, and social inequity with respect to child health result in negative externalities and rising burden of costs on the society. Some of the cost– called by some as costs of oppression[11]– are: psychological costs (loss of mental health and sense of self); social costs (loss and diminishment of relationships and recognition); intellectual costs (loss of developing full scale knowledge); Moral cost (loss of moral integrity); and material and physical costs (loss of security, resources, and quality of life). Many of these costs are overlapping and mutually reinforcing, they build and feed on each other, often in a vicious circle (Goodman, 2001).

Not all studies on nutrition seem free from biases. A analysis from researchers of the Children's hospital, Boston reveals that scientific studies elated to beverages funded solely by industry are for to eight times more likely to have conclusions favourable to sponsors' financial interest that research with no industry funding. Such biased findings have adverse impact on dietary guidelines and malnutrition intervention programmes. This should serve as an eye-opener for in countries like India where food habits are becoming urbanized and the household budget has been thinned out to buy less cereals and spend more on beverages (including soft drinks and juices), refreshments and processed foods (Gupta, 2007).

ISSUES, CHALLENGES AND SUGGESTIONS

Development to be meaningful and measurable should be seen both from quantitative and qualitative angles. For India to rise up in the index of human development particularly it is of urgent need that many trends in key indicators must accelerate if the national development targets are to be met. How can the country shine with rising economic growth rate but a low infant survival rate? Core issues therefore have to be addressed upfront in the realm of health and human rights in general and child rights in particular. Some key issues are as follows:

- We need to reduce IMR to below 40 by 2008. The target was to reduce IMR below 45 by 2007. Not only the speed of reduction but also the interstate disparities in the rate are an issue to be considered. In 2003, there was a 77 point difference between Orissa (87 per 1,000) and Kerala (10 per 1,000).
- Basic health of children has to be improved. Every kind of fever, anemia, malaria, diarrhea, etc. need timely and sufficiently attention.
- Problem of child malnutrition needs to be tackled using psycho-social as well as economic tools.
- Health administration needs to be tones up. Many a village has poor health care services by guides/ attendants and other medical personnel .Preventive, curative, and rehabilitative aspects of child health care need to be balanced for evolving a holistic approach to the problem.
- Problems of child labourers, street children, destitute, orphans, children of alcoholic parents, children of divorced parents and differently-abled children need special attention. Adoption and juvenile justice must be full proof.
- India at present needs more than 800,000 crèches for its children. Against this, we have been able to set up only 14,925 crèches.

- "All children in school by 2003" could not be accomplished. Another target is to reduce gender gap in literacy by at least 50 per cent by 2007.
- Government, NGOs and every one concerned with the good health and bright future of children have to take up challenge of improving the child health rights situation in the country. Literacy, education and participatory development techniques need to be integrated in child welfare schemes.

The Tenth Five Year Plan had very ambitious targets. So does the Eleventh Plan (2007-12). The biggest challenge is to ensure economic progress translate into social development. While children are counted their health should not be discounted. A broad conceptual framework of health should incorporate the needs and interests of those who perhaps cannot articulate them adequately or whose preferences cannot be properly determined. This is medical ethics as well as social justice.[12] The country badly needs a sound child budgeting. The budget should not only enhance investments on and incentives to promotion of child health, these should be based on rights-justice framework. What we do for our children is not a charity but a responsibility. Treating them as objects of charity and not as contributors amounts to denial of dignity and justice. On a pragmatic note a child budget in India may consider the following aspects:

1. Achieve all-round development of children in "children specific environment" approach and not a trickle down (from elders) approach. Let children have and enjoy their own rights and learn to exercise them judiciously.
2. Ensure that the benefits of Right to Information[13] permeate to policies, programmes and activities related to health care and welfare of the child: adequate and timely information on products and services related to heath and nutrition to be made available at all times, in every place.

3. Build and operate an efficient system of child health administration (including health infrastructure) with due emphasis on monitoring and evaluation to give momentum for good health of child starting from the womb, such as through the successful implementation of Safe motherhood programme and Reproductive Child Health Programme.[14]
4. Intensify the efforts at grass root level through personal contacts, information exchange, training, etc. to parents, teachers, students health workers, etc. in the finesse of child health and nutrition, and better utilization of child health services.
5. Raise the socio-economic status of women–particularly–rural so as to improve their interpersonal communication for better utilization of health services.[15]
6. Ensure optimum allocation of resources by Centre, between centre and states and between states and local governments for protecting children's rights to health, nutrition, education and so forth.
7. Devise public-private partnership for needs and rights based programmes in the light of national targets and dovetail them with the Millennium Development Goals (MDGs).[16]
8. Introduce flexibility, transparency and accountability in expenditure programmes for child health to ensure optimum utilization of services.
9. Develop a vigilance system for the production and distribution (including market and media) of all food and beverages meant for children as also on nutrition studies and reports.
10. Make a thorough mapping of children in need of health care and protection alongside those who face threats to the exercise of their rights.

CONCLUSION

There is a remarkable gap between expectations and rendering of social justice in India (Remakrishna, 2006), as far as children are concerned. This is substantiated by the inadequate implementation of policies and programmes to address the issues of child health and nutrition, despite a decade of New Economic Policy, India's Second generation reforms must, therefore, concentrate more on human resource development of which children are an integral part. A healthy sign is that social sector spending has picked up and total budgetary provisions for child health and protection programmes are also stepped up in recent years. Programmes are being expanded. But they are low compared to several developing countries. Moreover to secure children's rights effectively, adequate funding is necessary, but not sufficient condition. It is one of the ways of expressing concerns for addressing children's problems and promoting their rights. Increasing attention and allocation to children's issues allocation should go hand with increased awareness and participation in child health and rights development.

Child development programmes should have both vertical and horizontal equity and they should be vigorously implemented. Like in many other aspects of the economy the change in objective must be from effective 'control' to better 'management' with a balance in focus between input management and outcome monitoring. A knowledge-based advocacy can help create a favourable environment for this purpose.

When good policies are translated to good practices in the domain of child rights the country will be able to experience a healthy revolution of the younger generation. That is the meaningful outcome for all children that a civil society should expect and strive for. Child health has to move from the realm of social welfare to the realm of rights. The journey has already begun.

NOTES

1. A young Egyptian girl was asked, "What do you want to be when you grow up?" "Alive", she replied. (Benkappa, 1988), Quoted in Neeraja (2003: 1-2).

2. Child rights are rights of all persons below the age of 18. For the purpose of this paper child population is defined as the population in the age group 0-14 years, which is also the definition of the Child Labour (Prohibition and Regulation) Act, 1986.
3. In fact the Preamble the World Health Organisation (WHO) established in 1948 states: "The enjoyment of the fundamental *rights* of every human being without distinction of race, religion, political belief, economic or social condition." To this list unwittingly we may add: age, for the very objective of WHO is the "attainment of *all* people of the highest level of health". See for details, J.E. Park and K. Park, *Text Book of Preventive Medicine,* Jabalpur: M/s Banarasidas, 1991. Emphasis mine.
4. Emphasis mine.
5. The United Nations General Assembly agreed to adopt the Convention into international law on November 20, 1989. The Law came into force on September 2, 1990, after it was ratified by the required number of nations. The Convention generally defines a child as any person under the age of 18, unless an earlier age of majority is recognized by a country's law.
6. According to UNICEF, 193 states are party to the Convention, almost all the members of the United Nations.
7. Comment # 14, 2002. The Committee is the international body to monitor compliance to the International Covenant on Economic, Social and Cultural rights.
8. See P. R. Panchamuki, *Economic of Health and Nutrition,* CMDR, Dharwad, 1992; and Laxmi Devi (ed) *Encyclopedia of Economic Planning and Development,* Institute for Sustainable Development, New Delhi, 1996.
9. See Corrine H. Robinson and Marylyn R. Lawler, *Normal and Therapeutic Nutrition,* Mac millan Publishing Co., Inc, New York 1982, p. 4.
10. See P.V. Sukhatme, "Impact of Poverty on Public Health", *CARC Calling,* Vol. 8, No. 1, Jan.-March, 1995, pp. 2-5.
11. In many a society these costs are identifiable as costs of oppression to people from dominant groups. There is also the phenomenon of discrimination in health care.
12. For a detailed analysis of the relationship between health care and medical ethics see Dan Brock, "Quality of life Measures in

Health Care and Medical Ethics" in Nussbaum and Amartya sen (ed) *The Quality of Life,* New York: OUP.

13. The Right to Information Act (RIT), 2005 in India has come into effect from October 2006. The Act provides for the establishment of a Central Information Commission as well as State Information Commissions with a host of provisions for appeals, penalties, etc. with regards to enforcement of citizens' right to seek, receive and impart information.
14. An English proverb states, "the song of the mother to the baby at the cradle rings down to the body in the coffin". This aptly describes the extent to which the (mental) health of the child is largely dependent on that of the mother (see Neeraja, *op.cit,* p. 1).
15. The National Health Policy, 2000 has identified empowering women for improved health and nutrition as a strategic theme.
16. Nobel laureate Amartya Sen has said that an adequately capacious view of private and public actions is necessary for ensuring better health care in the country. He feels that a "fuller recognition" of health as a human right can follow from a realization that health is influenced not just by health care, but also by general economic prosperity and social cohesion, and ecoial and economic (in) equalities. [From excerpts of 14th KS Sajivi Endowment Lecture on "Health and Society" delivered by Prof. Sen at the Voluntary Health Services in Taramani, Tamil Nadu, on Saturday 09, February, 2007, NEWS: *The Hindu,* 11.2.2007, Vol. 130, No. 6, p. 8].

REFERENCES

Appaiah Parvathy, C. N. Shankar Rao and Jayanthi P. Shenoy (2006), *Human Rights, Gender Equity and Environmental Studies*, Mangalore: Jai Bharath Prakashana.

Baretto Duarte (1976), *India's Search for Development and Social Justice–Analysis of Indian Society-2.* The Indian Situation, Bangalore: Centre for Social Action.

Brock Dan (1995), "Quality of Life Measures in Health Care and Medical Ethics'. In Nussbaum, Marth C. and Amartya Sen, *The Quality of Life,* New York: Oxford University Press, pp. 95-131.

Deshta Sunil and Kiran Deshta (2003), *Fundamental Human Rights–The Right to Life and Oersonal Liberty,* New Delhi: Deep & Deep Publications, (P) Ltd.

Diwan Paras, and Peeyushi Diwan (1998), *Human Rights and the Law–Universal and Indian,* New Delhi: Deep & Deep Publications.

Goodman Diane J. (2001), *Promoting Diversity and Social Justice-Educating People from Priviledged Groups,* New Delhi: Sage Publications, Inc.

Gopalan C. (1984), "Child Survival and Child Nutrition", Archives of Nutrition Foundation of India.

Gupta Ritu (2007), "Co Twist to Nutrition Research", *The Economic Times,* Saturday, 27 January, ET Finance, p. 2.

Hans, V. B. (1997), *Nature and Scope of Health Economics–A Survey of Literature,* Unpublished M.Phil Dissertation, Department of Studies and Research in Economics, Mangalore University, Mangalagangothri.

Hans, V. Basil and G. V. Joshi (2006), "Marginalisation in the Midst of Modernisation–A Case of Health Status of Women in India". Paper Presented at the National Conference on 'Changing Social Order and the Marginalised Groups' by St. Aloysius College, NESA Bangalore and Mangalore Sociology Association, January 9-20, 2006.

Neeraja K. P. (2003), *Rural Women: Maternal Child Health and Family Planning Services,* New Delhi, Discovery Publishing House.

Ramakrishna Tata (2006), "Disability and Social Justice in India", *Participative Develoopment,* 5 (3 & 4), pp. 31-41.

Singh Surinder (1998), "Promotion and Protection of the Rights of Children", Embassy of India.

Subramanian, S. (1997), *Human Rights: International Challenges,* Volume One, New Delhi, Manas Publications.

Zaheer, Kamil (2007), 'INTERVIEW–India Needs to Feed its Children Better–UNICEF' By Reuters Saturday January 6, 08:56 AM. Available at *http: / / in.news.yahoo.com* (accessed on January 20, 2007).

WEBSITES

http: / / hetv.org

http: / / in.news.yahoo.com

http: / /mohfw.nic

http: / /nutritionfoundationofindia.res.in

http: / /www.cry.org

http: / /www.indianemassy.org

http: / /www.nhrc.com

http: / /www.unicef.org

http: / /youandias.org

http: / /www.indiatogether.org

Breast Feeding as Human Right of the Child

ALOK PANDEY*

> *"A nation's children are its supremely important assets and the nation's future lies in their proper development. An investment in Children is indeed an investment in nation's future. A healthy and educated child of today is the active and intelligent citizen of tomorrow. Bestow blessing on these little innocent lives bloomed on earth, who have brought the message of Joy from heavenly garden".*
>
> —R. N. TAGORE

Child development is integral to overall socio-economic development of a nation. Problems of child health and development present a formidable challenge. To meet this challenge every citizen of India has to make some contribution. It is obvious that hospital or the medical staff alone would not be able to cope with the growing needs of our children, without the active and positive involvement of the community. It is the mother who has to assume the role of a frontline health worker; and the doctors and others have only supplement and support her efforts, whether the issue involved is diarrhoeal dehydration or vaccine-preventable disease, low birth weight or malnutrition, infant death or childhood disability or the lack of attainment of full mental faculties. Since independence, India nearly 59 years ago, many changes have been brought about from one five year plan to another. The problems of children are multi-faceted and multi-

* B.Com., LL.M. Research Scholar of Law, Lucknow University, Lucknow (U.P.), 76A/4A, Jondhwal, Telyear Ganj, Allahabad-211004.

layered .They cover a wide range of fields from nutrition and education to development and protection so that they may become better human beings in later years.

The child has to be prepared for responsible life in a free society in the spirit of understanding, peace and tolerance, use of corporal punishment is antithetic to these values. We cannot subject the child to torture and still expect him to act with understanding, peace and tolerance towards others and be a protagonist of peace and love. It was probably for this reason Mahatma Gandhi said that "If we are to reach real peace in this world, and if we are to carry on a real war against war, we shall have to begin with children. And if they will grow up in their natural innocence, we won't have to struggle, we won't have to pass fruitless idle resolutions, but we shall go from love to love and peace to peace, until at last all the corners of the world are covered with that peace and love for which consciously or unconsciously, the whole world is hungering".[1]

The major health problems of children and high rates of mortality and morbidity, generally result from three interrelated conditions malnutrition, infection and the consequences of ill-times, closely spaced and too frequent pregnancies, without necessary health care.[2] They are often associated with poor socio-economic and social including scarcity of health and other social services. Breast-feeding has an important relevance to all these interlocking material and child health problems.

For the first few months of a child's life the best possible protection which any mother can provide for the baby's normal health and growth is exclusive breast-feeding. Breast-milk contains at least six anti-infective agents against some of the most common illness of infancy. It is also the most nutritious and hygienic food which any child can be given. So breast feeding is very important of the child for the first few months of life. Breast feeding is Human Rights of the Child.

Breast-feeding is a natural gifts and ideal type of feeding for the children, from birth to 6 months of life. Even in the most industrialized Societies. It has not been possible to replace breast milk, with formula feeds, without health risks. But depending on bottle and formula milks by poor people, living in unsanitary environment, bottle-feeding can be dangerous to the children, exposing them to severed malnutrition and deadly infections besides the unbearable economic burden on the family.[3]

The infant who does not receive colostrums, a marked fall in I.G. levels occurred on the fifth day after birth as compared to levels at birth. On the fifth day, levels of immunoglobulin are significantly higher in the serum of colostrums-fed infants than in those who do not receive colostrums. The immunoglobulin present in colostrums are to certain extent, absorbed from intestinal tract of new born infants, and this has got some physiological significance in the resistance to infection during the early neonatal period.[4]

Advantage of breast feeding to the nation reduce the incidence of marasmic-diarrhoea syndrome in the first 1/2 years of life. During period brain growth may get retarded and reduce protein gap. Breast milk most hygienic, so save the child from infection e.g., infantile eczema is much less in breast fed. It is a perfect food, so help in his growth and development and ready-made antibodies which protect against several common infectious diseases. Conductive to more healthy an happy relationship between the child an mother, leading to better personality development. It is economical and convenient and enjoyable and gives the emotional satisfaction to mothers. It helps in rapid involution of uterus and reduced the incidence of breast cancer among the mothers and very helpful of increasing the birth spacing.

Though breast feeding is a natural process and has been traditionally practiced since the origin of species there has been a decline in number of women (mothers) who go for in breast feeding due to the process of industrialization as well as the as the changing pattern of life style and also a large number of women now they work out side their homes, So they found feeding in convenient and impractical the availability of easy and attractive milk substitute contributed a lot towards the decline of breast-feeding practices. Maternity services and the attitude of health workers, however, unwittingly have created additional grounds for unblocking the process. Since the breast-feeding is a manifestation of human behaviour it is evident that the changing pattern of breast feeding should be viewed with in the sphere of socio-economic dynamic and changes in economic society.[5]

INTERNATIONAL LAW SUPPORT OF THE BREAST FEEDING

There has been great concern for the welfare of children at the international level culminating in the declaration of the Rights of the child adopted by the general Assembly of the United Nations. The Declaration in its preamble points out that the child by reason of his physical and mental immunity needs special safeguards and that mankind owes to the child the best it has to give and formulated several principles. It provided–the child shall enjoy special protection and shall be given opportunities and facilities, by law and by other means to enable him to develop physically, mentally, morally, spiritually and socially in a health and normal manner and in conditions of freedom and dignity. In the enactment of law for this purpose, the best interests of the child shall be the paramount consideration. Child shall also be protected from all forms of neglect, cruelty and exploitation.[6]

The right to adequate nutrition has been accepted since long in the normative instruments of International Law. The League of Nations in 1924 adopted the Geneva Declaration of Rights of the child. In 1948 General Assembly adopted 'Universal Declaration of Human Rights" The freedoms and right of children were implicitly included in this declarations which asserts, in Article 25 (1), that "everyone has the right to standards of living adequate for the health and well being of himself and his family including the food". This right has been reaffirmed in two major binding international conventions.[7]

The Universal Declaration of Eradication of Hunger and Malnutrition 1974,[8] which asserts in Article 6(2) the inalienable right of every man, woman and child to be free from hunger and malnutrition in order to develop their physical and mental faculties and fixes responsibility on the Government to work together for higher production and for more equitable and for more efficient distribution of goods between the countries and with in the countries.

The convention of the Right of child in order to maintain the standard of living adequate for their growth and development.[9] The Innocent Declaration on the Protection 1990, Promotion and support of Breast feeding was adopted by participants at a meeting on breast feeding held at the International child Development centre in Florence, Italy. The declaration started a variety of specific global goals including the goal that all women should be enabled to practice exclusive breast feeding and all infants should fed exclusively on breast mile from birth to four-six months of age.

The world submit for children held in year 1990 called for Empowerment of all women to breast feed their children exclusively for 4 to 6 months and to continue breast feeding with complementary food, well into second year. In 1992 the International conference on nutrition in Rome Pledged to reduce substantially within the decade, social and other impediments to optimal breast feeding. The fourth world conference on women 1995 in Beijing, promoting the benefits of breast feeding and International code of marketing of Breast Milk substitutes and facilitating of breast feeding by working women. In 1999 the 12th Session of the U.N. committee on Economic Social and cultural Rights released its general comment 1-2 on the right to adequate food. This statement by the committee constitutes definite contribution to International Juris Prudence.[10]

THE RIGHT OF BREAST FEEDING UNDER INDIAN CONSTITUTION

Children's programme should find a prominent part in our National Plans for the development of human resources, so that our children grow up to become rebuts citizens, physically fit, mentally alert and morally healthy, endowed with skills and motivations needed by society. Equal opportunities for development to all children during the period of growth should be our aim, for this would serve our larger purpose of reducing inequality and ensuring social Justice.[11]

In Indian Societies breast-feeding used to continue as long as the mother's milk was not exhausted either in natural biological course or consequent on another pregnancy. Today, the duration of breast-feeding, timing of the introduction of supplementary foods and the extent of reliance on foods other than human milk have changed a great deal.

The right of breast feeding in Indian constitution as not directly accepted but the above right included in different United Nation Charters, conventions has been duly accepted and recognized by our state who is the party to those covenants by in cooperating in the Directive Principles of State Policy.

Ordains that the children should be given opportunity and facility to develop in a healthy manner with proper freedom and dignity.[12] Further, it reiterates by giving importance raising the level of nutrition and of living of the people and improvement of public health.[13] Through the mode of improving the nutritional status of child has not be explicitly mentioned as a fundamental right in the Indian constitution, the Judiciary by the harmonious construction of the fundamental rights and the Directive Principles of State Policy has prescribed modalities of access to nutritious food including breast feeding and Right to life in Art 21 give the fundamental right including the life of child to live so breast feeding of the right of child therefore breast feeding is the human right of child.

CONCLUSION

Best food for the child is the mother's milk. Mother's milk is natural gift of the child so breast feeding is right of the child. Don't feed the child artificially unless you are sure that you have the money to buy enough milk. It is now known that breast-milk contains at least six anti infective agents against some of the most common illness of infancy. Breast feeding also the most nutritious and hygienic food. For the first few months of a child, life, the best food and best protection which-provide mother can for the baby's normal health and growth is exclusive breast feeding. The breast feeding is the very important to child growth and development. Breast feeding is the Human Rights of the Child. The following Suggestion is enumerated for effectuating the right of child in respect of breast feeding.

1. The Status should save the child from such unwarranted situation, by way making legislation for (specially the child respect of breast feeding)
2. Govt. N.G.O., Media, and Social workers, Religious Person, and famous person of the society Doctors etc. to create awareness to the importance of the breast feeding.
3. The Govt. should amend the existing maternity benefit by providing 6 months maternity leave benefits to the women, so that they can properly feed their children to meet their nutritional needs.
4. Embarrassment about burning the breast in front of other people. Working-class mothers are said to be more embarrassed by nudity. Breast-feeding break at work place should be provided and sufficient crèches should be created, so that the mother can be able to find sufficient time to breast feed their new born.
5. Generally women think that Breast feeding spoils the shape of the breast this is not true, for it is the enlargement of the breasts during pregnancy that stretches the skin and makes the breast more pendulous.
6. The Infant milk substitute feeding Bottle and Infant food (Regulation and control Act) 1992 should be implemented strictly and minimum sentence should be provided against those who violate the rules and

condition prescribed in the Act. Simultaneously all the artificial milk product sold in the marked must contain a brand the "breast feed is the best feeding".[14]

NOTES AND REFERENCES

1. Parents forum of meaningful Education Vs. Union of India (*AIR*, 2001 Del 212 at p. 218).
2. A. R. Omran: Health Benefits of Family Planning, WHO MCH/ 71.
3. R. Kumar (2002), 'Child Development in India', Vol. I.
4. O. M. Ellander: Vahlquist-B: Melbin T. (1959), Breast Feeding and Artificial Feeding Acts Paediac, Uppslain.
5. Dr. L. Khanede (1994), Breast Feeding is the Best Feeding, *Orissa Times*.
6. Satyavan Kottarakkara Vs. State, *AIR* 1997 Ker. 133 at p. 137.
7. International Convent on Economic Social and Cultural Right (1976), (ii) "Convention of the Right of Child, 1989".
8. Adopted on 16th November, 1974 by the World Food Conference and Endorsed by U. N. General Assembly in 1974.
9. Article 27 (1) "Convention of the Right of Child, 1989"
10. G. K. Mishra (2002), "Human Rights of Child Vs. Breast Feeding", *AIR, Journal*, 342.
11. *Supra*, 6.
12. Article 39 (g) of the Indian Constitution.
13. Article 47 of the Indian Constitution.
14. G. K. Mishra (2002), "Human Rights of the Child V. Breast Feeding", *AIR, Journal*, 342.

A New Paradigm for Law and Justice

J. P. Mishra*

INTRODUCTION

Strange is the world we live in. The more we try to make it better, the worse it becomes, or so it appears at least. The law, which was once the means to add value to our lives, has become a means to protect (commercial value of) things rather than man. The emergence of intellectual property rights presents a glaring example where the man stands next in importance to the things he creates. Examples are many. The justice, on the other hand, has become a thing desired by all but gettable by a chosen few. After a considerable run from pillar to post, either the quality of justice is robbed off by delay it permits or the justice is awarded in a way that leaves the awardees even more aggrieved.

It is ironical but true that we have become more educated (if one goes literacy rates), rich (going by per capita income or by the increasing number of rich person in our country), armed (taking into account the weapons of mass destruction that we have to our credit) and what not; but at the same time we are more ignorant (the way we fight for ourselves only, forgetting for the woes of our brethren), poor (going by the burgeoning number of poverty and hunger stricken mass of humanity) and unsafe (as is evident by unnatural deaths

* Faculty of Law, University of Allahabad (India).

owing to accidents, natural phenomena, or acts of aggression, insurgency or terrorism, etc). When we see the rich get richer with each passing day, and the poor more so; the words and phrases, used incessantly by the scholars of the times or the admirers of the system, in praise of law and justice simply become too hard to digest.

There is a manifold increase in corruption and terrorism, and decrease in human values. The world looks to have a great appetite for the rights which it wants to realize through any which means, paying scant care for the duties or, equivalently, the rights of others[1]. The systems of law and justice appear to have been missing some cardinal principles governing the life of man and his innate relations with the nature that preceded and pervades him.

Perhaps we need to change our vision of man and nature entirely, and adopt a universal and holistic view of things vital for our existence. In other words, we need look at things differently. The sections that follow touch these points only tangentially in an effort to hint at those values which may prove to be guiding forces in our quest for a new set of paradigms designed to make better the world we live in.

LAW AND JUSTICE

Law has been variously defined but still defies a complete definition. Having been viewed through spectacles of different ideologies it has got itself defined in as many ways. Accordingly, a sovereign[2], a society[3], common consciousness[4], norms[5], rules[6], nature[7], etc. have been brought to the aid of jurists in order that a complete definition may be woven. However, the fact remains that the concept of law pervades all these concepts but is enveloped by none. It is thus that the law has to take care of not only the changes in the various fields but also prepare itself to face the impact of these changes on the world we live in.

Justice, broadly speaking, is the balancing of interests either equally or equitably. This is done in the light of the law in force for the time being. This implies that there is a change in the facets of justice corresponding to changes in law with respect to a given field. However, the fact remains that the judiciary does more than merely applying the law to a case at hand; it also has to see whether law is worth its name, or whether the law is pertinent to the point under consideration, or whether the law sufficiently covers the matter under dispute, or finally, whether there is a gap in law that needs be filled for the administration of justice.

There have taken place tremendous changes during the past few centuries, particularly the 20th century, providing new frontiers of law-making[8] and broadening the canvas of justice[9]. As the law embraced human rights[10], environment[11], industrial property[12], intellectual property[13], cyber space[14] and biotechnology[15], etc; the new for a administration of justice emerged. The latter half of the last century witnessed the growing trend of globalization which, in turn, offered certain new platforms[16] not only to mobilize international support required for smooth functioning of law but also to ensure uniformity in the administration of justice, as far as practicable, at the domestic and international levels.

It may not be out of place to recall that even before globalization became a reality for us, the legal and judicial changes in one national kept on having their influence on other nations, India, whose constitution had been drafted in a way to have the best of several working constitutions of the world at that time, could not remain uninfluenced by several such changes taking place in Britain[17] and America[18]; but sometimes chose her own path[19]. The growing number of global agencies addressing various walks of life has created an atmosphere where every nation sees no option but to fall in line with latest developments in the field of law and justice characterized by these agencies.

Novel manifestations of our ever-changing perceptions of law and justice are marked by increasing numbers of independent nations who at the same time feel more and more dependent on others in their march towards development. On the other hand, globalization has landed all nations in a state where problem of one spreads like contagious disease to others very soon and what would otherwise have been confined to a specific region has become a global phenomenon. This spread of negative elements seems to have outsmarted the benefit that we once dreamt of deriving out of a state of globalisation.

The fear of nuclear catastrophe, the issue of terrorism, the dangers of biotechnological inventions, the increasing erosion of values in our life, the pollution of earth and the environment, the increasing gap between the poor and the powerful and the like are the problems the gravity whereof has increased exponentially even as the law and justice make their best endeavour to curb and remedy these for the welfare of mankind.

PARADIGM SHIFT

The march of mankind towards the future is always guided by the way it looks at the world. This world view has its base in certain patterns of thoughts and concepts that run through it. These patterns or standards or models are called paradigms. Viewed thus a vision of the world is woven around a set of such paradigms. Therefore when our world-view undergoes a drastic change, the underlying patterns of thoughts, concepts, etc. also change i.e. we adopt a new set of paradigms that replaces the existing one. This replacement of one set of paradigms by the other is called a paradigm shift. In this regard two things are noteworthy: first, that such a shift is an essential feature of man's progress towards fulfillment, and second, that such revolutionary changes as require a paradigm shift altogether do not occur every day.

The term 'paradigm shift' was first used by famous scholar Thomas Kuhn in 1962[20] in order to explain the scientific advancement and, according to him, it reflected that stage of transformation where 'one conceptual world-view is replaced by another'. However, the term is no more confined to the discipline of science alone; and is now frequently used for any set of thoughts and concepts that help us view the world in a more meaningful way than hitherto fore. For example, the view that sun revolves the earth gave way to the view that the earth revolves the sun; the view that the Universe had been created by the Almighty was dominated by the view that science along is true, etc. We can say that such revolutionary changes mark the paradigm shift from geo-centrism to heliocentric, creation to evolution, and faith in God to faith in Science respectively.

Why is it Needed Right Now?

We have a plethora of laws trying–or so they claim-to give us better rights/avenues for our development. Yet we are not happy people. The hunger stricken population runs in to hundreds of millions in India alone; supposing that we do not look at the world map and count countries like Somalia. And, things become unbelievably unpleasant once we think globally on a point. Our road accident deaths, for example, surpass the total death toll of any of the world wars[21].

The man for whom all this hullabaloo had been made seems to have been lost in the haze that the modern efforts have created. His aspirations lie buried under the carpet of the rich. The change of the world has meant for him almost the replacement of one system of oppression by the other with no respite in deed.

While there is no denying the fact that tremendous improvements have taken place for betterment of our life solely due to the application of sci-tech, advances in science and technology have given a new face to terrorism which has grown much more strong and ugly than what it was earlier. Law and justice both are trying desperately to overcome these ugly aspects of human action but their success is dismal. Also, there is the rising level of mass discontent reelected in the mass movements and social action litigations to fight the policies of the government[22].

On the premise that a certain section of our society remained downtrodden for long started the efforts of what is called protective discrimination theory; taking in its way the scheduled castes, scheduled tribes and, finally, the other backward classes. But the result is that the poorest of the poor do not have any caretakers and the lion's share of the state bounty given in the name of OBCs and the like is being swallowed by those who hardly need it, but thanks to the system, which showers all the abuses to a caste-based society but at the same time makes the caste the sole criterion for bracketing people for beneficial treatment. The ruling party breathlessly advertises its secular credentials but announces in the same vein to award reservations to the poor on purely communal grounds. Since no party wants to lose even one vote no party musters enough courage to oppose such unequal and discriminatory measures of the ruling class. The same politicians, however, look sideways on the issue of 30 per cent reservation to women in the Legislature.

Genetic engineering has emboldened the man to do things that disturb the state of nature. Japan's invention of genetically modified mouse that is able to see cat eye to eye is a harbinger of things to come[23]. In our enthusiasm to always do new things, we have tried to clone Einstein, etc. forgetting rudimentary rules of probability that out of innumerable co-ordinates of space and time that go in to making a person, the change of even a few of these may produce altogether a different person. But the most unfortunate point is that all over the world such efforts are flourishing- publically or privately-and so are the laws to prevent it. It is like what the phrase 'to create a ghost and fight with it' would have ever suggested.

India has adopted most of the British model minus, of course, the Crown. While India is trying to overcome the negativities of the system so adopted, UK looks all set to adopt a similar one. The Constitutional Reform Act, 2005 in Britain is a pointer to this direction. The UK will now have an Upper House (largely elected/ partly nominated), a system of courts headed by the Supreme Court, and, a set of human rights enforceable through these courts much like India; not to talk of the European Charter of Fundamental Rights which, as is the case with our Directive Principles of State Policy, is agreed in principle by all the members but is not binding on them. However, the matter of copying is only on the surface of our talk. What runs deeper than this is the meaninglessness of the system we adopt and discard and readopt and discard.

It seems the model of development or the idea of man, law and justice that we entertain at present have something patently basic (or, natural) lacking in them. If so, then, it is pertinent to ponder whether we have come to the last point on the path of that development which we had somehow modelled for us; and whether this pattern of things that we have developed is not going to deliver goods in anyway better than what it already has? We stand in the need of altogether a new set of paradigms for our further journey towards fulfillment because, as Thomas Aquinas assured us long ago, we are but a means in the schemed of some super-human legislator who wants to achieve certain ends through us like say, survival, continuity, perfection, etc.[24].

VALUES THAT WE NEED

Let us begin with an analogy. A tree is as strong as its roots. If the roots are hollow or rotten or without substance; the tree can not withstand winds, let alone the storms. But the most important factor is the ground on which the tree stands; from which its roots, trunk, branches and leaves get the food. A system of law and justice, likewise, is as good as the set of values it is supported by; and, of course, the philosophical foundation it has.

Our present system of law and justice is mostly based on materialistic values that focus on the physical comfort and encourage a cut-throat competition with pure and ultimate motive of becoming financially more well off than others. Since this does not ensure peace of mind and purity of thought as it obviously cannot, the man becomes desperate to accelerate his efforts little knowing that the model he is a slave to is inherently incompetent to provide him with the kind of pleasure and peace he is longing for. There are a few cardinal values a healthy, system cannot afford to ignore but which unfortunately our present system does not possess in their true spirit.

Ever since the emergence of positivist and other schools that sprang up in reaction to the natural law philosophy, the law stands divorced from *morality*. Minus its moral content, law becomes merely a collection of rules that govern our external conduct; because it is morality along that disciplines us internally..Living in such a system which is devoid of morality, a man tries to ensure that he acts in such a way that lets him go scot free[25]. Seldom does he pause to think whether he ought to do what he is going to. The lit must to check the validity of his actions, truly speaking, is whether it benefits him. And, the same criterion is there for a nation vis-à-vis other nations. The twentieth century witnessed a great debate known as the naturalist-positivist debate[26] but the fact remains that morality is more or less a forgotten value in the modern system of law and justice.

All are equal in the eyes of law. So goes the rhetoric, but the fact that law has often been used to serve the interests of few even at the cost of the interests of others shows that rhetoric is not always the reality. Sometimes the law is used to protect discriminatory action of state on the ground that *equality* allows reasonable classification of persons[27], at other times it is used to protect a caste as a class[28], and at still other times to treat even one person as a class![29]. Every system of law has a fairly good share of inequality; it is the quantum that differs. If the ancient system favoured one class, the modern system is favouring some other. Thus, it is certain that both systems have the same ending i.e. one particular class empowered, and others impoverished. Unless we profess as also follow the equality in its true sense, we cannot ensure the welfare of one and all. If we do not lose sight of the fact that equality is a relative concept rather than absolute, pragmatic rather than myopic, and inclusive rather than exclusive; law and equality can go hand in hand.

Closely related to equality is the value of *universality*. Presently, law of one country (or, region for that matter) hardly takes note of the law of other countries so long as her interests are protected. This has robbed the law of its universality. In this context, it may be noted that Zeno (350-260 B.C.) and his followers believed that entire universe was made up of just one element, that is, reason[30]. Reason is the spark of divine in man and hence all men of the world are equal. Arguing thus they inferred that since reason was an element universally present in every man, it was possible to make law universally applicable to all. However, Zeno's philosophy, which later provide ground for natural law theory that flourished in Rome and elsewhere for quite a long time, had echoed much earlier in India philosophy. Geeta informs us:

समम् सर्वेषु भूतेषु तिष्ठंतम् परमेश्वरम्। विनश्यत्स्वविनश्यंतम् यःपश्यति सःपश्यति।।

The present system of law and justice dwells primarily on the specifications of punishments that are to be awarded to the law-breakers, and pays almost no care to give incentives to those who have acted to uphold the law. As a result one comes to feel the presence of law and justice often through the medium of punishments only. Such things only arouse hatred between the man punished and the rest of the society. The promotion of *love for all* i.e. man and nature both does not form the subject- matter of law today. Forgetting this reality we ceaselessly try to find solutions to new challenges in new legislations.

Modern law and justice seldom encourage *a sense of duty*[31]. Our belief that legislation is the panacea of all ills manifests itself in the creation of newer rights like, say, human rights, intellectual property rights, fundamental rights and a host of other rights. This, at best, may and actually does result in creation of new for a for enforcement and adjudication of these rights. The state of affairs, however, remains almost the same if not worsens; because, as the sense of possessiveness of man increases, so does his greed for more and more rights.

CONCLUSION/SUGGESTION

The law of modern times is always seen under influence of some particular field which appears to be in fashion in the global market. This is why there is a phase when the thrust is entirely on environment, at other times the human rights, and at yet another time the intellectual property; often without having a look at our own system. For example, the human rights was an essential feature to be added to those nations of the world where either due to non-democratic systems or owing to some historical or conventional reasons the basic rights of man found no place in their law. But under the said impression of global fashionableness India too made law on human rights almost forgetting that there already existed fundamental rights under the Constitution which were capable of supporting every human interest. Now, India feels perturbed when the international organizations want her to support gay's rights, etc. under the garb of human rights[32].

Ulterior motives of politicians behind issues otherwise uncontroversial have created problems the nation finds hard to solve. The way the issue of social justice is being handled serves as an example. The reservation which once proved to be a powerful electoral weapon seems to have boom-ranged in the face of the politician who finds it difficult to solve the riddle why the castes or classes that were not backward, etc. in 1950 have become so after tasting the fruits of development for more than 50 years!

The justice delivery system of the modern times too is quite vulnerable in that it is not capable for focusing on more than one element at a time. This is why sometimes there is much hue and cry over the prisoner's rights; at other times the judiciary seems all out to punish the offender in the strictest possible terms. There was a phase when the judiciary was in a mood to break all the conventional rules of procedure which it felt were the barriers on the path of justice. At other times, the judiciary riding high on the bandwagon of judicial activism would not hesitate a bit in usurping the powers of the other two wings of the government.

The burgeoning cases of corruption, the rising crime graph, newer ways of committing crime, demands to protect immoral ways of life under the pretext of personal freedom, and the experiments in science and technology to play God and disturb the order of nature are all offshoots of the model of law and justice that we follow: a system which is based on and influenced by the Western model of the world view which is predominantly materialistic.

However, it is equally true that materialism cannot be written off from any model of world view once can think of because it is one of the four elements that according to Indian philosophy give meaning to ones beign[33] that is purushartha.

Therefore, it is suggested that the paradigm shift has to be from individuality to universality, from discrimination to equality, from ostensibly immoral demands to a sense of morality, and from a clamour for right to a sense of duty to name just a few. To say this is not to suggest to undo whatever has been or being done but to advocate for a change of point of thrust in our scheme of things rather than to reject the scheme altogether. That is to say, this paradigm shift is meant to ensure that fruits of development are tasted equally meaningfully by one and all rather than a chosen few-whether men or nations.

And this shift in paradigms must embrace law and justice first.

NOTES

1. As Kant says: "Act in such a way that the maxim of your action may be made the maxim of universal action; or, your action is right if it can co-exist with equal freedom of others."
2. Austin, for example, defines law as 'the command of the sovereign, backed by sanction'.
3. See, the views of scholars of the sociological school like Ehrlich, who says that the living law is that which the people obey in practice as against the law in the statute-books; Ihering, who feels that a law without purpose is no law; and Duguit, who asserts that law is good only if it promotes what he terms the 'social solidarity' *et al*.
4. The German scholar Savigny says that law is the product of the common consciousness (volkgeist) of the people; Gierke tries

to understand law in terms of the associations which, according to him, are based either on the theory of collaboration or domination; and Hegel is of the opinion that law is evolved out of the interaction between the opposites for example, the thesis and anti-thesis, etc.

5. Hans Kelsen says that law has a normative structure, and a norm is an ought-proposition; for example, if A commits theft, A ought to be punished. A norm derives its validity from a higher norm, which again derives its validity form still higher norm, and so on. The norm which gives validity to all the norms is called the grund norm. The grund norm validates all other norms but does not stand in the need of validation itself; because, as Kelsen said, the grundnorm is an ex-hypothesis. The grund norm of a country may be a constitution, a dictator's will or, simply, the socio-political reality.
6. HLA Hart presents a legal system as a system of rules; the primary rules creating rights and duties, and the secondary rules. The secondary rules are of three types, one for the identification, the other for the modification, and still other for the adjudication of the primary rules. Thus a legal system, says Hart, is the union of primary rules with the secondary rules of modification, identification and adjudication.
7. The naturalists see nature as the source of all law, and claim that since natural phenomena are the same everywhere, it is possible to derive natural norms of conduct that are universally applicable to man regardless of the co-ordinates of space and time. The theory was propounded by Zeno and his disciples who said that the entire universe is composed of but one element, that is, reason. The reason is the spark of divine in man, and since it is present in every man, all men are equal. Arguing thus, they presented cosmoplitan concept of law, which blossomed in the theories of St. Augustine and others and reached its perfection in the theory presented by Thomas Aquinas who declared; "Law is an ordinance of reason, made by one who has the care for the community, and promulgated."
8. The Human Rights Act, 1998; the House of Lords Act, 1999; Terrorism Acts of 2005 and 2006; Equality Act, 2006 and the Constitutional Reform Act, 2005, to name but a few, has introduced far-reaching changes in the UK law. The signing by Britain of the European Charter of Fundamental Rights on

December 13, 2007 has further enriched the legal fabric there. The American Constitution, originally have only seven Articles, has been amended 27 times so far (the last one in 1992 related to pay revision of the legislators). The Constitution of India is flexible enough to absorb the emerging demands of the changing times and has been amended 94 times (till June 12, 2006) including the amendments of far-reaching consequences, like, the abolition of right to property as a fundamental right, the introduction of fundamental duties, the anti-defection provisions, the reservation in jobs, etc. for the other backward classes, placement of environment in concurrent list as also in the Directive Principles, making right to education a fundamental right, etc.

9. In *Marbury b. Madison,* Justice Marshall established the efficacy of judicial review for all times to come; even though it had, literally speaking not been provided in the Constitution. American judiciary also evolved the concept of Social Action Litigation (SAL) to ensure that procedural technicalities of law might not come in a way of administering justice to people who really deserved it. In the UK. Enactments like Human Rights Act, 1998 and the Constitutional Reform Act, 2005 give a new face to the system of justice in UK because the latter provides for replacement of the House of Lords by the Supreme Court of Justiciary as the highest court of UK w.e.f. 2008 itself after the Act becomes effective.

   The judicial innovation of American courts galvanized the Indian courts and thus proved to be a precursor to judicial activism in India. Similarly, the policy of protective discrimination promoted by American judiciary in case of Blacks somehow helped the Indian judiciary uphold the policy of reservation to the other backward classes in order to achieve social justice. Justice Marshall's path-breaking judgment in *Marbury v. Madison* on judicial review echoed in the Supreme Court's decisions in *Keshavanand Bharati v. State of Kerala (1973,* the 'basic structure theory'), *Indira Nehru Gandhi v. Rajnarain* (1978, the judicial review is a part of the basic structure) and, recently, in *IR Coelho (Dead) by LRs v. State of Tamil Nadu* (2007, even the legislations placed in the IX Schedule of the Constitution are judicially reviewable).

10. Long after trying to replace the natural law theory with other theories the thinkers and politicians alike were convinced that

rights of an individual as a human being, irrespective of his religion, nationality, etc. should be protected. This global consciousness symbolized in the Universal Declaration of Human Rights (1948) soon got acceptance at the regional and national levels. The human rights jurisprudence so developed has become a part of modern jurisprudence.

11. It appeared almost paradoxical that the industries which aimed at betterment of our life were eating upon the environment so essential for our life. Stockholm Conference saw the issue blossom in to international environmental law while the concept of sustainable development became driving force for the Earth Summit. The green house effect, global warming, ozone layer depletion and climate change-the offshoots of pollution-have dominated the international debates ever since. The United Nations Conference on Climate Change in Bali-which concluded on December 14, 2007 is the latest such attempt which aims to prepare a roadmap for reduction of emission of green house gases, thus attempting to update Kyoto Protocol that expires in 2012.

12. The industrialization brought with it the prospects of huge production coupled with equally potential apprehension of missuse and malpractices in the creation, consumption, trade and commerce of the same .These prepared a ground for germination of industrial property rights.

13. The intellectual property laws, which are designed to protect the ideas with commercial value, quickly because the catch-world of modern legal system.

14. The world of machines-the cyber space- is where most of us today want to live in. Electronic laws, as cyber laws are often referred to, have made their presence felt in various walks of life, for example, e-governance, e-banking, e-commerce, etc; and have induced changes in other branches of law also.

15. While some of the biotechnological inventions do seem to augur well with the increasing pressure of population and incidental needs of food, shelter, etc.; the efforts for cloning man to create a cloned race altogether are worrying. The law on the point remained in a state of flux until TRIPs tried to evolve certain parameters for patenting, etc. of biotechnological inventions.

16. The United Nations and its various organizations in general and International Court of Justice in particular, the Universal

Declaration on Human Rights, the Trade Related Aspects of Intellectual Property Rights, the World Trade Organisation and its Dispute Resolution System are some of the prominent examples.

17. Justice in India got a fillip when the Supreme Court followed the *Ridge v. Baldwin* to invite the rules of fair hearing in to *Maneka Gandhi v. Union of India* interpreting the Article 21 (the right to life and personal liberty) which on the one hand marked a shift in the approach adopted by the Court in the previous cases but also metamorphosed the "procedure established by law" in to the "due process of law".
18. The impact of Justice Marshall's path-breaking judgment in *Marbury v. Madison* echoed in the judgment of Indian apex court when it ruled in *Indira Nehru Gandhi v. Rajnarain* that the Legislature can not take away the power of judicial review by inserting in to a piece of legislation phrases like "this shall not be called in to question in any court of law".
19. The Indian Supreme Court ventured to modify the rule of strict liability (laid down in *Rylands v. Fletcher* in 1868) in to one of absolute liability holding that the owner of the premises where handling of hazardous substances was being done owed an absolute and non-delegable duty towards anybody who got adversely affected due to such handling.
20. See. Thomas Kuhn's book "The Structure of Scientific Revolution", p. 10.
21. According to data released on the World Day of Remembrance for Traffic Victims, 1260000 people lost their life and 5000000 got injured while there was financial loss of about 1000 billion dollars during 2005-06. In India 100000 people lost their lives during this period. For further details, see Amar Ujala Allahabad Edition dated 18.11.2007.
22. For example, *Janadesh March* 2007 which prompted about 27000 landless people coming from 18 different states of India to walk on foot for several hundred kilometers and hold a rally in New Delhi on October 28, 2007 to arouse the government about their plights. Seeing that leaders of Congress, Left and other parties lost no time in sharing the platform with the activists, the Government sprang in to action with the Prime Minister announcing the setting up of two high power committees-one of these headed by himself-to look in to their demands.

23. See, *The Hindustan Times*, Lucknow Edition, dated 14.12.2007. In the same paper there is a news item showing the cats cloned by South Korean scientists. These cloned cats glow in the dark when exposed to ultra violet beams.
24. See, his book *Summa Theologia.*
25. See, the Bad man's theory suggested by famous realist Justice Holmes.
26. See, in particular, the debate between HLA Hart who admits that law should have a shared morality; and Leo Lon Fuller who strongly feels that law should not only have external morality (like patriotism and other lofty ideals) but also the internal morality (like resonableness, intelligibility etc.). Also see. The Concept of Law by Hart, and The Morality of Law by Fuller.
27. For example, see the judicial approach in pre-Maneka Gandhi phase.
28. Such was the approach in Indra Sawhney case
29. For Example, see the Court's approach in Chiranjit Lal Chaowdhury v. Union of India: AIR 1951 SC41.
30. See: Jurisprudence–The Philosophy and Method of the Law by Edgar Bodenheimer; Third Indian Reprint 2001, at p.13.
31. It took India almost three decades before she could write fundamental duties in her Constitution.
32. When some gay person were arrested on January 03, 2006, by Lucknow police, it was condemned by a non governmental organization 'Human Rights Watch which wrote to the Prime Minister about what it termed as "shameful" harassment of gay men. The United Nations agency on AIDS, UNAids also condemned the arrests. For more details, see BBC News, UK version at *http://news.bbc.co.uk/I/hi/world/south_asia/4602068.stm*
33. All the four purusharthas, namely, dhrama, artha, kama and moksha are collectively known as purushartha chatushtaya. The first three are collectively known as tivarga, and scholars like Manu and Vyas feels that the true observance of these relative values leads to the fourth, that is, moksha which is an absolute value. Of the three, says Manu, kama and artha must be rejected if contrary to dharma" (Manusmriti IV/176).

Role of the United Nations in the Development of Human Rights

KULJIT KAUR*

INTRODUCTION

Human nature is such that every society, even the most civilized one, is bound to witness disputes between man and man, man and society, man and state, and so on. It is true that human rights have intellectual roots reaching far back to the past, but it is generally recognized that the starting point of the evolution of an international human rights protection system coincides with the beginnings of an institutional framework for a permanent cooperation of States. The *League of Nations* and the International Labour Organisation (ILO), both created after the First World War, paved, though modest, the way for a process of defining human rights and their monitoring. Only with the foundation of the United Nations in 1945 one may mark the point from where the legal development of human rights and their protection on the universal plane gained a forceful dynamism.

Having experienced another World War with millions of dead and refugees, and the unprecedented violent outbreak of racism in Nazi Germany resulting in the Holocaust, the *UN Charter* pledged itself "to reaffirm faith in fundamental human rights, in the dignity and worth of the human person,

* Reader and Head, Department of Laws, Guru Nanak Dev University, Amritsar-143 005 .

in the equal rights of men and women and of nations large and small" (Preamble). Art. 1 of the Charter precisely defined as one of the principles of Organisation to promote and encourage "respect for human rights and for fundamental freedoms for all without distinction as to race, sex, language, or religion". Together with the General Assembly (GA), the Economic and Social Council (ECOSOC) became expressly entrusted with the task of promoting universal respect for, and observance of, human rights and fundamental freedoms[1].

THE UN INVOLVEMENT IN THE CREATION OF UNIVERSAL HUMAN RIGHTS

The Charter of the United Nations was the final turning point of the subject of human rights *vis-à-vis* international law. Realisation had dawned on the civilized part of the humanity that its future depended on establishment of a world community based on the principles of rights & equality of man and woman, one which enjoyed the rights as endowed to all living beings and one where there was no discrimination on any account, a community wedded to the goal of common good. The concept of human rights rested on the principle that they are sacrosanct bundle of rights vested in human beings so that they can live a dignified life "not by chance or choice but by being human". As put succinctly in the US Declaration of Independence, these spring forth from self-evident truths "that all men are created equal; that they are endowed by their Creator with certain inalienable rights; that among these are life, liberty, and the pursuit of happiness". Rules of international law designed to protect the human rights-as we now know, use or enforce-are by the large a phenomena created by the world order established by United Nations.

The most important of these rights arises out of the Universal Declaration of Human Rights, adopted and proclaimed by the General Assembly of the United Nation on 10th December, 1948. The Preamble of the Universal Declaration of Human Rights is of utmost importance. It envisioned "the foundation of freedom, justice and peace in the world" and in the wake of instances of 'barbarous acts which have out-reached the conscience of mankind showing "disregard and contempt for human rights", the need for "the advent of a world in which human beings shall have inherent dignity" and "equal and inalienable rights" enjoying freedom of speech and belief and freedom from fear and want.

Article 1 declared that all human beings are born free and equal in dignity & rights and are "endowed with reason and conscience ensured act towards one another in a spirit of brotherhood". Article 2 assured to all human beings all the rights & freedoms set-forth in the declaration without distinction of any kind such as race, colour, sex, language, religion, etc. The document declared various human rights which include the right to life; liberty and security of person; right against slavery or torture; rights against cruel, inhuman or degrading treatment or punishment; right of equality before the law and right to effective remedy against violation of fundamental rights guaranteed by the law, which includes right to fair and public hearing by an independent and impartial tribunal; the right to presumption of innocence till proved guilty; the right to privacy; the right to freedom of movement & residence; right to raise family; right to property; freedom of thought, opinion, expression, conscience and religion, etc.

The Universal Declaration of Human Rights governed part of the concerns about human rights. The principles proclaimed in the Charter of United Nations had shown recognition of "the inherent dignity and of the equal and inalienable rights of all members of the human family" as the foundation of freedom, justice and peace in the world. It naturally flowed from the Universal Declaration of Human Rights that the ideal of free human beings enjoying civil & political freedom and freedom from fear & want could be achieved only if conditions were created whereby everyone might enjoy his civil, political, economic, social and cultural rights[2].

With this in view, the International Covenant on Civil and Political Rights was brought in force on 23rd March, 1976 so that "universal respect for, and observance of, human rights and freedom" could be promoted as an obligation of the States. The civil and political rights declared in this Covenant are virtually an extension or enlargement of what had been originally declared in 1948 as human rights.

The International Covenant on Civil and Political Rights declared that all peoples "have the right of self-determination" and consequently to "freely determine their political status and freely pursue their economic, social and cultural development" and for such ends to "freely dispose of their natural wealth and resources" but this "without prejudice to any obligations arising out of international economic cooperation based upon the principles of mutual benefit".

Women and Children have almost always been the most vulnerable section of the society in the matter of human rights. History would bear testimony to the fact that, more often that not, it is they who fall victim to acts designed for exploitation. The Declaration on the Elimination of Discrimination against Women was transformed into a multi-lateral treaty through the Convention adopted by the United Nation's General Assembly in December 1979.

By adopting this Convention, the United Nations reaffirmed its faith "in fundamental human rights, in the dignity and worth of the human persons" of men and women alike. Taking note of the obligation of the State to ensure the equal rights of men and women in the matter of economic, social, cultural, civil and political rights on one hand and the continuation of extensive discrimination against women on the other, a measure was considered requisite to ensure that obstacles were removed in the participation of women alongside men, so as to promote the growth of prosperity of society and the family. Thus, in order to secure full development of the potentialities of women in the services of their countries and of humanity in the matters concerning & including food, health, education, training and opportunities for employment etc., United Nations declared its determination to implement the principles set-forth in the Detailed on the Elimination of

Discrimination against Women. Detailed provisions were made in the various Articles of this Convention so as to provide equality of opportunity and dignity in all spheres of life to women *vis-à-vis* men. It obliged the States to adopt measures to make the promises held out in the Convention real rights.

The UN human rights treaties are at the core of the international system for the promotion and protection of human rights. Every UN member state is a party to one or more of the seven major human rights treaties. It is a universal human rights legal system, which applies to virtually every child, woman or man in the world. The Covenants legally bind ratifying states to provide an effective remedy for those whose rights have been violated.

The successful implementation of the human rights treaty standards, whether at the international or national level, depend on their accessibility to the victims of human rights abuse. This means both familiarity with the standards and access to remedial mechanisms. International Treaties, Conventions or Declarations are a source of international law, the efficacy of which depends largely on the good-sense, cooperation and willingness of each member State to enforce it by legislative measures in the form of municipal law within its own territory, on one hand, and its willingness to be answerable and accountable at the international level with regard to its own trace record, on the other[3].

Although the Declaration, which comprises a broad range of rights, is not a legally binding document, it has inspired more than 60 human rights instruments which together constitute an international standard of human rights. These instruments include the International Covenant of Economic, Social and Cultural Rights and the International Covenant on Civil and Political Rights, both of which are legally binding treaties. Together with the Universal Declaration, they constitute the International Bill of Rights.

The Human Rights Commission is the only political organ of the UN that is exclusively involved in human rights matters. While originally its main function was the elaboration of

Conventions and Declarations (standard setting), later on the focus shifted more to the reaction to serious human rights violations. Particularly by the work of its Sub-commission on Promotion and Protection of Human Rights (formerly on the Prevention of Discrimination and the Protection of Minorities), composed of independent experts, the Commission achieved quite remarkable results in clarifying conceptual and substantial issues in the field of human rights. The annual six weeks public session of the Commission evolved into a genuine world's meeting place for human rights affairs with a participation of countless NGOs. On the other side, the degree of public attention is not always paralleled by the concrete outcome.

THE MAIN ACTORS AT THE UN LEVEL

Further, one of the most important actors in the field of human rights protection on the UN level is the *General Assembly*. We have already seen that the General Assembly, by its resolutions, instructed the Human Rights Commission to elaborate drafts of conventions, and after their discussion in the General Assembly's Third Committee, formally adopted them. Besides, in numerous declarations and resolutions, the General Assembly underlines the importance of human rights stressing the need of comprehensive observance.

Another Actor which certainly indicates a major development in public international law is the Security Council which has included a State's serious human rights violation in its assessment of whether a breach of or a threat to the peace is present. If the *Security Council* arrives at this conclusion, it may take any decision under Chapter VII or the UN Charter. Again, the composition of the Security Council inevitably will lead to politically motivated decisions, saving from condemnation and sanctions not only the permanent members themselves but their allies or political protégés alike. Thus rather in a broad sense the Security Council is contributing to the development of human rights and their protection.

Although individuals cannot apply to the *International Court of Justice* (ICJ), the jurisprudence of this principal judicial organ of the UN forms a cornerstone in international human rights protection. Allegations of human rights violations may be the basis of disputes between States submitted to the Court or the reason why an advisory opinion of the Court is requested[4].

An important strengthening of the cause of human rights became apparent by the establishment of *international criminal courts*. Since human rights violations are always committed by human beings, though acting as State organs, any redress of the most serious violations should embrace the personal responsibility of the individual perpetrators. After the activities of the Courts in Nuremberg and Tokyo (1945-48) it took decades before the idea got another impulse. Only the massacres in Bosnia-Herzegovina/Srbrenica and in Rwanda led to the establishment of two special criminal tribunals in the Hague (for former Yugoslavia) and Arusha (for Rwanda) by the Security Council in 1993/94 empowering the tribunals to bring to justice individuals having allegedly committed serious war crimes, acts of genocide and crimes against humanity. The results achieved by the tribunals are quite remarkable. Additionally, based on an international treaty (Rome Statute of 1998), the International Criminal Court (ICC) has been established. More than 100 States now have ratified the Statute. The ICC has just started its work.

The Conventions, Treaties, Declarations or Protocols remain mere paper promises till they are formally ratified by the member States and then acted upon by bringing about legislative measures in accordance with the Constitution of the country so as to translate the rights declared at the international level into real municipal rights. The journey from the stage of declaration in the international instruments to real enforceable rights in each Member State has been slow and tardy. In the matter of implementation, different countries have been selective in their approach. Further, mere declaration of a right in the domestic law of the country can never suffice. It has to be backed by effective machinery that can actually enforce the rights, bring to justice and punish those who violate these rights. Indeed, such machinery is required at two levels; one, to deal with violations by the subjects of the country within itself and the second, where these violations take place at the behest of one State against another State or against the subjects of the latter.

Thus, as far as state are bound by human rights obligations they cannot legally argue that the claim for respect of their commitments would interfere with their domestic jurisdiction. In this field, States cannot shield themselves from criticism and legal actions of other States. Experience has taught that States sometimes are either not willing or not capable to secure conditions where human beings may live in dignity. Making the respect and protection of human right an international concern, other States and the international community itself obtain the opportunity to press the State concerned to do its duty. However, at the end of the day, the success of the international protection of human rights still remains dependent on the willingness of all States to cooperate on all levels[5].

CONCLUSION

The concern of the United Nations with the promotion and protection of human rights and fundamental freedoms stems directly from the realization by the international community that "recognition of the inherent dignity and of the equal and inalienable rights of all members of the human family is the foundation of freedom, justice and peace in the world", and from the resultant pledge of States Members of the United Nations "to achieve, in cooperation with the United Nations, the promotion of universal respect for and observance of human rights and fundamental freedoms".

Today, the United Nations works to promote and protect human rights though a variety of approaches. Through the United Nations Technical Cooperation Programme in the Field of Human Rights, States may receive, at their request, technical assistance in the promoting and protection of human rights.

NOTES AND REFERENCES

1. Alfredsson, Gudmundur/Eide. Asbjorn (Eds.), The Universal Declaration of Human Rights: A Common Standard of Achievement, 1999.
2. Alston, Philip (Ed.), The United Nations and Human Rights: A Critical Appraisal, 1992 (Paperback 1996).
3. Bayefsky, Anne F. (Ed.), the UN Human Rights Treaty System in the 21st Century, 2000.
4. Mr. Eckart KLEIN, Professor, University of Ptsdam, 'The UN System', at 37th Annual Study Session, July 2006, Strasbourg.
5. *www.ohchr.org*

Problems of Refugee Women and the International Law

Ms. Suneet Kashyap*

There are currently fifteen million refugees and asylum seekers world wide[1]. More than 80 percent of the world's refugees are women and their dependent children. Violence against women is rampant during armed conflict. It is manifested through involuntary relocation, forced labor, torture, summary execution of women, forced deportation and racist state policies denying in limiting public representation health care, education, employment, and access to legal redress. Rape and other forms of sexual torture are used as strategies of war in order to shame and demoralize individual families and communities. Resettlement policies actively discriminate against women on ground of both race and gender. Refugee women are at greater risk than any other woman even for sexually transmitted diseases and infections (STI's) including human immunodeficiency syndrome (HIV). Migration increases the incidence of sexual and gender based violence (SGBV, e.g. Rape, forced impregnation, and forms of violence) which in turn promotes the spread of STI's. Refugee women like many migrant workers are frequently treated as second class citizen in their countries of destination. Racist state policies of host countries particularly on labor and immigration result in the exploitation of refugee and migrant women. The majority of trafficked people are women especially those bound for the world's sex industries.

---

* Lecturer, IGNOU, New Delhi.

Because the employment opportunity of these women are limited to domestic work or sex industry, therefore their right to work, freedom of movement, reproductive right, right to acquire, change, or retain their nationality, right to health and other basic human rights are violated. The result is that refugee women and their families are more vulnerable to religious, racial and gender discrimination and exploitation. Many of the victims are kidnapped and sold into slavery by their own families.[2]

Refugee women are normally the unacknowledged majority in the refugee camps. During their exile, it is this majority which undergoes the maximum hardship because of their gender, yet this fact remains hidden, unknown and unpublished[3].

Rape and other forms of sexual torture have become weapons in modern warfare, and have been used to an alarming degree by those who intent upon the destruction and genocide of large portions of humanity. However, these horrific events are carried out in the name of "ethnic cleansing" or are justified as moral imperative.

Both men and women refugees are vulnerable and require the same amount of protection, but women because of their gender need more protection as these women are more vulnerable and are subjected to additional physical and emotional risk of sexual abuse.

As per the UNHCR reports systematic sexual violence against women and girls of particular communities was one of the major causes for the flight of the refugees. The following account is drawn indirectly from an internal UNHCR field report based on information provided by members of one of the large refugee groups, which includes nearly 300,000 persons.

With little hesitation and great consistency both the men and the women interviewed stated that the reason for leaving their nation was to ensure the safety of their women. The surge in arrivals (in the country of asylum) appeared to be directly related to an increase in the incidence of rape. The victim's ages ranged from 15 to 52 years. The rape experience typically involved several perpetrators and often sexual incidents. Sometimes the military would take groups of women to their encampments. As many as thirty women would be taken at a time and kept from several days to a week. More often, however, the victims would be raped in their homes, sometimes while a male family member was present. The interviewers explained that in the face of heavily armed soldier, any resistance was futile. The rape was all the more horrifying as it almost invariably took place at night, and often the soldier would occupy sexual neighboring houses at a time, thus making escape to, or help from neighbors impossible. The soldiers were often reported to be drunk. Having taken over the use of the village place of worship for their encampment, the soldier would also take the women there and rape them.

It is to be noted that, although members of the military were involved, their abuse of power did not occur in the context of an armed conflict.

Some refugee women have sought asylum after being raped or otherwise sexually tortured with a view to facing their confession, or that of a male relative.

The refugee situations of women have put them at a greater risk from disease, displacement and exploitation. Women and children in conflict setting often face heightened health risk such as increase exposure to (violence, acute poverty disruption of health services) that facilitate the transmission of HIV/ Aids that leads to frequently lack access to safe condition for childbirth and emergency obstetric care.

Apart from physical wounds and starvation, these women develop symptoms of post-traumatic states disorder (PTSD) or depression. These long term mental problems can severely impede the functionality of these women in everyday situations and it makes matters even worse as they are confronted with a new environment and challenging situation.

A study shows that 28.3% of Bosnian refugee women had symptoms of PTSD three or four years after their arrival in

Sweden. These women also had significantly higher risks of symptoms of depression anxiety and psychological distress than Swedish born women.

The refugee women find difficult to get their health needs met. They describe a life of loneliness, despair and loss. Refugee's women suffer from severe stress, yet trying to communicate their needs is problematic. More than half of them suffer from depression. Most of them find the doctor's surgery unhelpful, as because they were unable to communicate their problem to the doctors because of language problem thus, the health services offered to them proved useless.

The sanitation provided in camps to these refugee women is inadequate. Being a woman they require separate toilets and bathrooms, however they are not provided with adequate toilets and other necessities and often have to share with them male counterparts. With no proper and inadequate toilet facilities, women have to go out and thus suffer from eve teasing.

In spite of the UNHCRs best efforts to deal with these problems a lot more is required to be done. These women should have access to health care (including care for both urgent and chronic needs) and also should be informed of the availability of these services in the most effective way. It should be noted that in many communities, women play a central role in providing other family members with health care, therefore access to health care for women can be broadly beneficial to the health of refugee communities.

Refugee women should have the opportunity to be attended by female medical professional if they:

Care should be taken to explain to women their choices concerning reproduction health and family planning, including information on the services available and the laws relating to abortion.

Additional psychological and physical care for survivors of trauma should be provided including counseling services for families as a whole where this is requested.

There is a vast discrimination against refugee women in providing education and skill training programme to them. As these women arrive in the host country most of them are illiterate and do not possess any skills for employment. Moreover, they do not get a chance for improving their condition as most of the time they are over hundred with household tasks and thus are unable to attend regular training countries the training and skill providing courses have a make focus. Due to ignorance and the erroneous assumption that heads of families are men, skill training programmes and income generating acting have been directed primarily at male refugees. However, this notion of aid agencies have left these women with any help or female heads e.g., widows, single mothers, or other unattached woman with no option.

It is thus to be noted that refugee women should be consulted by NGO and other authorities on the development of all training and education programmes or income generation projects, which are intended to meet their needs. A refugee woman frequently come from backgrounds where they have been economically active in the family and in the community and therefore it is essential that their skill and knowledge are recognized and developed through further training and education and utilized to their full potential.

The refugee women when settled experience this displacement and dislocation in a different way to male refugees. Their gender often functions to their disadvantage. While residing in host countries they experience the negative aspects of refugee hood (such as losing traditional roles, responsibilities and supportive networks) just like their male counterparts. They are uprooted from their social and cultural context, which previously structured their behavioral roles and value systems. However, displacement and dislocation for women often means the dismemberment of families, which produces drastic changes to family structures. Since they are unable to adapt to the host society because of their low formal education and lack of knowledge of new language they undergo through a traumatic experience. This hamper their social integration through community participation work, as it is not generally possible for them to attend language or training courses if child care is not provided. Isolation, loss of a frame of reference in the absence of traditional support system, and frequent family breakdowns aggravate the physical and emotional stress of being uprooted. Unable to meet her own needs the refugee women becomes increasingly dependent not only on her husband by also on her children to accomplish even the routine tasks of her life. The resultant feeling of depression and hopelessness damage not only the woman herself, but also the stability and integration of the family as a whole. Due to these problems refugee woman become invisible in settlement countries, and then specific needs go largely unnoticed although in recent years their problems have received some attention among government agencies much needs to be done.

The most fundamental problem that the refugee women face is the way they are looked upon by the host country. These women are treated as vulnerable and no effort is made to strengthen them or make them independent instead they are looked upon with revulsion and an object of pity. These women are not even consulted of any decision which affects their lives. Most of them become refugee because the male members of their family's political choices. However there are cases when women because of their own political involvement have to leave in exile as a price paid for such involvement. Once they are refugees, decisions are endorsed on them without their consultation.

Even in camps there are males who decide the refugee policy. There are male camp authorities; there are male refugee leader and male heads of the family with predictable resulting leas. However UNHCR has laid down some guidelines for the involvement of female protection staff and other areas where female should be involved, but low priority is being given in the involvement of women in prime areas of decision making and active participation.

The major reasons why refugee aid programmes are not successful is that women who are the bulk and who constitute the major portion of refugee are not included in the decision and policy making process[4]. Since the women constitute the major part and it is the women who can better sort out solution for their problem, but non involvement of women leads to making of such policy which are not gender friendly but male oriented since males do not try to understand women needs there policies and programmes are a total failure. Thus women should constitute a part of all refugee and programmes and in all decision making process refugee women should be included in the design management and implementation of assistance programme and this should become the criteria for all refugee aid policies.

Malnourishment is common to refugee in general but especially women and children suffer from it mostly. Normally in war conditions and in refugee camps in countries of first asylum women and children suffer from lack of proper food and nutrition. This occur in most of the cases because in many cultures the food goes primarily to the male family member who work to support the family, and the woman have to survive on the left over. In addition, through menstruation, women lose more nutrients (particularly iron) than men do. Breast feeding of infants is also an important factor because of which she is not provided with nutritional needs.

In the camps women are not provided with enough food, and these women tend to become weak because of the lack of minimum nutritional needs.

Refugee women also suffer from dehydration because water in refugee camps are rare and clean water is very difficult to obtain. Some women suffer from diarrhea and quickly become dehydrated. Although dehydration does not occur as frequently, once these women resettle in host countries of second asylum but the health provider should always look into the pre-existing problems. The needs of the refugee women and children are many. They need food, housing, clothing and health-care. Family planning, child care and education are also important as most of the women are of child-bearing age. Refugee organizations administer their own community's social services. There is consequently a pressing need for training in public and financial administration as refugee women are obliged to implement social development projects of a magnitude quite alien to their meager home budgets. Training should be given in the administration of other essential self reliance programmes viz. nutrition, food production, large scale manufacturing of children and adult clothes, mats, rugs and patch work blankets[5]. Relief agencies need to give more focus on the training of not only refugees but also of the nationals and expatriates working in camps. It has been found that most expatriated relief workers often arrive in the camps with very little preparation or orientation to what they will face.

The policy makers and the refugee aid planner are blind to the fact that refugee women needs are simply not the same as refugee man. These people have proved to be a total failure in providing protection and making policies for the specific requirement of women because of their gender.

A senior epidemiologist of UNHCR stated that "fifteen years ago, refugee women were viewed through a non dimensional lens as a mother. We did not see them as complete women as complicated human being with array of potential problems and not only childbirth" this situation of refugee women continued till 1980. After that, from the twentieth century onwards slow changes have taken place. Now to meet the gender challenge various women have been recruited in humanitarian organization. Specialized posts have been created for them too. Besides sensitization programmes have been developed for all staff and some budgets were rationalized to move nearer to equality.

Many of the people have the opinion that already a lot has been done to protect refugee women from sexual and other crimes, as national and international legislation has been made and also steps have been taken for the betterment of the lives of these refugee women, they have also been provided with craft and vocational training in the camps so that they could lead their life without the need of asylum even when they return home. However, some high officials have the view that it is 'counterproductive' to concentrate on women projects as they should be given chance to do things on their own.

NOTES

1. UNHCR, 'Who is a Refugee? ", Online: <*http: / / www.unhcr.ch*>
2. 'The World of Refugee Women at a Glance', *Refugee Magazine*, Nov., 2002, page 124.
3. Genevieve Campus-Jacques, 'Refugee Women: The Forgotten Majority', in Loescher *et. al*, Refugees and International Relation (1989), 141-158.
4. *Refugee Magazine*, 1998, Page 19.
5. *Refugee Magazine*, June 1985, Page 20.

The Limitations of Fundamental Human Rigths in Nigeria: A Critical Analysis

BASHIR LEKE IJAIYA*

INTRODUCTION

Man, undoubtedly co-exists in the society with some form of norms, traditional, beliefs, values and customs. These values include certain inalienable rights that are fundamental to the smooth functioning of man in the society. It is on this basis that these rights need to be safeguarded and protected for a just and egalitarian society; otherwise the society shall be reduced to a state of anarchy.

Notwithstanding these inherent in man, which though arise from the very nature of man as social animal and recognized and protected in a civilized legal order, they are not to be exercised to injure any other person, group or the society at large.

It is therefore intended in this paper to examine these rights as enshrined in the 1999 Constitution of the Federal Republic of Nigeria, and also to examine the extent to which an individual can exercise such right in the society. The paper is divided into five sections. Section one embodies the abstract and introduction to the paper.

Section two discusses the conceptual clarification of fundamental human rights. Section three discusses the

* Department of Private and Property Law, Faculty of Law, University of Ilorin, Ilorin, Nigeria.

fundamental human rights as embodied in the Constitution of Nigeria. Section four discusses the limitations of the fundamental human rights Provisions in the Constitution. The Conclusion is contained in the last section of this work.

CONCEPTUAL CLARIFICATION: FUNDAMENTAL HUMAN RIGHTS

What is a Right?

It is to be noted that, in spite of the inalienable and naturally endowed rights of man, such rights cannot exist in a vacuum. Put differently, for a man to cry for his right he must have been a member of a society. No person has rights except in the society of other person, for right implies a relationship between two persons. Right can be described as a relationship between person and person, and on that note, it is pertinent to note that there are several relationships and rights, which may exist, in a particular society.

Thus, there are moral relationships, and social relationships as well as moral rights and social rights. The legal basis of the society existence is predicated upon its moral and social value and so the legal rights are founded in the moral and social relationships which are the concerns of law or which the law recognizes as enforceable. Hence, it is pertinent to note that a legal right is not "a law" but a relationship, which is justiciable. This assertion as been adumbrated by Professor Montrose thus:

> *"Whereas "laws" are concerned with abstract possibilities of application, "rights" are concerned with the application of legal propositions to specific individuals"*[1]

The term right has several meanings. The concept of right as a human term appears in diverse contexts and situations and at different times and places. The term right, known as Rectors in Latin meaning straight, just and moral, has evolved to mean, simply, that which the law directs, approves or supports. It has been described as a liberty or power of possessing something, the disturbance or infringement for which there is a legal sanction. A right in its most general sense is either the liberty protected by law of acting or reacting in a certain manner, or the power (enforced by law) of compelling a specific person to do or abstain from doing or possessing a particular thing.

A legal right for our purpose is a capacity resident in one person of controlling with the support of the legal order, the action of others. In other words, a right could be something extracted from the fundamental basis of free will or sometimes based on legal relationship between person as determined by rule of law and sanctioned and protected by that legal order, or an interest, claim, privilege duly recognized and protected by a rule of legal justice[2].

The learned author has also described right in the following terms "Specifically it refers to that which is so directed for the protection and advantage of an individual or group and is said to be his or their rights"

It is pertinent to note that our jurisprudence has evolved to recognize that both natural and artificial person can have rights[3]; however, our discourse is more concerned about the rights of natural persons. The concept of right also goes along with its correlative duties because the existence of a right in favour of Y imposes a duty on Z to perform or to refrain from engaging in certain conduct that may affect that right of Y. A right therefore makes more meaning if the beneficiary is sufficiently enlightened about the existence of the right and has the means of enforcing the right.

From the foregoing analysis, it is important to note that human rights are therefore the demand or claims which individuals groups make on society, which are protected by law and have become part of EX-lege while others remained aspirations to be attained in the future[4].

Why are some Rights Fundamental?

It is pertinent to note that there are no specific rights or class of rights which can be ordinarily considered as fundamental.

Fundamental human rights are not a new morality just developing in contemporary society. They are rights inherent in man; they arise from the very nature of man as social animal and they are recognized and predicated in a civilized legal order.[5]

It is to be further noted that the word "fundamental" merely qualifies certain rights for reasons of emphasis or importance. Consequently, a right is a right to the extent that the legal order guarantees it as such. Therefore, to qualify a right as fundamental is a function of value rather than nature.

It must be noted that, whether a right is fundamental or not depends on the concession that has been reached, for the time being between the oppressors and the oppressed. And from a historical point of view, It is clear that what we today take for granted as inherent, natural and inalienable were in fact concession and the result of bitter battles fought and won by the oppressed against their oppressors down the ages. It is therefore not easy to explain why certain rights are regarded as fundamental and others are not so fundamental, at different countries at different times.

What is Fundamental Human Rights?

The term Fundamental Human Rights has been defined by Justice Kayode Eso JSC (as he then was) in *Ransome Kuti, V. Attorney General of Federation*[6] thus

> *"It is a right which stands above the ordinary laws of the land and which in fact is antecedent to political society itself. It is a primary condition to a civilized existence —— and what has been done by our constitutions since independence ——— is to have these rights enshrined in the constitution so that the rights could be 'immutable' to the extent of the 'non-immutability' of the constitution itself"*

Fundamental Human Rights, which are guaranteed in the constitution, are not privileges in the sense that they could not be withdrawn at the whims and caprices of the government of the day. They are rights, which the executive, the legislature and the judiciary are all enjoined to protect.

It is gratifying to note that there has never been successful attempt to alter any of the provisions of the Constitution relating to fundamental human right during the civilian regimes since their inclusion in our constitution.[7] Mr. Justice Chukwunwike Idigbe drew a distinction between human rights and fundamental human right in a scholarly paper which we agreed with when we noted that:

> *"—— It must be pointed out at this stage that these rights which are antecedent to the political society itself do not exist only in societies or states with written constitution. However, unless their existence or continued existence is guaranteed under the state's constitution they cannot with reference to that particular state or political society be described as fundamental rights. It is therefore my respectful view that a description of these rights as fundamental right ought to be confined to state or political societies governed by written constitution——"*[8]

The above opinion about the nature of fundamental human right was further clarified by Dr. Mudiaga Odje, SAN thus:

> *"It follows that while all rights enjoyed and asserted by human person may be described generally as human rights not all human rights can be termed fundamental rights or fundamental human rights under our classification unless they are entrenched in the constitution"*[9]

Nigeria has adopted political and civil rights rather than socio-economic rights because of her nature as a developing country. Several reasons have emerged for the origin of human rights provisions in our 1960 Constitution, among which is the popular recommendations of WILLINK COMMISSION ON MINORITIES.

It is pertinent to note that the fundamental human rights were enshrined in the Constitution in order to assemble the existing human rights in one entrenched chapter, which could not be easily amended.

Chief Obafemi Awolowo expressed his own view thus:

> *"Fundamental human rights are ordained not for the protection of ethnic minorities as such but for the protection of the citizen at large against executive and legislative tyranny or excesses."*[10]

In considering the above statement, it is therefore necessary to state that all fundamental rights are in the final analysis rights which impose limitation on executive government and are accordingly easily justiciable.

BASIC FUNDAMENTAL HUMAN RIGHTS IN NIGERIA

Following the report of Sir WILLINK COMMISSION, human rights were entrenched in Chapter III of 1960 Constitution and made justiciable. The adoption of fundamental rights followed a Royal Commission of 1958, the Minorities' Commission headed by Sir Henry Willink. Note further, that, these rights were reported verbatim in the Republican Constitution of 1963 and the subsequent 1979 and 1999 Constitutions.

The rights as contained under the 1999 Constitution are as follows:

(a) Right to life[11]

(b) Right to dignity of human person[12]

(c) Right to personal liberty[13]

(d) Right to fair hearing[14]

(e) Right to private and family life[15]

(f) Right to freedom of thought, conscience and religion[16]

(g) Right to freedom of expression and press[17]

(h) Right to peaceful assembly and association[18]

(i) Right to freedom of movement[19]

(j) Right to freedom from discrimination[20]

(k) Right to acquire and own immovable property any where in Nigeria[21]

(l) Compulsory acquisition of property[22]

RESTRICTIONS AND LIMITATIONS OF FUNDAMENTAL HUMAN RIGHTS

Be it noted that these rights are well protected by law; however there is a limit within which these rights can be enjoyed and protected. The 1999 Constitution provides for the restriction and derogation from fundamental human rights. These restrictions are spelt out in Section 45 of the 1999 Constitution. The Section is to the effect that nothing in the provisions of Sections 37, 38, 39, 40 and 41 of the Constitution shall invalidate any law that is reasonably justifiable in a democratic society —— (a) in the interest of defence, public safety, public order, public morality or public health; or (b) for the purpose of protecting the rights and freedom of other persons.

At this juncture, it is pertinent to note that inspite of the entrenchment of the rights to life in the Constitution as one of the fundamental human rights, the right is not absolute. The limitations of this right can be seen in the power of the sovereign state to prepare its citizen majority, those in the armed forces to defend the territorial sovereignty of the state in time of war. Therefore, if these members of the armed forces go to war to defend their state and die, this right becomes unenforceable as no one can be held responsible for the act of the infringement of this right. Hence, the right to life of members of the armed forces end where the rights of the sovereign state to order them to war commences. Whatever befalls the soldiers in the war field is an occupational hazard of the regular soldier. They have willingly chosen that profession and they must take it with all its hazards. Put differently, the situation is what is usually referred to *volunti non-fit injuria.* The maxim cannot, however, apply in the case of a man compulsorily forced to go to battle.

It is to be noted further that the right to life as guaranteed by the Constitution is not breached where it is done for the defence of any person from unlawful violence or for the defence of property. Where it is also to effect a lawful arrest or to prevent the escape of person lawfully detain or for the purpose of suppressing a riot, or insurrection or mutiny. From the proviso to Section 33 of the Constitution, it means any police officer or soldier who might have died in the course of his duty while suppressing riot or in the war front cannot enforce his fundamental right to life. In *Okonkwo V. The State*[23] *Akpabio J.C.A* observed as follows:

> *"Section 30 of the 1979 Constitution of the Federal Republic of Nigeria allows a person to use such force as is reasonably necessary for the defence of any person from unlawful violence or for the defence of property. A person is even entitled to kill in the defence of his property provided the force used is reasonably necessary in the circumstances"*

The legal implication of the above proposition as well as the proviso to Section 33 of the 1999 Constitution is that a person may be justified to deprive other persons of their lives under the circumstances discussed above.

It is to be further noted that the rights to private and family life though enshrined in the Constitution is by itself not absolute. The limitations of this right can be seen in the right and power of the state to interfere into the privacy of its citizens. This can be seen where the correspondence, telephone conversation and telegraphic conversation of a citizen can be tapped and intercepted where same is viewed to constitute and likely to constitute threat, and or affect the public safety, public order, public morality and public health. Also, the right can be limited in order to protect the right of others. A right should not and must not exist to the detriment of other members of the society. Hence, going by this, this right becomes restricted and the right of a person to private life ends where same is likely to affect the right of other members of the society.

There is also a right to freedom of Assembly and Association as guaranteed by the Constitution. The Constitution provides that every person shall be entitled to assemble freely and associate with other persons, and in particular he may form or belong to any political party, trade union or any other association for the protection of his interests. The right to peaceful assembly and association is guaranteed as long as assembly is peaceful. It allows individuals to come together to form political parties and only the gathering of people belonging to a recognized or registered political party will be regarded as peaceful.

However, this right becomes limited where the assembly and association is no longer peaceful and/or where people gathered together to form a political party and such is not registered or recognized by the Independent National Electoral Commission, the body vested with power to register for the recognition of political parties. The implication of an association or assembly of people, which is not legal or likely to be inimical to the public peace, indicates that the right is not absolute.

A person reserves the right to enjoy the right to peaceful assembly and association; however, where the right may spell doom to the peaceful co-existence of the society at large then, the right may be checked and restricted in its application. Specifically the right becomes limited and restricts the right of a person to enjoy same absolutely where the exercise of same will affect public safety, public order, public morality and public health. The right then becomes restricted and limited in the interest of defence.

The right to freedom of thought, conscience and religion could not have been much recognized in Christian Europe of the Middle Ages in view of the relish and ferocity with which the church hunted or was allowed to hunt for and punish dissenters. Even today one wonders whether in view of the English Act of settlement of 1701 a Professed Roman Catholic or Presbyterian would be allowed to ascend the throne of England.[24] In Nigeria, in spite of the recognition given the three major religions in Nigeria one wonders whether a member of Ogboni fraternity, a fraternity akin to traditional religion can ascend or be elected into a political office.

The Constitution guarantees right to the freedom of thought, conscience and religion. Specifically Section 10 of the Constitution makes Nigeria a secular state. The provision is to the extent that, government of the federation or a state shall not apply any religion as state religion. Therefore, Nigeria remains a secular state and secularity in this context requires giving the people of Nigeria religious, which are practiced in the country equal opportunity to flourish.

In *Jelebi Ojonge V. Aleyi Adegbudu*[25] the court held that no one can be forced to perform a native rite which is in conflict with his religion. This is indeed a freedom to practice any religion of one's choice.

However, in *Ojiegbi & Others V. Ubali*[26]. An election was fixed for Saturday December, 27, 1969 and because it was Saturday, the people of Seventh Days Adventist Church boycotted the election. They now went to court to challenge the fixing of election to Saturday because it violated their freedom of religion. The court decided against them on the ground that:

(a) That nobody is forced to vote in all election
(b) And that if the election was fixed for another date, the people in other religion could also sue of violation of their right.

The above decision of the court corroborates and affirms the principle that the right of a person to freedom of religion ends where others begin. That is to say no one should force another person to adopt a religion other than the one he chooses to practice.

More importantly, the fundamental right to acquire and own immovable property does not mean that property can be acquired by any means whether just or fraudulently. A man is entitled and eligible to acquire and own property but such property should not be acquired through illegal means; robbery. This right as provided under the Constitution further provides that one can do whatever one wishes with one's property but subject to several limitations either in the interest of the public, in general or in the interest of a Section thereof.[27]

It should be further noted that while it is true that a man may use his land the way he likes, such a man should not loose sight of the law of nuisance to the effect that such land should not be used in such a way as to cause injury to his neighbors. The neighbor though not co-owner of the land but are entitled to equal right to the use of the land for peaceful co-existence between one another.

The above analysis was illustrated in *Rylands V. Fletcher*[28]. The principle in this case is that if Mr. Z brings something unto his land, provided that, that thing is not naturally there and that thing by nature is capable of escape, and it escapes and causes damage to Y's land, Z is strictly liable to Yin damages, whether or not 'Z' has knowledge of the escape.

Also, the state may impose regulations relation to how individual may use property for example, by regulating the size of rooms, the size of doors and windows, the height of the building, the distance from the public highway and so on.

Also, the right to dignity of person is guaranteed by the Constitution and it is provided that no person should be subjected to torture or any inhuman or degrading treatment. Note however that this right is limited to members of the armed forces and the Nigeria police to perform a duty, which shall not be regarded as force labour. In addition, any such compulsory national service which forms parts of the education and training of citizen of Nigeria as may be prescribed by an Act of the National Assembly for example compulsory National Youth Service Corps training shall not be regarded as force labour.

Therefore, the right of a person to dignity is determined once a person becomes a graduate of University or Polytechnic and qualifies to participate in the exercise by virtue of his not being above the age of thirty years.

The right to personal liberty is also guaranteed in the Constitution. Every person shall be entitled to his personal liberty and no person shall be deprived of such liberty except where it is for the execution of sentence or court order in criminal matter .The personal liberty of a person ends where an order of a court is pronounced and imposed on a person. It is also the same where the right is breached for purpose of welfare and education of citizen below 18 years and also for the purpose of medical care for somebody who is suffering from contagious disease.

The right to individual the freedom of expression and press is also guaranteed in the Constitution. The Constitution specifically in Section 39 provides that every person shall be entitled to freedom of expression, including freedom to hold opinion and to receive and impart ideas and information without interference. Essentially, press freedom is a corollary of freedom of expression, which is itself a fundamental right without which genuine democracy cannot thrive.

It is to be further noted that in furtherance of the provision stated above with regards to freedom to hold opinion to receive and impart ideas. In the case of *New Patriotic Party V. Ghana Broadcasting Corporation*[29] *François. J.S.C.* has this to say on essence and purport of freedom of expression as follows:

> *"It is pertinent to observe that in the comity of nations where the democratic order secure the highest place of honour in the social fabric, the freedom of exchanging information and ideas appears to occupy the noblest point in the social scheme and serves as an essential point——"*

In spite of the above propositions, the freedom of expression and press is not absolute. Thus in the case of *Oyegbemi & Others V. Attorney Generation Of The Federation*[30], it was held that this right was not absolute subject to public safety, order, public morality, welfare of person and preventives of disorder and crime. The gist in the above cited case shows clearly that the freedom of expression and press ends where it will affect the public order and morality.

It is to be further stated that **Section 41** of the 1999 Constitution provides for the right to freedom of movement. The provision is to the effect that every citizen of Nigeria is entitled to move freely throughout Nigeria and to reside in any part thereof and no citizen of Nigeria shall be expelled from Nigeria or refused entry thereto or exits there from.

Thus, where the right of freedom of movement of a Nigerian will be inimical to the peace and order in the country such right becomes limited and no longer absolutely exercisable. The implication of which makes such a person's right terminable where that of public at large commence.

CONCLUSION

In the light of the foregoing, it is clear that though the 1999 Constitution guaranteed the fundamental human rights for all citizenry, however, there are limitations in exercising such rights. The purport of which can best be described as where the right of a citizen ends that of millions of other citizens begin.

NOTES

1. Quoted by M. Ikhariale infra, p. 8.
2. M. Ikhariale (1995), *"The Jurisprudence of Human Rights". Journal of Human Rights Law and Practice. Lagos Clon.*
3. Id.
4. Id.
5. Worley (1996), *"Human Rights and Duties and Legal Rights and Duties"*, Vol. 4.
6. (1995) 2 N.W.L.R (Pt 6), p. 230.
7. N. Aduba (ed) (1992), *Human Rights and Social Justice in Nigeria: Issues, Dilemmas and Options. In The Perspectives on Human Rights. Ministry of Justice Law Series.*
8. Idigbe J.S.C. (1982), *"Fundamental Right Provisions of the Constitution." All Nigeria Judges Conference, Paper delivered in Enugu, Nigeria.*

9. O. Mudiaga SAN (1986), *"Human Rights, Civil, Political, Social. Economic and Cultural. Their Place in the Future Political Order". The Nigerian Bar Association Journal,* Vol. 21, No. 3, p. 44.
10. *Quoted by* M. Ikhariale in "The Jurisprudence of Human Rights", *Journal of Human Rights Law and Practice*, Lagos, p. 11, 1995.
11. Section 33 of the 1999 Constitution.
12 Section 34 Id.
13. Section 35 Id.
14. Section 36 Id.
15 Section 37 Id.
16. Section 38 Id.
17. Section 39 Id.
18. Section 40 Id.
19. Section 41 Id.
20. Section 42 Id.
21. Section 43 Id.
22. Section 44 Id.
23. (1988) 4 N.W.L.R (Pt 544) 141 at p. 158.
24. A. A. O. Okunniga (1975), *"How Fundamental is Fundamental Human Rights"? Published unedited-Text of a Public Lecture Delivered in March 1975 at the then University of Ife now Obafemi Awolowo University Ile- Ife.*
25. (1983), 4N.C.L.R, p. 4924.
26. (1961), ALL NLR, p. 177.
27. A. A. O. Okunniga, *Op Cit.*
28. (1886), L.R. Ex. 265, (1866) L.R. 3, H.L. 330.
29. (2000), 20 W.RN.163 at p. 174.
30. (1982), 2 N.C.L.R, p. 35.

REFERENCES

A.A.O Okunniga (1975), *"How Fundamental is Fundamental Human Rights*? Published Unedited-Text of a Public Lecture Delivered in March 1975 at the then University of Ife now Obafemi Awolowo University Ile-Ife.

E. Burke and The Natural Law, *Natural Law Forum,* Vol. 6, 1961.

Idigbe J.S.C. (1982), "*Fundamental Right Provisions of the Constitution. All Nigeria* Judges Conference Paper delivered in Enugu.

M. Ikhariale (1995), "*The Jurisprudence of Human Rights". Journal of Human Rights Law and Practice*, Lagas: CLON.

M. Odje SAN (1986), "*Human Rights Civil, Political, Social, Economic and Cultural. Their Place and Protection in the Future Political Order. The Nigerian Bar Journal,* Vol. 21, No. 3.

N. Aduba (ed.) (1992), "Human *Rights and Social Justice in Nigeria: Issue Dilemma and Options", In The Perspectives on Human Rights. Ministry of Justice Law Review Series.*

Wortley (1996), "*Human Rights and Duties and Legal Rights and Duties*, Vol. 4.

Legal Aid and Justice: Panacea for Poverty Reduction

Bashir Leke Ijaiya*

INTRODUCTION

It is obvious that there are many problems aggravating poverty, one of which is lack of access to equal justice by the poor like the rich people. Poverty has been a tendency to degrade and condemn even when economic development improves the lot of the poor. Therefore any programme for using the law in at least reducing the effects of poverty will, necessarily require knowledge on who the poor are, what their problems are, and how they are related to the existing law and legal services. This question leads one to a discovery of the dimensions of poverty law and legal aid in relation to the idea of justice to the poor. It is significant to note that the social goal of legal aid is to make the delivery of legal services to the poor more effective, more accessible and more compatible with international standards and best practices all over the globe. Legal aid, in addition to providing better access to justice for indigent persons, is also an instrument for the alleviation of poverty and a provider of job opportunity for lawyers. Thus, legal aid is fashioned out in such a way as to be proactive and dynamic bulwark for the defence of the right of indigent and vulnerable people. It is aimed at operating like a proactive

* Department of Private and Property Law, University of Ilorin, Ilorin, Nigeria.

law firm adequately resource and endowed with ability to respond swiftly to the cries of the poor for help not only in criminal matters but also in civil, administrative and other matters where the intervention of a lawyer could make a difference. A situation where an indigent defendant is sent to prison or suffers an injury because he could not afford the services of a good lawyer is antithetical to democracy and there should an urgent need to strengthen the legal aid and put same in a position to handle more cases effectively and efficiently.

DEFINITION OF LEGAL AID

Legal aid has been taken to mean the organized effort of the bar, the community and the government to provide the services of lawyers free, or for a token charge, to persons who cannot afford to pay lawyer's fees. In the context of the existing constitutional demands and State obligations of some developing countries, it is obvious that, legal aid will have to assume a more positive and dynamic role which should include strategic and preventive services. Relieving "legal poverty"——the incapacity of many people to make full use of the law and its institutions——has now been accepted as a function of the welfare state. This function implies affirmative action from the State. Providing effective access to individuals and groups to avail themselves of legal entitlements is part of this affirmative function. How far the Government should go in this direction at any given time determines the definition and scope of legal aid at that time.[1] It can also be described as the right of every indigent and a constitutional obligation of the government. Further, the concept is to mean not only representation through lawyer at state expense in curt proceedings but will include legal advice, legal awareness, legal mobilization, public interest litigation, law reform and a variety of strategic and preventive services which, instead of assisting each individual on a case-by-case basis will help them as a class to avoid helplessness arising from poverty and promote equal access to justice. In this respect "legal aid" is a dynamic instrument of the 'war against poverty'[2]

It is well established that countries which have well-established and flourishing democracies have judicial system that are free, strong, well motivated and unbiased. The judicial systems in such countries are independent in every sense of the word and are well equipped to dispense justice to all and sundry without hindrance or prejudice. It is the belief of citizens that justice shall be done as stated by their courts (which are creations of their constitutions) that strengthens their constitutions and democracy. The judicial system of a country is the foundation or basis of the country's constitution and ultimately, democracy. The judiciary is the custodian of constitutional governance and democracy.

It is pertinent to note that the problems of judicial system in most developing countries are almost entirely that of administration of justice. Most constitutions of these countries provide clearly that all shall be equal before the law. Moreover, it is a right guaranteed under the constitutions of these countries that citizens shall have unrestricted access to the courts where they can conduct their cases either by themselves or by a legal practitioner of their choice. However, some of the impediments to a citizen's access to justice in developing countries include ignorance of the populace, poverty, corruption and bad or non-existent infrastructure for the administration of justice.

THE DEFINITION OF POVERTY

Poverty has been defined as lack of material well-being, insecurity, social isolation, psychological distress, lack of freedom of choice and action, unpredictability, lack of long-term planning horizons because the poor cannot see how to survive in the present low self confidence and not believing in one self.[3]

Schubert[4] saw poverty as either absolute or relative or both. Absolute poverty being that which could be applied at all time in all societies, such as the level of income necessary for bare subsistence, while relative poverty relates to the living standard of the poor to the standards that prevail elsewhere in the society in which they live.

In furtherance to the above definitions, Sengupta[5] saw poverty as not only an insufficient income to buy a minimum basket of goods and services but as the lack of basic capabilities to live in dignity. This definition recognizes poverty's broader features, such as hunger, poor education, discrimination, vulnerability and social exclusion. Also, In the light of the International Bill of Rights, poverty is defined as a human condition characterized by sustained or chronic deprivation of the resources, capabilities, choices, security and power necessary for the enjoyment of an adequate standard of living and other civil, cultural, economic, political and social rights.[6]

In furtherance of poverty, Hunt et al[7] saw poverty as either the failure of basic freedoms (from the perspective of capabilities), or the non-fulfilment of rights to those freedoms (from the perspective rights).Thus, from the human rights perspective. Poverty can be said to consist of the non-fulfilment of a person's human rights to a range of basic capabilities.

CAUSES OF POVERTY

The wide ranging root cause of poverty can be categorised into three broad groups: unequal distribution of assets; insecurity and vulnerability; and social exclusion and powerlessness. It was acknowledged that the persistence of high levels of inequality of income, assets and opportunities exacerbate poverty. High unemployment rates, lack of access to productive resources such as land, credit, market and information limits the productive capacity of the poor. Lack of access to basic services, such as education and health care, results in limited opportunities for the poor. Vulnerability and insecurity among the poor is made worse by weak social protection programmes. In addition, long term civil conflict and the breakdown of the rule of law put the poor at more risk. The poor suffer from social exclusion and powerlessness and are hereby unable to participate in decisions that affect their lives.[8]

The World Bank[9] identified the lack of voice, power and independences as causes of poverty which in effect subject the poor to rudeness, humiliation, shame, inhumane treatment and exploitation at the hands of the institutions of the state and society. In furtherance of the above, Narayan, et al[10] reiterates that lack of voice and power is experienced not only in interactions with the state, but also in poor people's interactions with the market, landlords, bankers, moneylenders and employers.

Yahie[11] observes that the factors that cause poverty include: (i) Structural causes that are more permanent and depend on a host of (exogenous) factors such as limited resources, lack of skills, locational disadvantage and other factors that are inherent in the social and political set-up; and (ii) the transitional causes that are mainly due to structural adjustment reforms and changes in domestic economic policies that may result in price changes, unemployment and so on. Natural calamities such as drought and man-made disasters such as wars, environmental degradation and so on also induce transition poverty.

The causes of poverty can also be viewed from the problem of urbanisation. According to Ward[12] the factors that cause poverty in most urban cities can be linked to the inner urban decay caused by poor urban public facilities because most infrastructure assets have been allowed to run down through lack of maintenance and investment. Facilities have broken down because local administrations have had insufficient resources and inadequate skills to maintain them. In addition, many amenities have been unable to cope with the increasing demands being placed on them. It is also observed that the local authorities over the years have cut expenditure on infrastructure development and raise tax rates that are counter-productive since this encourages the private firms to migrate and thus reduces employment.

CONSEQUENCES OF POVERTY

Discussing the consequences of poverty Narayan et al[13] observed that because of poverty, most households in the urban cities are crumbling. While some households are able to remain intact, many others disintegrate as men, unable to adapt to their failure to earn adequate incomes under harsh economic circumstance, have difficulty accepting that women are becoming the main breadwinners that necessitates a redistribution of income within the households. The result is often alcoholism and domestic violence on the part of men and a breakdown of the family structure. Women in contrast, tend to swallow their pride and go out into the streets to do demeaning jobs, or in fact, to do anything it takes to put food on the table of their children and husbands.

Von Hauff and Kruse[14] highlighted on three major consequences: (i) consequences for those affected. That is, for the people affected, poverty leads to physical and psychological misery, caused inter-alia by inadequate nourishment, lack of medical care, a lack of basic and job related education and marginalisation in the labour markets; (ii) consequences for the national economies of countries affected arising from the formation of slums in cities, a worsening of ecological problems particularly, as a result of predatory exploitation in the agricultural sector and through the failure to use the available human resources; and (iii) consequences for the political and social development of the countries affected. That is, mass poverty tends to preserve or reinforce the existing power structures and thus also the privileges of a minority of the population. In some cases this involves corrupt elite.

The World Bank[15] also observed that the consequence of poverty is the high level of vulnerability which is a constant companion of material and human deprivation given the circumstances of the poor and the near-poor. Instances have shown that most poor people usually live and farm on marginal lands with uncertain rainfall; live in crowded urban settlements where heavy rains can wipe not their houses; have precarious employment in the formal or informal sector; have a higher risk of diseases such as malaria and tuberculosis; have the risk of arbitrary arrest and ill treatment at the hands of local authorities (women in particular are risk of being socially excluded and victims of violence and crime). The risk that the poor people face as a result of these circumstances is the cause of their vulnerability. But the deeper cause is the inability to reduce or mitigate risk or cope with shocks-a cause that both draws from and feeds into the cause of other dimensions of poverty.

THE RATIONALE AND SCOPE OF LEGAL AID

Legal Aid is dedicated to the principle of equal justice for the poor. It envisages that the poor have easy access to courts and other government agencies on equal footing with others. It implies that the decisions rendered are fair and just taking account of the rights and disabilities of parties. Equal justice requires an approach responsive to inequalities and injustices existing in society and an interpretation that reflects the constitutional values and commitments and incorporates a humane, social-justice jurisprudence.

Equal justice is a system that works through adversary proceedings demands quality representation and advocacy, effective and meaningful remedies, progressive and people-oriented substantive laws and dynamic administration free from corruption and arbitrariness. In conditions where the poor are in majority and the government is democratic, one may argue that justice will mean a positive bias in favour of the poor both in substantive and procedural laws.

Historically, providing equal justice to the poor meant providing access to the courts and to fair treatment within the judicial process. This is the traditional rationale for legal aid to the poor. This view was based on the assumption that the legal system is otherwise sound, fair and effective and its integrity will suffer only if access to it is unequal. However, the concept of access has been undergoing transformation under the influence of democracy, collectivism and planned development. While there is no question that access to the courts is one necessary means of assuring equal justice for the poor, providing the indigent with a lawyer may have only a minimal effect in reaching that goal. New remedies, effective innovative strategies, competent advocacy, client participation as so on may become essential to achieve real equality. This may need substantial changes in legal proceedings, canons of interpretation, legal education, organization and methods of the legal profession and the technology of identifying legal issues and determination of social facts. Otherwise haw can equality be achieved by mere lawyer representation when the adversary commands disproportionate wealth, power and information. Governments or big commercial houses do have enormous staying power as compared to a poor litigant even if he has a capable lawyer. Therefore equal justice in the context of poverty implies not only legal services to enforce existing rights and beneficial entitlements of the poor but also use of legal services to develop new rights and entitlements by challenging unfair practices in society and government. In other words, legal aid in a developmental, social justice context implies that it is positively reformist in content and progressively egalitarian and activist in methods. Legal aid in this changed context requires confronting poverty and the conditions that produce poverty and challenging the individuals and institutions which perpetuate it.

In tracing the history and development of legal aid to the poor, Cappellatti[16] wrote that in each era the rationale for legal services to the poor has been directly related to the prevailing moral, political and legal philosophy. Thus, for many centuries throughout continental Europe and England, legal aid was given, if at all, as a charitable, but not a legal, obligation. The lawyer's duty was, for practical purposes, nominal rather than real; at best it provided "poor justice" for the poor. This was in tune with the prevailing religious notions and laissez-faire philosophy with minimal involvement of State in socio-economic programmes.

In some European countries, the egalitarian ethic of the French and American revolutions and the social democratic and labour regimes led to the establishment of legal aid as a matter of right (natural and, sometimes, statutory) to be paid for by the State.[17] Formal equality before courts was provided through statutory provisions. However, real equality or effective access eluded the poor and poverty remained unaffected by legal development. The use of law for reducing economic and social inequalities and promoting social justice by affirmative State action provided a new rationale for legal aid in most developing societies during the last three decades. For the first time, the relationship between legal services and poverty was recognized by advocates of legal aid only in 1960s. the development of the State funded legal services as part of the anti-poverty programme in the United States during Johnson administration focused the role and relationship of law, legal aid and poverty in that country.[18]

It will appear too preposterous to believe that given increased legal aid to the poor, poverty can be eliminated in the foreseeable future. The focus of legal aid is on distributive justice, effective implementation of welfare benefits and elimination of social and structural discrimination against the poor. Economic equality is a complex problem involving a variety of forces many of which are not yet susceptible to legal control. Therefore, the impact of even a dynamic legal services programme on poverty can only be marginal. It can make people aware of the socio-political processes and the role in them; it can increase opportunities for economic improvement; it can help implement government welfare schemes more effectively; it can mitigate structural imbalances in the legal system functioning against the poor; it can be an essential input in developmental planning and social justice administration. However, legal aid cannot be a panacea for all economic ills. Nonetheless, the potential is sufficient to warrant a significant place for legal aid in antipoverty programmes of the government particularly in developing countries.

THE LEGAL NEEDS OF THE POOR

To be poor means not having enough income to meet the basic needs of life. Measuring poverty in terms of the inadequacy of income to obtain a diet with the minimum number of calories considered necessary to maintain life. It is to be noted that poor in rural areas include landless agricultural labourers, small landholders, village artisans such as weavers, potters whereas the urban poor consists of the unemployed and severely underemployed, domestic and contract labour, disabled persons, pensioners et cetera. These groups generally have large families and poor education. The traditional social stratification based on caste system reflects and reinforces their general low incomes. Besides, women as a class are prone to destitution and exploitation when divorced, widowed or otherwise rendered homeless. The poverty of parents often forces children to hazardous labour or total destitution aggravating the poverty of the poor.

In the real sense, poverty can be understood only by the poor and not by the economists who study phenomenon or by the journalists who report on it or any other professional who study same according to the dictates of his professional understanding of the concept. Poverty robs the individual of his dignity and makes it impossible for the poor to share the fruits of freedom and democracy. They are reduced to the status of vote banks in election battles and often kept out of economic calculations. They are invisible to the human rights activists and the justice system is inaccessible to them.

Given the above perspective of poverty especially in some developing countries, one might ask whether the law has been helpless or ineffective in eliminating poverty or at least reducing its evil effects on human life and dignity. What is the relationship between law and poverty? Are not problems of the poor, legal problems? What are the factors which condition the utilisation of the legal remedies by the poor? What is the scope of the concept of equal justice under the law and how does the system provide for equality in legal services. These related questions form the concern of legal aid.

An honest attempt in answering the above questions will require some understanding of the legal dimensions of poverty and adequate knowledge of the people and their problems to be served through law. It will be interesting to know that the special problems of the rural poor and the urban poor separately and also to find how they compare with the legal problems of the non-poor living in rural and urban communities. Even among a given category of poor people there are likely to be differences between the problems of adults and children, men and women, tribals and non-tribals, scheduled castes and non-scheduled castes et cetera. An efficient organization of a legal services delivery system may have to take account of all these differences in legal needs of the poor and design the programme accordingly. However, one thing is certain that legal aid to the poor cannot be uniform in character, organization, and delivery.

The point to be emphasized here is that the legal needs of the poor are not the same at different places and at different times. A continuing assessment of the changing faces of poverty and the increasing involvement of the poor themselves in seeking their just rights and entitlements are essential to deliver justice in an unequal society. All that legal aid can possibly do is to help identify the problems, bottlenecks and the injustices and provide appropriate the problems machinery for access to the legal system.

EQUAL ACCESS TO JUSTICE

The concern for the poor has been a part of legal development in all democratic and progressive societies. This is manifested in the passing of the various welfare laws and allocations of funds for the welfare needs of the poor. In developing countries, planned development based on the principle of "growth with social justice" has been the pattern for more equitable distribution of resources, opportunities and incentives. Constitutional devices such as reservation for weaker sections and affirmative governmental action based on protective discrimination in favour of poorer sections have been introduced to make the system work in favour of the under-privileged and long exploited groups. However, for a long time it was not realized that the utilization of these legal benefits by the poor depended on the availability of legal services and that a variety of historical, sociological. Cultural and economic constraints limited the scope of access to legal services for the poor beneficiaries. One obvious result of this situation has been either the non-implementation of welfare laws or the cornering of the benefits by the better organized, vocal sections of the beneficiary groups to the detriment of poorer sections amongst them, illiteracy, destitution, economic and social bondages, cultural inhibitions, and bureaucratic and political corruption seriously impaired the accessibility and assertiveness of the poorest of the poor resulting often in total denial of justice to them. They continued to be invisible to the formal legal system excepting as accused and defendants in harsh and insensitive judicial proceedings. The high cost of litigation and the inordinate delay involved in the process ruined the life of many of those who attempted to resist the injustices and bought legal services at great sacrifice including their livelihood. In the resultant situation the poor came to use the legal system only when so compelled by being drawn into it as accused and defendants.

In addition, another interesting development of the limited use of the legal system by the poor (and perhaps the over-use of it against the poor) is the structure and organization of the legal profession itself. The nature of services provided, the concentration of services in courts, the cost of services, the style of pleadings and advocacy have all been influenced by the question of who hired lawyers for what and against whom.

Against the backdrop of the foregoing and in a scathing indictment on the denial of legal services to the poor and in a bold attempt to make courts accessible to the poor, the Supreme Court of India in People's Union for Democratic Rights & Ors V. Union of India & Ors[19] observed as follows:

> "......... The rule of Law does not mean that the protection of the law must be available only to a fortunate few or that the law should be allowed to be

> prostituted by the vested interests for protecting and upholding the status quo under the guise of enforcement of their civil and political rights. The poor too have civil and political rights and the Rule of Law is meant for them also, though today it exists only in paper and not in reality. If the sugar barons and the alcohol kings have the Fundamental Right to carry on their business and to fatten their purses by exploiting the consuming public, have the 'charmas' belonging to the lowest strata of society no Fundamental Right to earn an honest living through their sweat and toil? The former can approach the court with a formidable army of distinguished lawyers paid in four or five figures per day and if their right to exploit is upheld against the government under the label of Fundamental Right, the courts are praised for their boldness and courage and their independence and fearlessness are applauded and acclaimed. But, if the Fundamental Right of the poor and helpless victims of injustice is sought to be enforced by public interest litigation, the so called champions of human rights frown upon it as a waste of time of the highest court in the land, which, according to them should not engage itself in such small and trifling matters. Moreover, these self-styled human rights activists forget that civil and political rights simply do not exist for the vast masses of our people."

The Supreme Court through this opinion gave a warning to the judicial system of the country as well as to the legal profession in particular that they must shed their character as upholders of the established order and the status quo. They must be sensitized the need of doing justice to the large masses of people to whom, justice has been denied by a cruel and heartless society for generations. It may appear ironical that the highest court of the land had to confess its inaccessibility to the poor and initiate steps overlooking the objections of a certain section of the Bar which is obliged under its rule of ethics to render equal services to the poor. Has there been a collective institutional failure in denying justice to the poor? Or is it a failure of law itself to match up to the new values and aspirations of the Constitution? Or is it the result of a deliberate refusal on the part of the poor to avail themselves of legal remedies even when provided free? Whatever be the answers to these questions, one thing is certain that the utilization of the legal system by the poor has been marginal all these years. One of the consequences of this is that the judicial system operated unfairly to the interests of the poor. Put differently, our courts have been responsible and have contributed immensely to the unequal access to justices between the poor and the rich.

SUMMARY AND RECOMMENDATIONS

It is significant to emphasize here that not having enough and sufficient income to sustain one means of livelihood is not only what is poverty, but poverty can also be seen for the lacking of many other varieties of life. Where the rights of a man who though not ordinarily poor is infringed upon and such a man is unable to have access to the courts– the custodian of justice, where such rights can be remedied, it goes without saying that such a man may be subjected to losing valuables and thereby resulting into poverty. Equal access to justice to all through legal aid therefore will go a long way in checking and ameliorating the abject poverty which has now become endemic in most of the developing countries.

To this end, governments of developing countries are called upon to ensure that all citizens irrespective of political, social and economic status have equal access to justice. The legal aid scheme should be reinvigorated to meet the varieties needs of the poor instead of offering legal services alone; it should be broaden to include not only legal services but also to legal awareness, legal mobilization, public interest litigation, law reform and a variety of strategic and preventive services which in themselves will go along way to reduce poverty. Also related to this is adequate and proper funding and recruitment of qualified staff into the judiciary so as to increase access to justice by indigent members of the society.

On the other hand, the poor on their own should endeavour to avail themselves with all the available opportunities provide by the government to see that their rights when infringed are remedied through legal aid. The lackadaisical attitude of not willing to press home ones rights should be discouraged as more as possible. This will greatly assist the poor to get justice and hence reduction of poverty. The principle of alternative dispute resolution should be encouraged so that disputes and conflicts are resolved through mediation rather than going to court.

More importantly, our courts are commended to relax its rules that are always characterised with rigidity so as to give equal access to justice to all without any technicality or rigidity. Most poor are always reluctant to seek for justice in the court of law because of the nature of the proceeding which take too much time before it is concluded. The time consuming and cumbersomeness of the litigations should be done away with by our courts so as to avail the poor the rights to obtain justice within a reasonable period of time. Access to court by the indigent should be made less cumbersome and less expensive so that it becomes easy for all and sundry to have access to court.

Also important is that the government should ensure that people of high integrity and other good qualities should be considered in the appointment of judges. Their appointment into the judiciary should be made open and transparent. There should be good and handsome remuneration for the judicial officers and their staff. Above all there should be financial autonomy to the judiciary as well as the legal aid scheme.

Finally, there should be law-related education in the school system. Legal education should be taken to the people and most importantly, there should be a national commission that should be vested with power to oversee civic education and other related matters.

NOTES

1. N. R. Madhava Menon (1988), "Legal Aid and Justice for the Poor (ed.).
2. Garibi Hatao.
3. Narayan, D., Patel, R., Schafft, K. Rademacher, A. and Koch-Schulte S. (2000), *Voices of the Poor: Can Anyone Hear Us?* New York: Oxford University Press.
4. Schubert, A. (1994), *Poverty in Developing Countries:* Its Definition, Extent and Implication. Economic, Vol. 49/50, p. 17-40.
5. Sengupta, A. (2003), Poverty Eradication and Human Rights. In *Pose T. (ed) Severe Poverty as a Human Rights Violation.* New York: UNESCO.
6. United Nations (UN) (2001), *Substantive Issues Arising in the Complementation of International Covenant of Economic, Social and Cultural Rights: Poverty and the International Covenant of Economic, Social and Cultural Rights.* New York: UN.
7. P. Hunt, S. Osmanis and M., Nowak Summary of the Draft Guidelines in a Human Rights Approach to Poverty Reduction Strategies. *http / / www.uhuchrich / development / poverty.html.*
8. A. M., Romero-Lozada, Conclusions of the High-Level Roundtable on Eradication of Poverty, (2005) 1.
9. World Bank (note 7 above).
10. D. Narayan, *et. al* (note 12 above) 33.
11. Yahie, *The Design and Management of Poverty Alleviation Projects in Africa: Evolving Guidelines Based on Experience.* World Bank EDI Human Resources Division (1993).
12. M., Ward (1999), 'Perceptions of Poverty: The Historical Legacy.' *IDS Bullentin*, Vol. 30, No. 2: 23.
13. D. Narayan, *et. al* (note 12 above) 35
14. M., Von Hauff and B. Kruse (1994), "Conceptual Bases for a Consistent Poverty-Oriented Policy", Vol.49/50:41-55.
15. The World Bank (note 7 above)
16. M. Cappellatti and B. Garth (ed) *Access to Justice*, Vol. 1, Sijthoff (1978).
17. *Ibid.*
18. *Ibid.*
19. A. I. R. (1982) S. C. P. 1473-1477.

Status of Women Domestic Workers in Tirunelveli City- A Study

R. Ezhil Jasmine*

INTRODUCTION

Domestic service or the employment of people for wages in their employer's residence was sometimes simply called "service". Domestic workers perform domestic chores such as washing, ironing, shopping, cooking and cleaning the house. In India, in ancient times, domestic work was largely performed by 'Serfs' belonging to the 'Shudras', who were denied access to education. The emancipation of middle-class women in the late twentieth century and their entry into the professional workforce has given rise to a sharp increase in the employment of domestic workers in India. According to 1991 census, 5.76 lakh women were engaged in the domestic services industries. Due to a large gap between the urban and rural incomes and lack of employment opportunities in the countryside, even an ordinary middle class urban family can afford to employ a full-time domestic worker. As such the household workloads are shifted to the domestic workers. These workers belong to the lower stratum of the society and are often considered as cheap labour. The problems of women domestic workers are complex and huge in its magnitude.

* Lecturer in Commerce, Government Arts College for Women, Sivagangai.

NEED FOR THE STUDY

Tirunelveli city is the headquarters of Tirunelveli district in the state of Tamilnadu (South India). It is a 2000 year old city located on the banks of the perennial Thamirabarani River. It has a population of 4,11,298 (2001 census) spread over an area of 128.65 sq.kms. As there is a high demand for domestic workers in Tirunelveli city, women from the nearby rural villages are moving to the city to serve as domestic workers for the urban population. Poverty and unemployment are the primary reasons for women domestic workers entering into labour market. These women workers are routinely denied basic rights. Lack of social security, poor wages and long hours of work are the most pressing problems faced by them. Hence an attempt has been made to study the status of women domestic workers in Tirunelveli city.

OBJECTIVES OF THE STUDY

The study intends to pursue the following objectives:

- To study the reasons for why women domestic workers enter into labour market.
- To find out the socio-economic conditions of the women domestic workers in Tirunelveli city.
- To know the occupational diseases (if any) of the women domestic workers.
- To study the problems of women domestic workers in Tirunelveli city.
- To study the job satisfaction of women domestic workers in Tirunelveli city.

METHODOLOGY OF THE STUDY

As the women domestic workers are not well conversant with social science investigations, interview schedules were administered as a primary tool for the purpose of collecting primary data from them. The interview schedule was based on the objectives and parameters of the study. Several attempts were made to interview the domestic workers in their work spot and at their homes. Some of them hesitated to respond because of the fear that their employers might terminate them, while others readily responded to the questions. Observations sheets were also used to record relevant and useful observations. The interview schedule was pre-tested and modified (wherever necessary) before actual collection of data.

SAMPLE SIZE

For the sake of the study, 124 women domestic workers were selected by adopting purposive sampling method. Due care has been taken to include samples from different parts of Tirunelveli city namely Junction area, Vannarpettai, Murugankurichi, Melapalayam, Maharajanagar, Samathanapuram, Thyagarajanagar, Perumalpuram, N.G.O. Colony, Kulavanigarpuram and other important locations.

Table 1
Age-wise Classification of the Women Domestic Workers

Age in years	*No. of domestic workers*	*Percentage*
Below 20	14	11.3
20-40	56	45.2
40-60	37	29.8
Above 60 years	17	13.7
Total	124	100

Source: Primary data.

The study highlights that majority of the women domestic workers (45.2 per cent) belong to the age group of 20 to 40 years, 29.8 per cent of the workers belong to the age group of 40 to 60 years, 13.7 per cent of the workers are above 60 years and the remaining 11.3 per cent of the workers are below 20 years.

The educational status of the women domestic workers is also studied and presented in the following Table:

Table 2
Education-wise Classification of the Women Domestic Workers

Education level	*No. of domestic workers*	*Percentage*
Illiterate	2	1.6
Below SSLC	81	65.3
SSLC	35	28.2
Higher Secondary	6	4.9
Total	124	100

Source: Primary data.

It was found out that majority of the women domestic workers (65.3 per cent) are educated below SSLC level, 28.2 per cent of the workers are SSLC holders, 4.9 per cent of the workers are Higher Secondary holders and 1.6 per cent of the workers are illiterates. A remarkable point is that they do not have awareness regarding new avenues of employment. Besides it is difficult for them to train themselves in any skill other than domestic work. But a few of them learn typewriting, embroidery, handicrafts and computer courses. They have a concrete plan of switching over to a better type of employment. One of the workers stated that her employer sponsors her higher studies.

Table 3
Religion-wise Classification of the Women Domestic Workers

Religion	*No. of domestic workers*	*Percentage*
Hindu	91	73.4
Christian	28	22.6
Muslim	5	4.0
Others	-	-
Total	124	100

Source: Primary data.

The study reveals that majority of the women domestic workers (73.4 per cent) are Hindus followed by Christians (22.6 per cent) and Muslims (4 per cent). The domestic workers belonging to Muslim religion generally prefer to work in the houses of Muslim employers.

Table 4
Caste-wise Classification of the Women Domestic Workers

Caste	*No. of domestic workers*	*Percentage*
Scheduled Caste	43	34.7
Schedules Tribe	19	15.3
Other Backward Caste	45	36.3
General	17	13.7
Total	124	100

Source: Primary data.

Majority of the women domestic workers (34.7 per cent) belong to Scheduled Caste, 15.3 per cent of the workers belong to Scheduled Tribes, 36.3 per cent of the workers belong to Other Backward Caste and 13.7 per cent of the workers belong to General category.

Table 5
Marital Status of the Women Domestic Workers

Marital status	*No. of domestic workers*	*Percentage*
Married	101	81.5
Un married	23	18.5
Total	124	100

Source: Primary data.

Out of 124 women domestic workers taken for the study 81.5 per cent are married and the remaining 18.5 per cent are unmarried. Full time domestic work is mostly taken up by unmarried women and they reside in their place of employment ie., in the house of the employers. They are young and energetic, capable of doing any kind of domestic work and are extremely vulnerable to sexual abuse of various kinds. They grieve that they become the prey for each and every member of the employer's house. They are totally powerless and do not have easy access to legal protection. In fact they are scared to disclose the roguish activities of their employers chiefly due to lack of job security.

Table 6
Family Size of the Women Domestic Workers

Size of family	*No. of domestic workers*	*Percentage*
1-2 members	8	6.5
2-4 members	55	44.4
4-6 members	49	39.5
More than 6 members	12	9.6
Total	124	100

Source: Primary data.

The study reveals that majority of the women domestic workers (44.4 per cent) have 2 to 4 members in their families, 39.5 per cent of the workers have 4 to 6 members, 9.6 per cent of the workers have more than 6 members and only 6.5 per cent of the workers have 1 to 2 members in their families. Some of them are bread winners. They are widows and deserted women who had to support their families with the income they earn. Some of them have pathetic conditions in their family which includes unemployed members, handicapped and mentally retarded children, drunkard husband or father, sick parents and over debt.

Due to the changing conditions, most of the women domestic workers in Tirunelveli city are living in nuclear families. Only a few of them live in joint families. Besides they have also realized the importance of small family and are gradually adopting the family planning concept.

Table 7
Number of Children of Women Domestic Workers

No. of children	*No. of domestic workers**	*Percentage*
1-2	46	45.5
2-4	44	43.6
More than 4	4	3.9
No Children	7	7.0
Total	101	100

Source: Primary data.
*Only 101 domestic workers (101/124) are married.

Majority of the women domestic workers (45.5 per cent) have 1 to 2 children, 43.6 per cent of the workers have 2 to 4 children, 3.9 per cent of the workers have more than 4 children and 7 per cent of the workers have no children. Though the domestic workers are educated only up to school level, their children are studying in schools, colleges and renowned institutes. Some of their children are studying in Engineering colleges and Polytechnic colleges on merit basis.

Table 8
Number of Earning Members in the Family of Women Domestic Workers

Earning members	*No. of domestic workers*	*Percentage*
One *	25	20.2
Two **	72	58.1
Three **	18	14.5
More than three **	9	7.2
Total	124	100

Source: Primary data.
* Respondent herself
** Including the respondent

The study reveals that 58.1 per cent of the women domestic workers have two earning members in their family, 20.2 per cent have only one earning member (worker its self), 14.5 per cent have three earning members and 7.2 per cent have more than three earning members in their families. The male members of their families are mostly auto drivers, hawkers, construction workers, carpenters, peddlers, hotel employees, hospital employees and scavengers.

The women domestic workers have taken up domestic work due to various reasons. The primary reasons are analyzed and shown in the following Table:

Table 9
Reasons for Taking up Domestic Work

Reasons	*No. of domestic workers*	*Percentage*
Economic cause	56	45.2
Bread winner	25	20.2
Safe work environment	8	6.5
Non-marketable skills	28	22.6
Flexible working hours	7	5.6
Total	124	100

Source: Primary data.

ECONOMIC REASONS

It was found out that 45.2 per cent of the domestic workers have selected domestic work due to economic reasons. Poverty and unemployment are the basic reasons for this attitude. Guruvammal, a domestic worker in Tirunelveli city stated her husband who is a Plumber, seldom brings home money and she was forced to go for domestic work.

BREAD WINNERS

The study reveals that 20.2 per cent of the workers have opted domestic work because they have no other source. They are single earners (bread winners) who entirely depend on the income from domestic work. With no social security or health coverage and very little administrative support, the domestic workers manage to survive and find their way out of hunger and homelessness.

SAFE WORK ENVIRONMENT

The study shows that 6.5 per cent of the domestic workers have chosen domestic work for the sake of safe work environment. They state that their family members leave their houses early in the morning and return only in the evening after the day's work. Hence, instead of sitting idle, they prefer to take up domestic work in the houses located in surrounded area. They stated that they are safe in the work environment.

NON-MARKETABLE SKILLS

22.6 per cent have chosen domestic work mainly because of their non-marketable skills. They are largely people from lower castes and have no access to any type of training that could open new avenues of employment. In fact they could not afford to get themselves trained. Domestic work is the only area in which they could excel.

FLEXIBLE WORKING HOURS

The study shows that 5.6 per cent of the women domestic workers prefer domestic work due to flexible working hours. Especially part time domestic workers could fix their working hours under different employers according to their convenience. Some of them go back to their houses after completion of morning duty and return to work in the evening.

Table 10
Nature of Employment of the Domestic Workers

Nature	*No. of domestic workers*	*Percentage*
Full time	19	15.3
Part time	105	84.7
Total	124	100

Source: Primary data.

Full time women domestic workers could be accessed by the employers at any time irrespective of day or night. Hence it becomes difficult to identify their working hours. They have to wake up even during midnight hours especially when a guest arrives. Besides the full time women domestic workers are prone to sexual exploitations by members of the employer's family, frequent guests, relatives, neighbours and friends. They experience a tremendous sense of loneliness. Conversation with other domestic workers is often strictly forbidden.

Part time domestic women domestic workers have stipulated working hours. They have to be very punctual and sincere in doing the specific tasks assigned by their employers.

Table 11
Number of Employers Served by the Women Domestic Workers (Per day)

No. of employers	*No. of domestic workers*	*Percentage*
One	23	18.5
Two	32	25.8
Three	41	33.1
Four	22	17.7
More than four	6	4.9
Total	124	100

Source: Primary data.

It is apparent from the study that majority of the women domestic workers (33.1 per cent) serve for three employers, 25.8 per cent workers serve for two employers, 18.5 per cent workers serve for one employer, 17.7 per cent workers serve for four employers and 4.9 per cent workers serve for more than four employers. Due to poor wage structure, the part time women domestic workers serve for more than one employer and strive hard to earn money.

Table 12
Number of Hours Worked by the Women Domestic Workers (Per day)

Working hours	*No. of domestic workers*	*Percentage*
1-2 hours	9	7.3
2-4 hours	18	14.5
4-6 hours	31	25.0
6-8 hours	47	37.9
Full time	19	15.3
Total	124	100

Source: Primary data:

It is clear from the Table that 37.9 per cent women domestic workers work for 6 to 8 hours per day, 25 per cent workers work for 4 to 6 hours, 15.3 per cent workers work on full time basis, 14.5 per cent workers work for 2 to 4 hours and 7.3 per cent workers work for 1 to 2 hours per day. The part time workers are fully engaged in their duties especially during morning and evening hours. But the full time workers are expected to work round the clock. The typical tasks include cooking, washing, sweeping, ironing, shopping and looking after the children of the employers.

Table 13
Experience of Women Domestic Workers (in years)

Experience (in years)	*No. of domestic workers*	*Percentage*
Less than 5 years	21	16.9
5-10 years	23	18.6
10-15 years	22	17.7
15-20 years	32	25.8
More than 20 years	26	21.0
Total	124	100

Source: Primary data.

The table indicates that 25.8 per cent of the women domestic workers have 15 to 20 years experience, 21 per cent workers have more than 20 years experience, 18.6 per cent workers have 5 to 10 years experience, 17.7 per cent workers have 10 to 15 years experience and 16.9 per cent workers have less than 5 years experience in doing domestic work.

Table 14
Personal Income of the Women Domestic Workers (Per month)

Income (in Rupees)	*No. of domestic workers*	*Percentage*
Below 500	10	8.1
500-1000	36	29.0
1000-1500	59	47.6
1500-2000	15	12.1
Above 2000	4	3.2
Total	124	100

Source: Primary data.

The study shows that 47.6 per cent of the women domestic workers earn Rupees 1000 to Rupees 1500 per month, 29 per cent workers earn Rupees 500 to Rupees 1000, 12.1 per cent workers earn Rupees 1500 to Rupees 2000, 8.1 per cent workers earn below Rupees 500 and 3.2 per cent workers earn above Rupees 2000 per month. In fact, most of the domestic workers stated that they seldom get their wages at the beginning of the month. Withholding wages is a common attitude among the employers.

Table 15
Family Income of Women Domestic Workers (Per month)

Income (in Rupees)	*No. of domestic workers*	*Percentage*
Below 1500	33	26.6
1500-3000	39	31.5
3000-4500	44	35.5
Above 4500	8	6.5
Total	124	100

Source: Primary data.

It is clearly evident that 35.5 per cent of the women domestic workers have a family income Rupees 3000 to Rupees 4500, 31.5 per cent workers have a family income of Rupees 1500 to Rupees 3000, 26.6 per cent workers have a family income below Rupees 1500 and 6.5 per cent workers have a family income above Rupees 4500. The women domestic workers felt that they find it highly difficult to their run their family with such a meager income. Some of them are single earners entirely depending on the income from domestic work.

Table 16
Type of Residence of the Women Domestic Workers

Type of residence	*No. of domestic workers*	*Percentage*
Own house	8	6.5
Rented house	113	91.1
Leased house	3	2.4
Total	124	100

Source: Primary data.

The study shows that 91.1 per cent of the women domestic workers reside in rented houses, 6.5 per cent workers reside in their own houses and 2.4 per cent workers reside in leased houses. The domestic workers residing in rented houses are often forced by the landlords to vacate their houses. The workers struggle to search for another house within the short span of time given by the landlords. The house rent takes away a considerable portion of their income and leave little residual income to meet other necessities.

Table 17
Expenditure Pattern of the Women Domestic Workers
(Per month)

Expenditure	*Percentage of monthly income*
House rent	26.6
Grocery	50.9
Clothing	0.8
Loan Repayment	9.8
Education	10.4
Health	0.3
Savings	0.7
Miscellaneous	0.5
Total	100

Source: Primary data.

- The expenditure of every women domestic worker is converted in to percentage and averages are thereby taken.
- Only 102 women domestic workers are living in rented houses.
- Only 94 women domestic workers are married.

HOUSE RENT

The women domestic workers spend 26.6 per cent of their income for paying the house rent. As they work in urban area, they reside in small houses or portion of a small house which is located in a walkable distance from the employer's residence. The house rent in urban locality is rather high which the domestic workers could not afford. Besides most of the landlords demand rent on the first day of every month and the domestic workers borrow from money lenders to tackle the situation.

GROCERY

The study shows that the women domestic workers spend majority of their monthly income on grocery items (50.9 per cent). Most of them buy grocery items on credit from the shops close to their residence and they settle their account in the beginning of every succeeding month. Generally, rice, sugar, kerosene and wheat are bought from ration shops.

CLOTHING

Most of the women domestic workers are poverty stricken and that they could afford to buy clothes. Some of the employers provide them clothing especially during festivals and special functions. Besides they also get free saree and dhoti (once a year) from Government of Tamilnadu (Public Distribution system) through ration cards.

LOAN REPAYMENT

Paucity of finance is a challenge that characterizes the lives of women domestic workers. They borrow from money lenders if any unforeseen expenditure suddenly arises. But they struggle to repay the loan. One of the workers stated that she suffers from the clutches of money lenders for the past ten years. The study found out that 9.8 per cent of their income has been spent for repayment of loan.

EDUCATION

The women domestic workers spend 10.4 per cent of their income for the education of their children. Some of them have received advance money from their employers in this regard. A few stated that their children are studying in colleges especially on merit quota. This indicates the keen interest of domestic workers in educating their children. Most of them are aware of the significance of education and they do not want their children to become domestic workers.

HEALTH

Only a negligible amount (0.3 per cent) was spent by the women domestic workers for health care. Some of them get medical treatments from Government hospitals while some other get treatments in private hospitals. The medical expenses of part time women domestic workers are not met by their employers. Only a few full time workers stated that their employers meet their medical expenses.

SAVINGS

All domestic workers have the eagerness and desire to save money for their future commitments. As they earn a poor income, they could save only 0.7 per cent (average) of their income per month. The full time workers are able to save more money than the part time workers.

Table 18
Occupation Diseases of Women Domestic Workers

Disease	*No. of domestic workers*	*Percentage*
Back pain/body pain	19	15.3
Skin disease	5	4.0
Anaemia	18	14.5
Ringworm	4	3.2
Wheezing/bronchitis	11	8.1
Indigestion	8	6.5
Ulcer	12	9.7
Rheumatic problem	8	6.7
Any other disease	10	8.1
No disease	29	23.3
Total	124	100

Source: Primary data.

Occupational diseases pose a serious problem to the women domestic workers. Exposure to smoke, unhygienic methods of floor cleaning and toilet cleaning, irregular food consumption, continuous exposure to water and washing powder and lack of nutritious food causes different types of occupational diseases. Majority of the workers suffer from body pain/back pain/leg pain, anemia and ulcer.

Table 19
Details of Insurance Coverage of Women Domestic Workers

Insurance coverage	*No. of domestic workers*	*Percentage*
Covered	5	4.0
Not covered	119	96.0
Total	124	100

Source: Primary data.

It is clear from the study that 96 per cent of the women domestic workers are not covered by insurance and only 4 per cent are covered by it. The primary reason for not insuring is that they could not afford to take insurance policy. Secondly they are least interested in insuring because death seems to be a distant phenomenon for them. Instead they are particular in solving their immediate and day-to-day problems. Some of them have saved a small portion of their income in the ways:

Table 20
Mode of Savings of the Women Domestic Workers

Preferred Institution	*No. of domestic workers*	*Percentage*
Bank	17	13.7
Post office	16	12.9
Chit Fund	36	29.0
Employer	16	12.9
No savings	39	31.5
Total	124	100

Source: Primary data.

As far as women domestic workers are concerned, the access to formal institutions of savings such as banks and post offices is generally very low. Majority of the domestic workers (29 per cent) save money through private Chit Funds,

13.7 per cent through Banks, 12.9 per cent through Post Office, 12.9 per cent through their employers and 31.5 per cent have no savings at all. Some of the workers have borrowed money from money lenders and are unable to repay the same. Hence savings seems to be a dream for them.

Table 21
Problems of Women Domestic Workers

Problems	*No. of domestic workers*	*Percentage*
Lack of job security	11	8.9
Sexual exploitation	9	7.3
Abuse	17	13.7
Poor wages	36	29.0
Heavy work load	14	11.3
Long duration of work	8	6.5
Occupational disease	12	9.7
Lack of leave facility	5	4.0
No retirement benefit	4	3.2
Lack of medical facility	2	1.6
Charges of theft	6	4.8
Total	124	100

Source: Primary data.

LACK OF JOB SECURITY

Job security is absent in the case of domestic work. Hence the workers could not rely on their monthly income. They always fear that they could be terminated at any time without notice. Only those workers who have a long service under one or two employers and who had gained the trust of their employer are relieved from their problem.

SEXUAL EXPLOITATION

The principal reasons for sexual exploitation of women domestic workers were acute poverty, lack of employment, unorganized labour force and lack of community support. Besides, the domestic workers borrow money from their employers in times of dire need. The employers take it as an advantage and sexually exploit them. Full time workers are more prone to sexual exploitation as they reside in the house of the employer.

ABUSE

This a very common problem faced by the women domestic workers. In this study, 13.7 per cent women domestic workers consider abuse as the most severe problem. They stated that their employers use filthy languages, harsh words, constant threats and insults without any reason. An innocent worker lamented that her employer often gets irritated whenever she is neatly dressed. She added that her employer never allows her to take rest. A remarkable point is that women employers are crueler towards women domestic workers. Another worker stated that her employer always scolds her in English and call her a bitch. In fact, most of the domestic workers do not know that they could approach the legal professionals and police personal for redressing their grievances.

POOR WAGES

The women domestic workers in Tirunelveli city are paid poor wages. According to study, poor wages is the basic problem of 29 per cent of the workers. The employers often cheat them by not giving the promised wages. Some of them stated that their employers frequently go for tour and deduct their wages proportionally for the leave days. This shows that the domestic workers could not depend on their income.

HEAVY WORK LOAD

Heavy work load seems to be a major problem for 11.3 per cent of the women domestic workers. The workers stated that their employers do not have humanitarian concern on them. They felt that they were treated just like a commodity. Especially when a guest arrives, their work load becomes heavy and the employer seldom pay any extra amount.

LONG DURATION OF WORK

Long duration of work is a crucial problem for 6.5 per cent of the women domestic workers. Especially full time workers have no stipulated working hours. Irrespective of day or night, they have to discharge any type of work assigned to them. In fact, long duration of work spoils the health condition of the workers. One of the workers stated that her family members are not permitted to meet her at the employer's residence during working hours. This in turn affects the family well being of the workers.

OCCUPATIONAL DISEASE

Occupational disease seems to be the greatest threat for 9.7 per cent of the women domestic workers. One of the workers stated that her employer frequently asks her to burn several heaps of papers and plastic covers. Another worker stated that her employer gives several buckets of clothes for washing (per day). The inhuman activities of the employers are the basic reasons for the occupational diseases of domestic workers.

LACK OF LEAVE FACILITY

Leave facility is essential for the women domestic workers. Especially maternity leave is inevitable. But the employers hesitate to grant even maternity leave to the workers. Sometimes the workers are terminated even if they take leave for genuine reasons. Besides whenever the workers return after taking casual leave, the employers accumulate as many tasks as possible and assign them. The women domestic workers, who were already poor and weak, get psychologically affected. Hence lack of leave facility is the biggest problem for 4 per cent of the domestic workers.

NO RETIREMENT BENEFIT

Even after putting up long years of service, the women domestic workers do not get any retirement benefits. In fact, most of them are not aware of such benefits. They simply expect a better wage from their employers so as to satisfy their immediate wants and needs. Hardly 3.2 per cent of the workers are very specific that they should be entitled to retirement benefits like that of organized workers.

LACK OF MEDICAL FACILITY

The women domestic workers pay the medical expenses (if any) from their own pocket. Only a few employers reimburse such expenses. In case of life threatening diseases, the workers borrow money from money lenders or relatives or friends to get treatment in private Hospitals. Huge debt accumulates before they get recovered from the disease. As such, lack of medical facility seems to be a great problem for 1.6 per cent of the domestic workers.

CHARGES OF THEFT

The women domestic workers are always suspected for the valuable things or cash missing in the employer's house. Even trustworthy workers are sometimes charged as thieves. In this context, if the innocent worker/workers take leave, then the employers confirm that they have really stolen and start torturing them in different ways. Some times they are taken to the Police Station and blamed as culprits.

Table 22
Job Satisfaction of the Women Domestic Workers:

Opinion	*No. of domestic workers*	*Percentage*
Highly satisfied	19	15.3
Satisfied	32	25.8
Not satisfied	73	58.9
Total	124	100

Source: Primary data.

The study shows that 15.3 per cent of the women domestic workers are highly satisfied with domestic work, 25.8 per cent are satisfied and the remaining 58.9 per cent are not satisfied. Some of them stated that their neighbours and relatives always suspect them as immoral. Besides they felt that their employers never appreciate them. Instead they always find fault with them. Hence they are not satisfied with domestic work. But some of them are highly satisfied. They state that their employers are kind, generous and broadminded.

FINDINGS

- The study shows that 84.7 per cent of the women domestic workers serve on full time basis and 15.3 per cent workers serve on part time basis.
- Majority of the women domestic workers (33.1 per cent) are serving for three employers.
- It was found out that most of the women domestic workers work for 6 to 8 hours per day.
- There is no agreement between the employer and the women domestic workers. Hence the domestic workers are frequently exploited by their employers.
- As for as Tirunelveli city is concerned, there is lack of improvement in the wages of domestic workers. If the workers demand for more wages, the employers simply terminate them and look out for new workers.
- The women domestic workers have no legal status. There is no scheme or legal provisions in force to regulate the employment of domestic workers. Hence they are cheated by the employers by levying overwork than what is actually agreed upon (orally). Besides under-payment and non-payment of wages are also faced by the workers.
- Majority of the women domestic workers in Tirunelveli City belong to the age group of 20 to 40 years.
- The study shows that most of the women domestic workers are educated below SSLC level. Some of them are ignorant and are too innocent to understand the behaviour of the employers. Anyway they are keenly interested in educating their children so that they may have a bright future.
- It was found out that 81.5 per cent of the women domestic workers are married. Most of them have 1 to 2 children in their families.
- Majority of the women domestic workers (44.4 per cent) have 2 to 4 members in their families.
- The study reveals that majority of the women domestic workers are Hindus (73.4 per cent) followed by Christians (22.6 per cent) and Muslims (4 per cent).

- Majority of the women domestic workers (34.7 per cent) belong to Scheduled Caste, 15.3 per cent of the workers belong to Scheduled Tribes, 36.3 per cent of the workers belong to Other Backward Caste and 13.7 per cent of the workers belong to General category.
- The women domestic workers have taken up domestic work mainly due to economic reasons. They toil from the clutches of moneylenders, unable to repay the long existing debts.
- It is clear from the study that most of the domestic workers (58.1 per cent) have two earning members in their families.
- The personal income of most of the domestic workers ranges from Rupees 1000 to Rupees 1500 per month. The workers who are single earners find it difficult to manage their family with the poor income. But the family income of the most of the workers ranges from Rupees 3000 to Rupees 4500 per month.
- The study shows that 91.1 per cent of women domestic workers live in rented houses.
- The women domestic workers spend a huge portion of their income for rent and grocery.
- The women domestic workers suffer from various occupational diseases like ulcer, wheezing, back pain, leg pain, body pain etc.
- Majority of the women domestic workers (96 per cent) do not have insurance coverage. This is mainly because of the fact that they could not afford to pay the premiums. Some of them are ignorant of the benefits of insurance.
- It was found out that majority of the women domestic workers (29 per cent) prefer to save their money in private Chit Fund agencies.
- The domestic workers in Tirunelveli city are not recognized as workers. They have no right to worker's compensation, weekly holidays and minimum wages.
- The low social and economic status of the occupation adversely affects the marital prospects of women domestic

workers. Their marriage proposal often gets cancelled due to the fact that they are not recognized as labour. Instead they are often suspected to be immoral and indecent.

- The full time women domestic workers are more subject to sexual exploitation than the part time workers.
- The domestic workers get medical treatment from Government Hospital situated at High Grounds, Tirunelveli. But they complained that they do not get proper treatment in the Government Hospital. Most of them could not afford to get treatment in private hospitals. Only a few could afford.
- Besides wages, the domestic workers are not given any other benefits either by the employer or by the Government to take care of their health, safety and future.
- Domestic workers are not registered and are not shown in employment statistics.

SUGGESTIONS

- A separate Act should be passed by Government of Tamilnadu to regulate the employment of domestic workers especially women.
- The employers should pay at least one month's pay as bonus once in a year. This would help the domestic workers in several ways.
- Regular meals should be given by the employers to the women domestic workers irrespective of the nature of work performed.
- The domestic workers in Tirunelveli city should create awareness among themselves to form Union so that they could fight for their problems. A membership fee of at least Rupees 10 per year should be fixed for this purpose. A great deal of progress could be achieved through collective action of the Union.
- The organized labour in Tirunelveli city should encourage the unorganized domestic workers to get themselves organized.

- The local Government of Tirunelveli city should compel the domestic workers to wear identity cards stating their name, address, age, name of the employer/employers and other important details regarding their employment.
- While employing domestic workers, the employers should enter into written agreements stating the nature of domestic work, duration of work and remuneration details.
- Minimum wages of domestic workers should be fixed by the Government based on the cost of living index in Tirunelveli city and the employers should be compelled to contribute towards Provident Fund and Gratuity benefits of the workers.
- Maternity leave should be provided for women domestic workers atleast for first two children. Otherwise the employers should be heavily fined.
- The domestic workers should be given two week paid leave (per year) in addition to weekly off. This would enable them to maintain health and take care of their family.
- The domestic workers should compulsorily take insurance policy atleast for a small amount. The employers should share the premium amount.
- The minimum age for women domestic workers should be fixed at thirty. This may avoid frequent incidents of sexual harassments.
- The employers should remit an advance deposit in the bank/post office in the name of domestic workers while recruiting them .The workers could utilize the amount in times of emergency.
- The employers should give valid reasons for terminating the domestic workers. A reasonable period of notice should be given in the event of termination so that the workers could seek another employment. Sudden termination should necessarily be accompanied by huge and immediate compensation without any excuse.

- The employers should be instructed by the labour office to pay the remuneration of domestic workers through Bank or Post Office.
- Extra payment should be given to the domestic workers while assigning extra work other than what is actually agreed upon.
- It is of paramount importance to provide annual increment benefits to the domestic workers.
- The brutal activities of the employers towards women domestic workers must be punished instantly without any delay.

CONCLUSION

The study reflects that women domestic workers in Tirunelveli city suffer a great deal of mental trauma in their life. They remain the most vulnerable and exploited groups even after five decades of independence. Though the constitution guarantees them the right to equality and right against exploitations, their condition akin to slaves is apparent. In fact, the contribution of domestic workers to the economy is ignored and deprived of social benefits and workers' rights. Hence there is a great need to create an awareness in the society of the plight of women domestic workers. If the domestic workers are given the same status as of regular workers, there will be betterment in their working conditions which in turn would lift their status in the society.

REFERENCE

Boserup, Ester (1970), Women's Role in Economic Development, St. Martins Press, New York.

Towards Equality: Report of the Committee on the Status of Women in India, Department of Social Welfare, Ministry of Education & Social Welfare, Government of India (1974) December, New Delhi.

ILO (1984), Introduction to Social Security, Geneva, International Labour Office.

Occupational Health Issues of Women in the Unorganized Sector (1998) Report of the Task Force on Health, National Commission on Self Employed Women, February.

Yadhav N. Kashyap, Rani (1998), Working Women and their Constraints, *Journal of Social Research*, Delhi, Jan-March.

Mittal, L. N. (1998), Women the Worse Hit, *Social Welfare*, January.

Koli. P. A. (2005), Economic Development and Environment Issues, Serials Publications, New Delhi.

Nambiar, A.C.K (2005), Population Development and the Environment, Serials Publications, New Delhi.

Sujata Gothoskar (2005), New Initiatives in Organizing Strategy in the Informal Economy Case Study of Domestic Workers Organizing in India, Committee for Asian Women, Bangkok.

Debasree Laheri (2007), Abuse of Child Domestic Workers in India: Crises and Challenges, *The Indian Police Journal*, Vol. LIV No. 4, October-December.

South Asia Workshop on home-based Work, (2007), A Home Net Report, December, Ahmedabad.

www.labourfile.org/newsmore.aspz?Nd=23

www.indiatogether.org/2004/nov/hrt-domhelp.htm

www.globaljusticecenter.org/papers2005/ally_eng.htm

www.kishorecariappa.blogspot.com/2007/09/maids-get their-due.htm/

www.teresas.ac.in/main/Domestic%20workers%20meel.asp

http://en.wikipedia.org/wiki/Tirunelveli

http://www.hindu.com/2007/07/15/stories/2007071554480600.htm.

Organizational Performance Assessment: Effectiveness, Efficiency, Productivity

RITA REZAEE*

Two important topics receiving considerable attention in policy circles and within academe today are productivity and efficiency. As enrollments in higher education continue to expand, public funding is becoming increasingly scarce, particularly as competition increases from other recipients of public funds such as healthcare and corrections. In light of this many policymakers have found themselves asking if higher education institutions are using their resources productively. Over the past decade, questions of this kind have given rise to a number of studies seeking to assess productive and cost efficiency.

Productivity, in the most straightforward sense, may be defined for any given firm, organization, or operating unit as simply the ratio of output produced to physical inputs used. In higher education, examples of single-input and single-output productivity measure might include the number of students (educated) per faculty member or the number of journal articles published per researcher. While measures like these are interesting and useful in certain contexts, they are quite limited for describing the aggregate productivity of an institution like a university that uses several (m) inputs to produce several (n) outputs. Here, in order to arrive at a single-

* Faculty member of Shiraz University of Medical Sciences, Iran.

valued productivity measure. This is done by developing composite, or virtual, inputs and outputs by attaching some relative importance, or weight, to each input and output. From this it is possible to derive a Total Factor Productivity measure.

In sum, productivity measures are nothing more than rank-free indicators of the rate at which inputs are translated into outputs.

How then does efficiency relate to productivity? In the most straightforward sense, the former can be seen as an index of the latter. If one were to calculate productivity estimates for a set of institutions (in keeping with the higher education focus) and seek to identify the most (least) productive unit, efficiency can be defined as the index used to rank the different productivity values. Productivity then, is a *value* assigned to the rate at which inputs are converted into outputs and efficiency is a *ranking* of different values.

Most questions that organizations probe through evaluation are in three categories:

What did we do?

How well did we do it?

What difference did our program make? (What changes occurred because of our program? (Earl, Sarah *et al*, 2002)

Assessment of organizational performance is defined as the measurement of organizational performance that assessment users evaluate in relation to reference points for the purpose of supporting their requirements and expectations. It is therefore very important for educational leaders to clarify for assessors (1) who their important external assessment users are, (2) the types of assessment information they need, (3) the types of decisions they make based on assessment results, and (4) the potential impact those decisions have on the organization's capacity to perform. High-quality assessment programs are robust and capable of providing the right information at the right time in the right format to meet ever-changing needs of all the organization's important assessment user groups.

There are two types of groups who use assessment results in higher education: external and internal. External user groups are governing boards; governmental agencies; potential students, donors, employees, and contractors; organizations that affirm; and external academic peers. Based on their evaluation of assessment findings, these groups make important decisions that greatly affect the following organizational aspects:

Operating and capital resources; Research grants and contracts; Program mix and pricing structures; Student financial aid; Sanctions for noncompliance; Accreditation; Rank; Eligibility; Censure; Future enrollments; Future workforce

DONATIONS AND GIFTS

Internal user groups exist inside the institution. There are three types of internal user groups: senior leaders, administrators and managers, and faculty and staff. Internal user groups use assessment for the following purposes:

- To account to others
- To manage strategy
- To allocate resources
- To manage and control quality of processes and organizational culture
- To improve programs and services
- To support personnel decisions
- To advocate causes

Internal assessment user groups operate inside the institution. As noted earlier, there are three types of internal assessment users, defined by position and job responsibilities: senior leaders, administrators and managers, and faculty and staff. These groups use assessment to account to others, manage strategy, and build learning organizations that strengthen innovation, allocate resources, control quality, improve programs and services, and support personnel decisions.

Accountability: External assessment users, such as governing boards, government agencies, and major donors, hold senior leaders accountable for the performance of their organizations. Senior leaders use assessment to account to these important stakeholders in terms of mission achievement (performance outcomes), progress toward strategic goals, efficient use of resources, quality of institutional resources, programs and services, accreditation, ranking, compliance, and so forth. Internal auditors assess performance on behalf of senior leaders.

They evaluate performance against internal policies and procedures and sometimes against external laws, rules, standards, and criteria. Internal auditors report assessment findings to senior leaders through audit reports.

It is the responsibility of senior leaders to identify and clarify all the unique needs of the organization's important external assessment users. It is the responsibility of assessment leaders to build a robust assessment program that enables senior leaders to fulfill their accountability responsibilities.

Managing Strategy: Senior leaders use assessment results to manage strategy in specific ways, namely, to frame strategy; to clarify, operationalize, and align strategy; and to monitor strategy achievement.

Framing Strategy: Senior leaders use strategic planning processes to frame strategies that determine an organization's competitive advantage and place in the environment. Strategic thinking requires objectivity and an honest assessment of how an institution is doing and where it is heading. Educational leaders must not only know what the organization is setting out to do but also when it has succeeded or failed.

McNamara (1999) explains that leaders use a variety of strategic planning models, including goals-based, issues-based, organic, or scenario-building models, to frame strategies. Leaders select the model best suited for their "organization's leadership, culture of the organization, complexity of the organization's environment, size of the organization, expertise of planners," and other factors.

Strategic planning typically starts with an analysis of an organization's external and internal environment—a process known as a SWOT analysis (SWOT is an acronym for "strengths, weaknesses, opportunities, and threats.")

Assessment is also helpful in exposing institutional strengths and weaknesses. Through assessment, senior leaders can discover a great many things, including these:

- Nature and scope of student learning
- Quality of research
- Quality of programs and services
- Levels of satisfaction of employees, students, and important stakeholders
- Quality of partnerships with important suppliers and service partners
- Quality of critical resources
- Quality of work processes
- Current levels of productivity and efficiency
- Scope of innovation
- Financial health and well-being of the institution

Institutional strengths and weaknesses, combined with external opportunities and threats, help senior leaders frame strategies to bring their institutions closer to their vision of performance excellence.

Senior leaders also use assessment to support resource allocation decisions. Good decision making is usually supported by reliable and valid decision support data, much of which comes from assessment.

Senior leaders face many challenging, sometimes unpopular, decisions to ensure the future success of their organizations.

Senior leaders recognize that for an organization to "learn," all members of the organizational community must understand where the organization is headed and how much progress is being achieved. The organizational community needs regular, accurate, and timely feedback on progress toward strategic goals. In a true learning organization, members use assessment to answer the performance question "How are we doing in relation to our performance goals?" Senior leaders, as well as administrators and managers, use assessment to enable the organization to learn from its past performance within the context of its desired future. For purposes of assessment, administrators and managers are defined as all individuals who manage the operations of an organization or a "unit of analysis" whose performance is under review. In higher education, administrators and managers generally include assistant vice presidents, assistant deans, directors, coordinators, and department chairpersons. As mentioned before, many administrators and managers perform leadership functions, and many senior leaders perform management functions. The important point is that people engaged in management activities use assessment somewhat differently than when they are engaged in leadership activities.

The expression "unit of analysis" is used in assessment to define an organization, program, or process whose performance is under review. A unit of analysis can be an entire institution, a college such as the College of Arts and Sciences, a school such as a law school or medical school, an academic department such as the Chemistry Department, an administrative office such as Admissions or Information Services, a program such as General Education or Writing Across the Curriculum, or a cross-functional process such as payroll. When properly used in assessment, a unit of analysis whose performance is under review has very clear boundaries. Boundaries can be delineated through traditional administrative and budgeting structures or other boundary-defining entities. When a unit of analysis is a cross functional process such as payroll, the unit requires a clear beginning and ending and clear lines of responsibility and ownership.

Like senior leaders, administrators and managers use assessment to account to important stakeholders for their unit's overall performance, manage goals and objectives, support resource allocation decisions, and strengthen organizational culture to encourage innovation. However, in their managerial role, they also use assessment to monitor and control operations; improve programs, services, and processes; and support personnel decisions.

One of the most important uses of assessment is to improve programs, services, and processes. In most organizations, improvement is a shared responsibility.

Performance management is a means of auditing and managing system-wide activity. Organizations are encouraged to raise their levels of performance, and manage their staff and customers more tightly to achieve better outputs and outcomes and avoid appearing at the bottom of a league table. Its core assumptions are that performance levels in the public sector can be raised; that this is desirable and necessary; and that evaluation on both an individual and comparative basis will promote improvement.

What is new in the current reform movement is the emphasis on the use of performance assessments for systematic, school-wide, instructional and curricular purposes at the school-level and, in addition, for accountability purposes at the district- and state-levels. In some instances, proponents of assessment reform view performance assessments as the lever for systemic curricular and instructional reforms at any level of the educational hierarchy.

EFFICIENCY AND EFFECTIVENESS OF EDUCATION SYSTEMS

Measuring efficiency and effectiveness in education is of great importance considering that resources are usually limited, while needs for such resources are often limitless. The underlying objective of making best use of resources devoted to education requires a drive to maximizing both the efficiency and effectiveness. Thus, these concepts are applied in order to monitor and evaluate how well resources are used in an educational system and to priorities the use of such resources.

The determination of the effectiveness of an organization has been identified as one of the objectives for any organization especially in Higher Education, and, indeed, it may be more properly thought of as an evaluation objective. It is a crucial element of organizational assessment and has received considerable attention in the professional literature. Wallace and Van Fleet, (2001) identifies a number of criteria for effectiveness at the organizational level and then describes several models for measuring organizational effectiveness. Those models and their "key questions" are as follows:

(a) *Goals:* Have the established goals of the organization been met?

(b) *Critical Constituencies:* Have the needs of constituents been met?

(c) *Resources:* Have necessary resources been acquired?

(d) *Human Resources:* Is the organization able to attract, select, and retain quality employees?

(e) *Open Systems:* Is the organization able to maintain the system, adapt to threats, and survive?

(f) *Decision Process:* How are decisions made and evaluated?

(g) *Customer Service:* How satisfied is the costumer with the organization?

Multidimensional approaches to organizational assessment date back at least fifty years. Despite its duration, however, there has been little agreement on basic definitions and approaches. Kanter and Brinkerhoff proposed that the most interesting questions related to organizational assessment are not technical, but rather conceptual. How to measure effectiveness was less interesting to them than what to measure, the selection of definitions and techniques, and how effectiveness is linked to an organization's structure, functioning, and environmental relations (Kanter and Brinkerhoff, 1981).

schooling compares to other potential public and private uses. e.g. comparing the earnings of technical-vocational graduates with the earnings of students graduating from academic subjects. By measuring outputs in monetary values, it is possible to compare educational programs directly to other potential uses of society's resources.

There are a number of techniques that are often employed in order to measure the efficiency of education systems. These include: parametric or regression based estimators; non-parametric analysis; cost benefit analysis; cost-effectiveness analysis; measurement of rates of return to education. A number of conceptual problems are faced in attempting to undertake a meaningful measurement of efficiency. These include:

Difficulties with the identification of the components of the education system that is relevant to the analysis;

Determining how the components will be measured,

Difficulties in measuring costs–this includes the problems of collecting data on private costs of education both inside and outside of educational institutions; a lack of agreement on the type of costs that should be included;

Methodological issues concerning the measurement of educational outputs and outcomes. For example, there are questions about how to incorporate cognitive as well as affective aspects in a measurement instrument. When determining the efficiency of a system the outputs are normally limited to aspects such as the number of graduates in a course or the average grades in a course. Measurement of long-term effects or outcomes is almost never taken into account.

To meaningfully measure the efficiency of an education system, the inputs and the process have to be related to the effects, which are based on the outputs and the outcomes. The education system can be viewed as consisting of four main components.

Inputs: These are the real resources used in education, e.g. the characteristics of learners, educators, curricula, textbooks, facilities and equipment, and financial resources.

The Goal Attainment Model;

The Systems Resource Model;

The Internal Processes Model; and

The Constituency Satisfaction Model. (Cameron, 1981)

Cameron also isolated five major factors as predictors of organizational effectiveness:

External environment;

Institutional structure;

Institutional strategy;

Institutional demographics; and

Institutional finances. (Cameron, 1986)

Cameron concluded by proposing that:

The most critical of these five factors are "the external environment" and "institutional strategy."

Proactive institutional strategies that address the external environment are more successful than those geared toward internal institutional matters; and

Multidimensional management strategies are required to improve higher education institutions' organizational effectiveness. (1986)

Projected outcomes can be used to measure the efficiency of a Higher Education Institute (HEI). If all of an HEI's students qualify within the expected time (in three years for a three-year full-time course, for example, or six years for a three-year half-time course) the institution would be 100 per cent efficient. However, some students may repeat a year for various reasons and will take longer to complete. Others will drop out. This cause the efficiency figure to drop. The efficiency of an institution is defined as the ratio of the time students should ideally take to obtain a qualification, to the time they are projected to take on average (taking account of repeat years and drop-outs). (HEFCE, 2001).

Efficiency and effectiveness in (higher) education were defined as follows:

Efficiency– "An ability to perform well or achieve a result without wasted resources, effort, time, or money (using the smallest quantity of resources possible)" ..."Educational efficiency can be measured in physical terms (technical efficiency) or in terms of cost (economic efficiency)".

Effectiveness– "An output of specific review/analyses that measure (the quality of) the achievement of a specific educational goal or the degree to which a higher education institution can be expected to achieve specific requirements".

In distinguishing between efficiency and effectiveness, the following concepts have often been citied and used:

Internal Efficiency– A system is more internally efficient than another if, in order to produce the same level of output, it is less costly. It refers to a comparison of learning (a non-monetary outcome of education) to the costs of educational inputs. Internal efficiency addresses the question of how funds within the educational sector should be best allocated.

It is concerned with obtaining the greatest educational outputs for any given level of spending.

External Efficiency– For measuring the external efficiency of education system one tries to ascertain the impact which the school, college, university graduates i.e. the product of education system are making on the society. Items such as community gains (i.e. community activities), political (i.e. government activities), personal gains (i.e. return to individual and his/her family), students achievement at higher levels of education, the life time income as well as the social stability are taken into account. It refers to the ratio of monetary outcomes to monetary inputs.

Internal Effectiveness– A system is more internally effective (technically efficient) than another if, in order to produce the same level of output, fewer of at least one input is/are used.

External Effectiveness– External effectiveness is concerned with the relationship between non-monetary inputs and monetary outputs, or how the overall use of money for

Balk 1974 cited productivity as "encompassing efficiency, effectiveness, and their symbiotic relationship". In another model, productivity was but one of ten organizational assessment indicators (Macy and Mirvis, 1976).

Kanter and Brinkerhoff proposed three kinds of effectiveness:

(a) Task effectiveness or goal attainment, including output, results, efficiency, etc;

(b) Appropriate organizational structure and process, including organizational characteristics, member satisfaction, motivation, communication links, internal conflict resolution, absence of strain between subgroups, etc; and

(c) Environmental adaptation, including flexibility in the face of change, resource acquisition, and longer-term adaptation and survival.

Cameron's important work in the 1980s sets a useful context for understanding the importance of organizational effectiveness, especially for managers. Earlier academic literature on the subject had criticized organizational effectiveness studies on the grounds those they:

Failed to adequately identify indictors of effectiveness;

Relied too much on single indicators of effectiveness, ignoring relationships between multiple factors;

Failed to create an adequate level of specificity; and

Over-generalized when considering dissimilar organizations or subunits. (Goodman, Atkins, and Schoorman, 1983).

Cameron dismissed these inadequacies as researchers' concerns and argued for the importance of organizational effectiveness measures when managers, consumers, and others have important choices or judgments to make. Cameron also concluded that criteria of effectiveness are especially ambiguous in organizations that lack clearly defined goals. (Cameron, 1986).

Cameron acknowledged four dimensions for organizations to reflect their effectiveness:

Processes: These are the interactions between learners and inputs, between different inputs themselves, and between teaching/learning processes, e.g. attendance/participation, absenteeism, etc.

Outputs: These are the direct and more immediate results or effects of education, e.g. learner's completion/certification.

Outcomes: These are the ultimate or eventual effects of education, e.g. increased earnings, employment, contribution to productivity, improved health, and other non-monetary outcomes. (European Research Associates, 2006).

Evaluation is the process of gathering information on the results of past activities for the purpose of making decisions about them. Organizational Performance Evaluation occurs when this process is applied to assessing the state of the organization as whole. Typically, this refers to how well it is achieving its stated mission and involves looking at its goal attainment as well as how efficiently it has performed. (This is different from Program Evaluation in which the focus is on one specific part of the organization.) .Evaluation can occur in a formal, systematic way through the application of a professionally designed evaluation program or it can be carried out with varying degrees of informality ranging from gathering a few reports to completely impressionistic estimates about how things have been going.

REFERENCES

Balk, W. L. (1974), Why Don't Public Administrators Take Productivity More Seriously? Public Personnel Management, 3 (4), 318-325.

Cameron, Kim. (1978), Measuring Organizational Effectiveness in Institutions of Higher Education, *Administrative Science,* Quarterly 23 (December), 604-33.

Cameron, Kim S. (1981), Domains of Organizational Effectiveness in Colleges and Universities, *Academy of Management Journal,* 24(1) 25-47.

Cameron, Kim S. (1986), A Study of Organizational Effectiveness and Its Predictors, *Management Science*, 32 (1) 87-112.

Cameron, Kim and Smart J. (1998), Maintaining Effectiveness Amid Downsizing and Decline in Institutions of Higher Education, *Research in Higher Education,* 39 (1): 65-86.

Earl, Sarah *et al.* (2002), Outcome Mapping: Building Learning and Reflection into Development Programs. International Development Research Centre (Canada).

European Research Associates (2006), Key Education Indicators on Social Inclusion and Efficiency.

Higher Education Funding Council for England (HEFCE) (2001), Guide to Performance Indicators in Higher Education, from: *www.hefce.ac.uk*

Kanter, R. M., Brinkerhoff, D. (1981), Organizational Performance: Recent Development in Measurement, *Annual Review of Sociology,* Vol. 7. 331.

McNamara, Carter (1997), Basic Guide to Program Evaluation. Authenticity Consulting, LLC. Copyright 1997-2007. Adapted from the Field Guide to Nonprofit Program Design, Marketing and Evaluation.

Wallace, D. P. and Van Fleet, C. (2001), Library Evaluation: A Casebook and Can-do Guide. Englewood, CO: Libraries Unlimited.

Overview to Evaluation: Types, Methods and Strategies

Rita Rezaee* & Shirain Iranfar**

INTRODUCTION

Evaluation is a methodological area that is closely related to, but distinguishable from more traditional social research. Evaluation utilizes many of the same methodologies used in traditional social research, but because evaluation takes place within a political and organizational context, it requires group skills, management ability, political dexterity, sensitivity to multiple stakeholders and other skills that social research in general does not rely on as much. Evaluation is the systematic collection of information about a program that enables stakeholders to better understand the program, improve its effectiveness, and/or make decisions about future programming. Evaluation can be described as a systematic process for judging the value or worth of something. In general, evaluation involves establishing criteria, collecting evidence, and making a judgment. (Rennekamp *et al.* 2007) A simple definition of evaluation defines it as the art of judging something or determining its value. It is also the process of collecting, analyzing and interpreting information to determine the adequacy and effectiveness of a program. (IMLS, 2000).

Evaluation is defined as the systematic way to assess the extent to which a program has achieved its intended results.

* Faculty member of Education Development Center, Shiraz Medical School, Iran.
** Faculty member of Kermanshah University of Medical Student, Iran.

Evaluation is done in different ways and for different purposes. Evaluation processes occur for internal organizational reasons of budget justification, expenditure justification, program improvement, and to assess program or service accomplishments. Evaluation can be used to establish baseline data for future comparison, to gauge user satisfaction and to assess staff performance. Evaluation processes can also be triggered by administrative requirements, including requests from governing bodies.

Weiss defines evaluation as "the *systematic assessment* of the *operation* and/or the *outcomes* of a program or policy, compared to a set of *explicit* or *implicit standards,* as a means of contributing to the *improvement* of the program or policy" (1998).

Griffiths and King (1991) identify some principles for good evaluation that still bear repeating: (1) Evaluation must have a purpose; it must not be an end in itself; (2) Without the potential for some action, there is no need to evaluate; (3) Evaluation must be more than descriptive; it must take into account relationships among operational performance, users, and organizations; (4) Evaluation should be a communication tool involving staff and users; (5) Evaluation should not be sporadic but be ongoing and provide a means for continual monitoring, diagnosis, and change; (6) Ongoing evaluation should provide a means for continual monitoring, diagnosis and change; (7) Ongoing evaluation should be dynamic in nature, reflecting new knowledge and changes in the environment.

TYPES OF EVALUATION

There are many different types of evaluations depending on the object being evaluated and the purpose of the evaluation. Perhaps the most important basic distinction in evaluation types is that between ***formative*** and ***summative*** evaluation.

Formative evaluation includes several evaluation types:

- *Needs assessment* determines who needs the program, how great the need is, and what might work to meet the need;

- *Structured conceptualization* helps stakeholders define the program or technology, the target population, and the possible outcomes;
- *Implementation evaluation* monitors the fidelity of the program or technology delivery;
- *Process evaluation* investigates the process of delivering the program or technology, including alternative delivery procedures.

Summative evaluation can also be subdivided:

- *Outcome evaluations* investigate whether the program or technology caused demonstrable effects on specifically defined target outcomes;
- *Impact evaluation* is broader and assesses the overall or net effects, intended or unintended of the program or technology as a whole;
- *Cost-effectiveness and cost-benefit analysis* address questions of efficiency by standardizing outcomes in terms of their dollar costs and values;
- *Secondary analysis* reexamines existing data to address new questions or use methods not previously employed;

Meta-analysis integrates the outcome estimates from multiple studies to arrive at an overall or summary judgment on an evaluation question (Earl, Sarah *et al.* 2002).

Evaluation should be part of any organization's overall planning process and integral to the assessment of current services and resources, the development of strategies for change, and the monitoring of progress toward goals and objectives. Indeed, in order to be valid, an evaluation must reflect the organization's mission, goals, and objectives. In planning the evaluation of a specific program, the evaluator should first gather relevant background information. This activity might well include reviewing the professional literature, identifying professional standards and guidelines, and networking with colleagues. Next, the evaluator should decide what he or she actually wants to know, that is, focus the evaluation. This requires a determination of the purpose(s) of the evaluation specific to the program being examined.

After focusing the evaluation, decisions must be made about the overall design of the study, the method(s) to be used, and the measurements to be made. In other words, the evaluator should decide what must be measured, choose an evaluation method, select the data collection techniques to be employed, plan the construction and/or purchase of data collection instruments, plan the data analysis, develop a budget for the evaluation study, and recruit personnel. As is often the case in research studies, it is a good idea to utilize more than one method so as to increase the reliability and validity of the study and its findings. Haynes (2004), for example, argues for mixed-method evaluation, which combines user-centered with system-centered paradigms and qualitative with quantitative methods.

EVALUATION METHODS

There is selected evaluation methods mentioned below:

Input Measurement

Input measures are measures of the resources that are allocated to or held by an organization and represent the longest-standing, most traditional approach to assessing the quality of organizations and their resources and services.

Output/Performance Measurement

Output or performance measures serve to indicate what was accomplished as a result of some programmatic activity and thus warrant being considered as a type of evaluation research. Such measures focus on indicators of output and effectiveness rather than merely on input; are closely related to the impact of the program on its community; and, all evaluation methods should be related to the organization's goals and objectives.

One critical element of performance measurement is effectiveness; another is user satisfaction.

Impact/Outcomes Assessment

Rossi, Lipsey, and Freeman (2004) point out that outcome must relate to the benefits of products and services, not simply their receipt (a performance measure). However, given the increasing call for accountability, it is becoming imperative to measure outcomes or impact. Indeed, "outcomes evaluation has become a central focus, if not the central focus, of accountability-driven evaluation" (Patton, 2002).

Some authors use the terms *impact* and *outcome* synonymously; others see them as somewhat different concepts. Patton (2002) suggests a logical continuum that includes inputs, activities and processes, outputs, immediate outcomes, and long-term impacts.

Service Quality

Service quality, briefly defined, is "the difference between user's expectations and perceptions of service performance" (Nitecki, 1996). As a concept, it dates back to at least the 1970s and has some roots in the total quality management (TQM) movement. TQM is characterized by the implementation of standards of quality, the encouragement of innovation, the measurement of results, and the taking of corrective actions as needed. TQM emphasizes the use of a team approach to maximizing customer satisfaction.

Process Evaluation

The second stage in Patton's (2002) continuum described in the section on impact/outcomes assessment was *processes* or activities. "A focus on process involves looking at *how* something happens rather than or in addition to examining outputs and outcomes". Process data permit judgments about the extent to which the program or organization is operating the way it is supposed to be operating, revealing areas in which relationships can be improved as well as highlighting strengths of the program that should be preserved (Patton, 2002). Process evaluation focuses on "what the program actually *does*" (Weiss, 1998). It is the most frequent form of program evaluation (Rossi, Lipsey, & Freeman, 2004). Process indicators are somewhat similar to performance measures, but they focus more on the activities and procedures of the organization than on the products of those activities.

Benchmarking

One of the relatively recent approaches to measuring the performance of organizations is benchmarking. Benchmarking tends to fall into the "Total Quality Management" category. Benchmarking represents a structured, proactive change effort designed to help achieve high performance through comparative assessment. It is a process that establishes an external standard to which internal operations can be compared. (Jurow, 1993).

There are several types of benchmarking, one of which is referred to as competitive or performance benchmarking. Performance benchmarking utilizes comparative data gathered from the same field or the same type of organization. The data are usually derived from analyses of organizational processes and procedures. Benchmarking can be used to establish best practices, identify changes to improve services, evaluate opinions and needs of users, identify trends, exchange ideas, and develop staff. Peischl (1995) points out that, candidates for benchmarking include the services or products of an organization, internal work processes, internal support functions, and organizational performance and strategy.

Standards

Standards refer to a set of guidelines or recommended practices, developed by a group of experts that serve as a model for good service. Some general types of standards, as identified by Baker and Lancaster (1991), include technical standards, performance standards, output measures, input measures, qualitative standards, and quantitative standards.

Quantitative Evaluation

Any evaluation method that involves the measurement of quantitative/ numerical variables probably qualifies as a quantitative method, and many of the methods already examined fall into this broad category. Among the strengths of quantitative methods are the evaluators can reach conclusions with a known degree of confidence about the extent and distribution of that the phenomenon; they are amenable to an array of statistical techniques; and they are generally assumed to yield relatively objective data (Weiss, 1998).

Experimental Methods

Usually, but not always, deal with quantitative data and are considered to be the best method for certain kinds of evaluation studies. Indeed, "the classic design for evaluations has been the experiment.

It is the design of choice in many circumstances because it guards against the threats to validity"(Weiss, 1998). The experiment is especially useful when it is desirable to rule out rival explanations for outcomes. In other words, if a true experimental design is used properly, the evaluator should be able to assume that any net effects of a program are due to the program and not to other external factors. On the other hand, experimental methods are relatively weak in producing findings that can be generalized to other situations because they are usually conducted in rather controlled settings. Also, experiments tend to be used to test the effects of one component of a program at a time rather than the entire program. Another limitation of the true or randomized experiment is that it is not well suited for evaluating programs in their early stages of implementation. If the program changes significantly before outcomes are measured, it will be difficult to determine which version of the program produced what effects (Rossi, Lipsey, & Freeman, 2004).

Survey Methods

Survey methods *are* often quantitative in nature but lack the experiment's ability to rigorously test the relationship between a program or service and its outputs or impact.

Questionnaires and interviews, and observation to a lesser degree, represent the most commonly used survey data gathering techniques. Other quantitative methods covered by the *Encyclopedia of Evaluation* (Mathison, 2004) include concept mapping, correlation, cross-sectional design, matrix sampling, meta-analysis, panel studies, regression analysis, standardized tests, and time series analysis.

Cost Analysis

Simple cost analysis is basically a descriptive breakdown of the costs incurred in operating an organization. Cost-related techniques more concerned with the assessment of whether monies are being spent in an optimal fashion usually fall into one of two groups—cost-effectiveness studies and cost-benefit analysis. "The term 'cost-effectiveness' implies a relationship between the cost of providing some service and the level of effectiveness of that service. Cost-effectiveness analyses can be thought of as studies of the costs associated with alternative strategies for achieving a particular level of effectiveness" (Lancaster, 1993). Some examples of cost-effectiveness measures include the cost per relevant informational resource retrieved, cost per use of a resource, cost per user, and cost by satisfaction level (Lancaster, 1993; Matthews, 2004).

Cost-effectiveness analysis can be seen as "a truncated form of cost-benefit analysis that stops short of putting an economic value on outcomes [benefits] of programs" (Klarman, 1982). "'Cost-benefit' clearly, refers to a relationship between the cost of some activity and the benefits derived from it. In effect, a cost-benefit study is one that tries to justify the existence of the activity by demonstrating that the benefits outweigh the costs (Lancaster, 1993).

Other kinds of cost analysis discussed by Weiss (1998) and Matthews (2004) include the following:

1. Cost-minimization analysis: seeks to determine the least expensive way to accomplish some outcome
2. Cost-utility analysis: considers the value or worth of a specific outcome for an individual or society

3. Willingness-to-pay approach: asks how much individuals are willing to pay to have something they currently do not have
4. Willingness-to-accept approach: asks individuals how much they would be willing to accept to give up something they already have
5. Cost of time.

EVALUATION STRATEGIES

There are four major groups of evaluation strategies:

Scientific-experimental models are probably the most historically dominant evaluation strategies. Taking their values and methods from the sciences—especially the social sciences—they prioritize on the desirability of impartiality, accuracy, objectivity and the validity of the information generated. Included under scientific-experimental models would be: the tradition of experimental and quasi-experimental designs; objectives-based research that comes from education; econometrically-oriented perspectives including cost-effectiveness and cost-benefit analysis; and the recent articulation of theory-driven evaluation.

The second class of strategies is ***management-oriented systems models***. Two of the most common of these are **PERT**, the **P**rogram **E**valuation and **R**eview **T**echnique, and **CPM**, the **C**ritical **P**ath **M**ethod. Both have been widely used in business and government. It would also be legitimate to include the Logical Framework or "Log frame" model developed at U.S. Agency for International Development and general systems theory and operations research approaches in this category. Two management-oriented systems models were originated by evaluators: the **UTOS** model where **U** stands for Units, **T** for Treatments, **O** for Observing Observations and **S** for Settings; and the **CIPP** model where the **C** stands for Context, the **I** for Input, the first **P** for Process and the second **P** for Product. These management-oriented systems models emphasize comprehensiveness in evaluation, placing evaluation within a larger framework of organizational activities.

The third class of strategies is the ***qualitative/anthropological models***. They emphasize the importance of observation, the need to retain the phenomenological quality of the evaluation context, and the value of subjective human interpretation in the evaluation process. Included in this category are the approaches known in evaluation as naturalistic or 'Fourth Generation' evaluation; the various qualitative schools; critical theory and art criticism approaches; and, the 'grounded theory' approach of Glaser and Strauss among others.

Finally, a fourth class of strategies is termed ***participant-oriented models***. As the term suggests, they emphasize the central importance of the evaluation participants, especially clients and users of the program or technology. Client-centered and stakeholder approaches are examples of participant-oriented models, as are consumer-oriented evaluation systems.

There is no inherent incompatibility between these broad strategies each of them brings something valuable to the evaluation table. In fact, in recent years attention has increasingly turned to how one might integrate results from evaluations that use different strategies, carried out from different perspectives, and using different methods.

CONCLUSION

Evaluation can be an effective way to:

Provide constant feedback on the extent to which the projects are achieving their goals.

Identify potential problems at an early stage and propose possible solutions.

Monitor the accessibility of the project to all sectors of the target population.

Monitor the efficiency with which the different components of the project are being implemented and suggest improvements.

Evaluate the extent to which the project is able to achieve its general objectives.

Provide guidelines for the planning of future projects.

Influence sector assistance strategy. Relevant analysis from project and policy evaluation can highlight the outcomes of previous interventions, and the strengths and weaknesses of their implementation.

Improve project design. Use of project design tools such as the log frame (logical framework) results in systematic selection of indicators for monitoring project performance. The process of selecting indicators for monitoring is a test of the soundness of project objectives and can lead to improvements in project design.

Incorporate views of stakeholders. Awareness is growing that participation by project beneficiaries in design and implementation brings greater "ownership" of project objectives and encourages the sustainability of project benefits. Ownership brings accountability. Objectives should be set and indicators selected in consultation with stakeholders, so that objectives and targets are jointly "owned". The emergence of recorded benefits early on helps reinforce ownership, and early warning of emerging problems allows action to be taken before costs rise.

REFERENCES

Baker, S. L., and Lancaster, F. W. (1991), The Measurement and Evaluation of Library Services (2nd ed.). Arlington, VA: Information Resources Press.

Earl, Sarah *et al.* (2002), Outcome Mapping: Building Learning and Reflection into Development Programs. International Development Research Centre (Canada).

Griffiths, J. M., and King, D. W. (1991), A manual on the Evaluation of Information Centers and Services. New York: American Institute of Aeronautics and Astronautics Technical Information Service.

Haynes, A. (2004), Bridging the Gulf: Mixed Methods and Library Service Evaluation, *Australian Library Journal,* 53(3), 285-307.

IMLS. (2000), Managing Program Outcomes: Measuring Program Benefits of National Leadership Grants. The Alliance Group.

Jurow, S. R. (1993), Tools for Measuring and Improving Performance. In S. Jurow & S. B. Barnard (Eds.), Integrating Total Quality Management in a Library Setting (pp. 113-126). New York: Haworth.

Klarman, H. E. (1982), The Road to Cost-effectiveness Analysis. Milbank Memorial Fund Quarterly: *Health and Society*, 60(4), 585-603.

Lancaster, F. W. (1993), If you want to Evaluate your Library . . . (2nd ed.). Champaign, IL: University of Illinois, Graduate School of Library and Information Science.

Matthews, J. R. (2004), Measuring for Results: The Dimensions of Public Library Effectiveness. West Port, CN: Libraries Unlimited.

Mathison, S. (Ed.) (2004), Encyclopedia of Evaluation. Thousand Oaks, CA: Sage Publications.

Nitecki, D. A. (1996), Changing the Concept and Measure of Service Quality in Academic Libraries, *Journal of Academic Librarianship*, 22(3), 181-190.

Patton, M. Q. (2002), Qualitative Research and Evaluation Methods (3rd ed.). Thousand Oaks, CA: Sage Publications.

Peischl, T. M. (1995), Benchmarking: A Process for Improvement. Proceedings of the First International Conference on TQM and Academic Libraries (pp. 119-122). Washington, DC: Association of Research Libraries.

Rossi, P. H., Lipsey, M. W., and Freeman, H. E. (2004), Evaluation: A Systematic Approach (7th ed.). Thousand Oaks, CA: Sage Publications.

Weiss, C. H. (1998), Evaluation: Methods for Studying Programs and Policies (2nd ed.). Upper Saddle River, NJ: Prentice Hall.

Relevance of Humanrights in the 21st Century

P. MUTHAIYAN* & K. SELVANATHAN**

INTRODUCTION

Liberalization and Globalization have presented new challenges and opportunities to Indian economy. Up gradation of technology and Human Resource Development are the best solution to meet the challenges and utilize the opportunities to the best advantage. The Human Resource Development in terms of quantity and quality much depends on education. In the context, of Liberalization the higher education sector has to be re-oriented as market driven and education policy requires to be reexamined.

The objective of acquiring higher education by an individual, in the present context is mostly job oriented i.e. 'Education for job' therefore the individual is expected to demand certain types of courses which may provide the necessary skills which are demanded the labour market. As on date there is an heavy demand for engineering, medical and Paramedical courses as they promise employment opportunity not only in India but also abroad. This kind of bias though justified at individuals points of view, may not be conductive for the development of all sectors of economy, since the manpower mix will be lopsided. Therefore, the educationalists and policy makers to come out with new

* Reader, Department of Economics, Pondicherry University, Pondicherry, India.
** Registrar, Pondicherry Engg. College, Pondicherry, India.

policies to encourage the students to enroll themselves in other than professional courses. It is expected that the development of service sector at a faster rate compared to other sectors will alter the course mix and enrollment in higher education.

In this context this paper examines the necessity to introduce new courses in the emerging areas which will be useful to the students and to the society at large. On such area is Human Rights.

THE IMPORTANCE OF HUMAN RIGHTS

The globalization and privatization within the economy of a country has led to some bad effects on the society in terms of violation of human rights, development which does not take care of all the constituents of the society will not be a real development. Therefore, economists are now emphasizing the need for incorporating strategies to develop the nation in all areas. Including economic inequality crated has led to poverty, malnutrition, disease, etc., among the weaker sections of the society. In the political arena violation of rights against weaker sections of the society has emphasized the need for upholding human rights in the political field also. The concept of human rights help us to understand human beings and communities and as a set of legal norms rooted in the rule of law, human rights should be an important tool for analyzing and remedying the abuses of power local , national or international levels by individuals, groups, government and inter-governments.

DEFINITION OF HUMAN RIGHTS AND AWARENESS

Human rights besides civil, political includes economics, social and cultural rights such as right to food, clothing, housing, medical care and education. A broader working definition of human rights education consists of four levels of human rights awareness.

Level One

Unconditional and critical submission of violations of human rights.

Level Two

Reflecting awareness of human rights. But there is a refusal or lack of interest to ascertain the rights due to fear, risk, etc.

Level Three

Reflecting to exercise the human rights, prevention or seeking redress of their violation through commonly accepted bays, filing complaints to the proper authorities.

Level Four

Active and independent defense of human rights through organized collective efforts.

HUMAN RIGHTS GROUPS

Since the proclamation of the universal declaration of human rights 1948 and subsequent treaties thousands of human rights organization world wide, have come up. The concept of human rights has made an important contribution to efforts to redress and remedy. For example, injustice within the country and between the countries. The objective of these organizations both government and non-government are to promote, guarantee and protect the human rights and make accountable the persons, group or section which is responsible directly or indirectly for violation of human rights.

Human rights educator must be capable of critical thinking and learn to analyze the situations with the holistic frame work of human rights about the political, civil, economic, social and cultural etc.

VIOLATION OF HUMAN RIGHTS

The following are the traditional human rights which are emphasized, protected and promoted.

(a) Political rights, individual rights, civil rights of individuals and groups, gender rights and ethnic rights, minority rights, etc., Human rights activists consider the following areas which need urgent attention.

(b) Poverty-as a violation to numerous rights, death by mal nutrition or preventable disease or subsistence poverty that offend human dignity or deemed to be more important matters of human rights concern.

(c) Inequality structural adjustment programmes, privatization and marketisation has further widened the gap between rich and the poor especially in the developing and underdeveloped countries.

HUMAN RIGHTS EDUCATION

Numerous non-government organizations have come up in all the countries to take up the cause of protection of human rights areas, health, education, housing, environment, basic work standards, etc. the interaction between human rights activists and academicians has encouraged the educational institutions to introduce new programme in the area of human rights in developed countries. The following are the some of the graduate and under-graduate programmes run in the colleges.

(a) Introduction of Human Rights
(b) Domestic human rights
(c) Philosophy of human rights
(d) Theology of human rights
(e) Humanitarian law and human rights
(f) International human rights and business laws
(g) Human rights and non-governmental organizations

The contents of human rights courses and syllabi for teaching of courses on human rights is a more of inter-disciplinary in nature. The human rights courses tend to reflect the field of political economists, philosophy, women rights and anthropology and so on. The subjects of study are drawn from various disciplines, arts science and professional.

NECESSITY OF INTRODUCING OF COURSES IN HUMAN RIGHTS IN INDIA

There are be right job opportunities for graduates in the various human rights organizations within India and also in other countries. The established organizations like legislature, executive, judiciary of the government due to various reasons cannot protect human rights. Therefore human rights organization established by government and non-government institutions have taken up the responsibility of spreading human rights awareness among the various groups of society and also has taken up actions to promote and protect human rights in various areas. In carrying out such activities, lot of trained personnel to have knowledge on the subjects of law, business, political system, sociology, anthropology, etc are needed. Therefore, the higher educationists in India should come forward to introduce courses on human rights.

CONCLUSION

The need of the hour is to introduce new courses in the colleges in diversified areas so as to provide job opportunities for the students. On such course to be introduced in human rights. The UGC and such other bodies of Government of India should encourage the Universities and Colleges to start courses on human rights by providing specific grants to such institutions.

Index

A

Accountability, 274
Administration,
  Free from Corruption and Arbitrariness, 235
  Of Justice, 179
Administrative System, 26
Afghanistan, 16, 18, 34
Africa, 20, 21
Africa and CASWANAME, 15
African Convention, 39
Aid Agencies, 80
Aliens Act, 1905, UK, 58
Alma-Ata Declaration, 1978, 1, 3, 5
  Of Health for All (HFA), 155
American Convention of Human Rights, 1969, 62
Angola, 18
Anti-Infective Agents, 170
Armed Conflicts, 145
  And Social Violence, 13
Asia and Pacific, 20, 21
Asylum
  Claims, 74
  Countries, 16, 18, 20, 30
  Seekers, 21, 74, 91-98, 203
  Seekers Claims, 21
Austria, 22
Azerbaijan, 23

B

Balkans, 13
Balwadi Nutrition Program, 156
Bangladesh, 34, 75
  Liberation War, 49
  Struggle for Freedom, 49
Bangladesh-India Border, 49
Basic Human Rights Details, 134
Benchmarking, 290
Bengali Refugees in India, 49
Bengalis and Pakistanis, 75
Bhore Committee, 3
Bilateral Negotiations Policy, 14
Biotechnological Innovations, 180
Biotechnology, 179
Birth Spacing, 171

Bonded Labour, 146

Bosnian Refugee Women, 205

Bottle Feeding, 171

Breast

- Cancer, 171
- Feeding in Indian Societies, 174
- Feeding, 169-175
  - Human Right of Child, 170
  - Practices, 172

Brussels (1910) Convention, 65

Burundi, 17, 18

Buxa Transit Camp, (West Bengal), 34

C

Calcutta Declaration, 1999, 1

Canada, 22

Capital Resources, 273

Caste System, 238

CASWANAME, 20, 21

Central Africa, 13

Ceylonese Universities, 77

Chad, 16, 18

Charter of Child Rights (CRC), 155

Child

- Budgeting, 161
- Development Program, 163
- Exploitation, 146
- Health Administration, 162
- Health and Nutrition, 163
- Labour (Prohibiton) Act, 155
- Labour, 137, 140, 146
  - Exploitation, 140
  - Worst Labour, 137
  - Yardsticks, 1'37
- Labourers, 160
- Malnutrition, 160
- Marriage Restraint Act, 155
- Rights, 135
- Rights Structure, 154

China, 74

Chorzow Factory Case, 125

Civil and Political Rights, 196, 197

Commission for Social Development, 113

Committee on Economic, Social, and Cultural Rights, 5, 152

Compensation, 129

Compensatory Damages, 127

Constitution of Nigeria, 214

- Rights Details, 218-225
- Rights under-, 218

Contemporary International Law, 59

Convention

- Against Torture & Other Forms of Cruel—Treatment or Punishment, 109, 124
- On the Elimination of All forms of Discrimination against women, 109
- On the Rights of Child, 109
- On Elimination of all Forms of —Women, (CEDAW), 32

On Reduction of Statelessness, 32
On Refugee Status, 67, 73
On the Prevention and Punishment of the Crime of Genocide, 32
On the Rights of the Child, 32
Relating to Status of Refugees, 1951, 29, 39, 91, 93
Relating to Status of Stateless Persons, 31
Convention—Status of Refugees, 56
Core Labor Principles, 135
Corporal Punishment, 170
Corruption, 178, 186
Political, 240
Criminal Tribunals, 199
Crude Death Rate, (CDR), 4
Cubans, 64
Customary International Law, 58, 96
Cyber Space, 179

D

Dalai Lama, 34
Daycare Scheme for Working/Ailing Mothers, 156
Decade of Disabled Persons, 114
Declaration of
Human Rights, 2
Elimination of Discrimination against Women, 196, 197
Rights of Mentally Retarded Persons, 113
The Elimination of Violence against Women, 6
The Rights of Disable Persons, 113
Democratic Republic of Congo, 18, 19, 44, 74
Denmark, 30
Destruction of Eco-System and Eco-Infrastructure, 85
Developing Countries, 19, 16, 150, 163, 239, 242
Dharmshala, Tibetan Govt. Seat in Exile, 35
Directive Principles, 174, 183
Discriminations, 6, 7, 73
Displaced Persons, 74
Displacement, 55
District Tirunelveli, 246
Domestic
Labour, 146
Services Industries, 245
Violence, 234
Workers, 245
Workers in India, 245
Drug Trafficking, 146
Drugs and Vaccines, 4

E

East Pakistan, 49
Economic
And Social Council (ECOSOC), 60, 111, 113, 115, 194

Development, 229

Economy,

Indian, 297

National, 72

Education, 5, 71, 143, 144, 151, 156, 203, 245, 257

Higher, 271, 273, 278, 297

Law Related, 243

Medical, 3

System, 277

Environment, 179

Environment and Degradation, 85

Ethnic Cleansing, 2104

European

Charter of Fundamental Rights, 182

Convention on Extradition, 66

Immigration Law, 61

Evaluation, 285-295

Methods, 287-289

Strategies, 293

Types, 286, 290

Expulsion and Deportation, 68

External User Group, 273, 274

Extra Territoriality Principle, 63

F

Federal Republic of Nigeria, 213, 217, 220

Five Year Plan

(5th), 4

(6th), 4

(7th), 4

(8th), 4

(10th), 161

Framing Strategies, 274

French and American Revolutions, 236

Fundamental Human Rights, 7, 213, 214, 216, 217, 219

Rights, Defined, 216

In Nigeria, 213, 218

Fundamental Rights, 3, 174, 186, 195, 222

G

Gandhi, Indira, Prime Minister, 49, 77

Gandhi, Mahatma, 170

Gandhi, Rajiv, former PM of India, 77, 79

General

Assembly, (UN), 194, 198

Communication, 5

Genetic Engineering, 182

Geneva Declaration of Rights of Child, (1958), 31, 65, 150, 172

Genocide, 40, 73, 204

German Leaders, 40

Germany, 22

Global

Markets, 186

Refugee Population, 15-17

Refugee Program Administrator, 91

Refugee Trends, 13
Globalization, 179
Globalization and Privatization, 298

H

Haitan Refugee Centre, 94
Haitians and Indo-Chinese, 65
Health
Administration, 160
And Family Planning Services, 4
And Nutrition, 149
Care, 203
Legislation, 10
Of Women and Children, 149
Policy, 9
Policy in India, 3
Programme, 7
Services, 7
System, 1, 8
Workers, 172
High Commission
for Refugees, 57
for Russian Refugees, 41, 44
HIV, 203
HIV/AIDS, 7, 205
Human Development Policies and Programmes, 1
Human Resource Development, 297
Human Rights, 1, 68, 69, 71-73, 77, 85, 88, 97, 106, 121, 133-146, 149, 179, 186, 193, 194, 297-301
Abuse, 79
Agenda, 27
And Refugee Law, 25-36
And Refugees, 42, 43
Awareness, 298
Classification, 106
Collective, 55
Commission, 197
Conventions/Declarations on Refugees Details, 44-45
Defined, 298
Education, 300
Groups, 299
Humanitarian Law, 106
Instruments, 5, 111, 123, 197
Law, 57, 106, 107, 121
Law Development, 106
Litigation, 122
Of Child, 133-146, 175
Of Refugees, 28-29, 39
Principles, 2
Standards, 98
Traditional, 299
Tribunals, 124
Violations, 13, 25, 72, 84, 121, 126, 129, 198, 299
Violation Victims, Remedies under International Law, 121-129
Humanitarian Assistance
Program, 75
In Iraq, 75

I

ICESCR (International Convention in Economic, Social and Cultural Rights), 108
ICMR-ICSSR Joint Panel, 3
Immigrant
 Countries, 19
 And Migrants, 9
Immigration Policy, 40
India's Security, 77
Indian
 Elections, 35
 National Congress, 3
 Troops, 87
Indo-Sri Lanka Accord, 76-78
Industrial Property, 179
Industrialized Countries, 19
Industry, 171
Infant Mortality Rate (IMR), 4, 160
Infantile Eczema, 171
Infections, 171
Infections Diseases, 171
Information Technology, 156
Institutional Strengths/Weaknesses, 275
Insurgency/Terrorism, 178
Integrated Child Development Scheme (ICDS), 156, 159
Intellectual Property, 179
Intellectual Property Rights, 177
Inter-Ethnic Conflicts, 85
Internal
 Assessment, 273
 User Group, 273
Internally Displaced Persons (IDPs), 22, 23, 44, 79, 83, 85
International
 Aid, 20
 Bill of Rights, 197, 232
 Child Development Centre, Florence, Italy, 173
 Committee of Red Cross, 88
 Convention on
  Civil and Political Rights, (ICCPR), 108, 124, 195, 196
  Elimination of All forms of Racial Discrimination, 109, 124
  Protection Rights, 110
 Court of Justice (ICJ), 93, 125, 199
 Covenant on
  Civil and Political Rights, 34
  Economic, Social, and Cultural Rights, 34
 Crimes Victims, 125
 Criminal
  Court, 125, 199
  Law, 55
  Tribunals, 199
 Day of Disabled Persons, 114
 Human Rights, 5, 10
  Law, (IHRL), 110, 116, 121

Protection, 199

Protection System, 193

Humanitarian Law, 57, 72

Labor Organization (ILO), 111, 112, 134, 193

Report on Child Labour, 139

Law, 5

Monitoring Committee, 106

NGO, 106

Peace Law, 62

Refugee Law (IRL), 14, 55, 58, 91

Refugee Organization, 44, 111, 112

Standards of Protection of Refugees, 14

Tribunals, 122

IPEC, 142

IPEC Rapid Assessment of Trafficking in Girls, 140

Iraq, 17, 18, 74, 75

Iraq's Invasion of Kuwait, 75

Islamic Republic of Iran, 16, 18, 74

J

Jayawardene, JR, 77

Johnson Administration, 237

Judicial System, 241, 242

Judiciary, 186, 243

Justice Delivery System, 186

Juvenile Acts, 155

K

Karunanidhi, K, CM Tamil Nadu, 78

Kashmir Valley, 73

Kashmiri Pandits, 73

Key Participation Rights, 136

Kofi Annan, UN Secretary Gen., 135

Kottaram Camp, 85

L

Labour

Market, 297

Regimes, 237

Lankan Tamil Refugees—Repatriation, 83

Law

and Justice, 177-187

and Legal Services, 229

Reforms, 242

League of Nations, 43, 44, 57, 193

General Assembly, 150

Legal Aid

And Justice, 229-243

Scope, 235

Legal System, 235, 240, 242

And Cultural Traditions, 143

Liberalization and Globalization, 297

Liberation Tiger of Tamil Eelam (LTTE), 76, 77, 79, 82, 84-87

Ban in India, 78

Terrorists, 72

Life Expectancy, 4

M

Main Countries which Resettled Refugees, (MCR), 19
- Australia, 19
- Canada, 19
- Denmark, 19
- Finland, 19
- Norway, 19
- Sweden, 19
- USA, 19

Management Oriented System Model, 293

Managing Strategy, 274

Mannar Island, 83

Massacres in-, 199
- Bosnia-Herzogovina, 199
- Rwanda, 199
- Serbia, 199

Mental Health Care, 114

Migrants, 40

Migration, 55, 56, 61, 95, 203

Migration Control, 55

Millennium Development Goals, 162

Minorities, 8, 10

Missarami Transit Camp, 34

Montenegro, 23, 44, 74

Montivideo Treaty, 1889, 62

Morbidity, 170

Mortality, 170

Mukti Bahini, 49

Municipal Law, 63, 66

N

Nansen
- International Office, 41
- Passport, 41

National
- Charter for Children, 158
- Election Commission (Nigeria), 221
- Fund for Child Care Services, 156
- Health Policy (NHP), 3, 4
- Institute—Child Development, 158
- Legal Rights, 134
- Nutrition Policy, 158
- Security, 32
- Youth Service Corps, 223

Natural Calamities, 233

Nepal, 34, 140

Netherlands, 22

Network of Slaves, 141

New Economic Policy (NEP), 103

Nigeria,
- A Secular State, 222
- Major Religions in-, 221

Non-Governmental Organizations (NGO), 57, 72, 75, 80, 88, 116, 161, 175, 207, 247, 300

Nuclear Catastrophe, 180

Nuremburg Trial, 40

Nutrition and Education, 170

O

OBC, 182, 249

Optical Protocol, (OP), 142

  Child Pornography, 142

  Child Prostitution, 142

  On Sale of Children, 142

Organization of African Union (OAU), 64

Organizational

  Community, 276

  Performances, 271-283

P

Pakistan, 75

Palk Straits, 83, 84

Para Medical Workers, 3

Participant-Oriented Model, 294

Persecution, 56, 92, 97

Polices and Legislation Measures, 158

Political Asylum, 14

Political Terror, 13

Port-Au-Prince, 94

Poverty, 2292-232, 234-238, 300

  Causes, 232-233

  Defined, 230-231

Primary Health Centre (PHC), 4

Principle of

  Non-Extradition of Political Offender, 59

  Non-Refoulment, 55-69, 91-96

  Public International Law, 61

Problems of Children, 169, 170

Productivity, 271

  Measures, 272

Pubic Health System, 4

R

Racism in Nazi Germany 193

Racist State Policies, 203

Radical Groups, 77

  ERRLR, 77

  PLOTE, 77

  TELO, 77

Rajiv Gandhi Assassination, 78

Rameshwaram, 83

Rape/Sexual Torture, 203, 204

RDP, Development of International Standards, 105-116

Reform Movement, 277

Refugees, 8, 13, 15, 17-19, 20-23, 25-36, 33, 39-53, 55-69, 71-88

  Afghan, 16

  Aid Program, 209

  Bangladeshis, 56

  Burmese, 56

  Camps, 49, 80, 81, 85, 87, 204

    Assam, 49

    Bihar, 49

    India, 76

    Meghalaya, 49

    Tripura, 49

    West Bengal, 49

  Citizenship, 20

Classification of-, 40
Convention, 1951, 39, 62
Crisis in India, 68
Depends on International Aids, 20
Displaced Persons, 13
From-, 14, 17
Afghanistan, 14
Angola, 17
Bangladesh, 14
Bosnia and Herzogovina, 17
Iraq, 17
Liberia, 17
Montenegro, 17
Mynamar, 14
Pakistan, 14
Serbia, 17
Sri Lanka, 14
Gender and Age, 21
In Australia, 41
In Europe, 41
In Latin America, 41
In North America, 41
Law, 25, 26, 57, 91
Legal Status, 20
Mass Exodus, 91
Movement, 56
Nationalities, 17
Political, 62
Population, 15
Problems, 13, 44
Producing States, 53
Protection, 75
Reduction in Europe, 15
Rwanda and Kosovo, 95
Sri Lanka, 56
Status, 26
Women, 203, 204, 206, 207, 209
Discrimination, 207
Problems, 203
Rehabilitation of Disabled, 112
Relief Agencies, 209
Repatriation, 18
Republic of Tanzania, 16, 17
Research Grants, 273
Reservation for Weaker Sections, 239
Resettlement, 18, 59
Resettlement Policies, 203
Right to
Birth Registration, 136
Health Criteria, 6
Health, 1, 3, 5
Health of Child, 150, 153
Protection—Exploitation, 136
Rights of
Children, 149, 173
Disable Persons, (RDP), 105-116
Refugees, 60, 62
Rights under Refugee Convention, 49

Rights, 2
  Civil, 2
  Cultural, 2
  Economic, 2
  Political, 2
  Social, 2
Royal Commission, 1958, 218
RSD Procedure, 97
Russian Federation, 74
Rwanda, 75

S

Scheduled Caste/Tribes, 182
Science and Technology, 155, 187
Security, 55
  Council, 198
  Council Resolution, 95
  National, 91, 97
Serbia, 23, 44, 74
Sex Industry in China and Taiwan, 141
Sexual
  Exploitation, 146
  Orientation of Health Policies, Program and Strategies, 8
Sexually Transmitted
  Diseases (STDs), 203
  Infections, 203
Shelter and Rehabilitation, 35
Sierra Leone, 18
Sinhalese, 76
Sino-Indian Border, 1962, 34
Siracusa Principles, 10
Skill Training Program, 207
Slavery, 146
Social
  Justice, 239
  Research, 285
  Stratification, 238
Society (ies), 2, 7, 8
  Caste Based, 182
  Developing, 237
  Industrialized, 170
Socio-Economic
  Program, 236
  Rights, 217
Sokha Committee, 3
Somalia, 18, 74
South Africa, 22, 26
Soviet Union, 13
Sri Lanka, 18
  Armed Forces, 77
  Refugees, 81-83, 87
  Tamil Refugees, (SLTR), 71-88
  Tamils, (SLT), 71
Standard Rules—Disabilities, 115
Standards, 290
Status of Refugees, 62, 96
  Under International Law, 43
Stowaway;s Refugees, 64
Stowaway's Asylum, 64

Sub-Saharan Africa, 139
Sudan, 18
Supreme Court of India, 240-241
Sustainable Development, 1
Sweden, 22
Swiss and Dutch, 61
Systematic
  Discrimination, 56
  Sexual Violence, 204

T

Tamil
  Insurgencies, 77
  Militant Group, 76
  Refugees (TR), 71, 76, 78
  United Liberation Front (TULF), 77
Technology,
  Communication, 105
  Up-gradation, 297
Territorial Asylum, 95
Terrorism, 178, 180, 181
Terrorist Organization 73
Terrorists, 95
Tibet, 34
Tibetan (s), 25-26
  Refugees, 34, 35
  Refugees in India, 34
Tiger Rebels, 86
Tirunelveli City, 245-269
Total Quality Management, 290
Trafficking and Prostitution, 140, 141
  In Africa, 141
  In Sudan, 141
Trafficking in Children in-, (TC), 142
  Laos, 142
  Mynamar Border, 142
  Thailand, 142
Trafficking of
  Adivasi Girls in India, 141
  Girls in-, (TG), 141
    Burma, 141
    Cambodia, 141
    Indonesia, 141
    Thailand, 141
Training and Education Program, 207
Transparency, 10
Tribal Population, 8
Turkey, 74

U

UNCHR Bureau for CASWANAME, 16
UNESCO, 112, 124, 143, 144
UNICEF, 135, 156
United Nations, 29, 33, 41, 43, 44, 59, 60, 73, 88, 93, 106, 110-112, 114-116, 121, 133, 200
  Charter, 74, 108, 112, 174, 193, 195, 198
  Committee on Educational, Social and Cultural Rights, 173

Convention on Right of Child, 151, 152
Convention on the Status of Refugees, 14
Conventions, 61
Creation of Universe of Human Rights, 194
General Assembly, 23, 75, 106, 151, 172
High Commissioner for Refugees, (UNHCR), 14, 15, 18, 19, 20-23, 26, 34, 35, 44, 57, 72, 74-77, 79, 82-88, 91, 94, 96, 98, 124, 155, 204, 206, 208, 210
    Assets Program, 76
    Beneficiary, 19
    Global Appeal on Sri Lanka, 84
    In Lanka, 79
    Programmes, 16
Human Rights, 197
    Committee, 126
        Specified Remedies, 1126
International Children Fund, 111, 112
Organs, 127
Relief and Works Administration, 88
Role in Development of Human Rights, 193-200
Security Council, 121
Social Commission, 111, 112
System, 124
    Technical Cooperation Programme, 200
United States, 22, 41, 65, 77
    Declaration of Independence, 1194
    Supreme Court, 94
Universal
    Declaration of
        Eradication of Hunger and Malnutrition, 172
        Human Rights,45, 93, 134, 151, 194, 195
    Immunization, 4
Urbanization, 233

V

Vienna Declaration of Human Rights, 152
Violence Against Women, 203
Voluntary Organizations, 3

W

Welfare Laws, 239
Willink Commission on Minorities, 217
Willink, Sir, Henry, 218
Women Domestic Workers, (WDW), 245-269
    Caste Wise, 249
    Educational Status, 247, 248
    Expenditure Pattern, 258
    Marital Status, 249
    Mode of Saving, 259
    Occupational Diseases, 259, 262